A Mystagogy of Sacrament

Saying Amen

A Mystagogy of Sacrament

Saying Amen

Kathleen Hughes, RSCJ

Foreword by Gabe Huck

LITURGY
TRAINING
PUBLICATIONS

Acknowledgments

SAYING AMEN: A MYSTAGOGY OF SACRAMENT © 1999 Archdiocese of Chicago: Liturgy Training Publications, 1800 North Hermitage Avenue, Chicago IL 60622-1101; 1-800-933-1800, orders@ltp.org, fax 1-800-933-7094. All rights reserved.

Visit our website at www.ltp.org.

Sources of texts cited in this book may be found on page 207.

This book was edited by Victoria M. Tufano. Audrey Novak Riley was the production editor. The book was designed by Pete Pona, and Mary Bowers was the production artist. Tracy Walker provided the art for this book. The typefaces used in this book are Berkeley, University Roman and Carpenter. It was printed in Canada by Webcom Limited.

Library of Congress Cataloging-in-Publications Data
Hughes, Kathleen, 1942-
    Saying amen : a mystagogy of the sacraments / Kathleen Hughes ; foreword by Gabe Huck.
       p. cm.
    Includes bibliographical references.
    ISBN 1-56854-239-9
    1. Sacraments — Catholic church. 2. Mystagogy — Catholic Church. 3. Catholic Church —
Liturgy. I. Title.
    BX2200.H79 1999
    264'.0208 — dc21
                                  99-17446
                                      CIP

ISBN 1-56854-239-9
SACBK

05 04 03 02 01   6 5 4 3 2

Contents

Foreword

Only after reading Kathleen Hughes' entire manuscript did I notice the four words with which it begins. "But we had hoped . . ." (Luke 24:21) stands at the head of her introduction, and no one need wonder why.

Those four words echo in my memory, and not in just any voice. In August of 1960, early in the short papacy of John XXIII and still two years before Vatican II began, the 21st North American Liturgical Week was held in Pittsburgh. I had worked that whole summer following my first year in college so I could take a bus from Nebraska to Pennsylvania and attend the North American Liturgical Week. I was there at the Mass celebrated by Cardinal John Wright, then archbishop of that city and a strong advocate of Catholic renewal. It is Cardinal Wright's voice I have heard ever since then whenever Luke 24:21 is read. And at other times, too, for in his homily that verse was like a refrain. Again and again Cardinal Wright used the word Luke puts on the lips of the two traveling to Emmaus. I say "the word," not "words," because in Latin it is a single word. "*Sperabamus,*" Wright intoned throughout the homily — and his tone made it sound like what it said. Each time he would add the English: "We used to hope . . ."

Just now I found Wright's homily in the proceedings of that Liturgical Week:

> We used to hope that the charity of Christ would wipe out war. We used to hope that the mercy of Christ would cancel the tormenting memory of sin. We used to hope that the majesty of Christ would so transcend the boundaries of racial, national, and religious divisions as to unify, fervently and forever, the scattered tribes of men. We used to hope that peace and plenty and the strength of every kind we crave would surely be ours if only we followed Christ and bore his name. We used to hope that faith would be untroubled and freedom be untrammeled. . . . *Sperabamus!* We used to hope.

That is the power of a word—for four decades it has articulated some part of this world for me, has given me a way to take hold, to hold on, to remember that *sperabamus* is not new and it is not the last word. Such remembering has always had at least a little awareness of the conclusion of Wright's homily:

> All these [dialogue, study, work for unity] are good and Christ walks with us in them all. But they are not enough. It is in the breaking of the bread that we must again come to know Christ. It is in the eating of the bread that we are truly united to him. It is in living by the power of this bread that we grow in the life more abundant and the love undying that the liturgy was given us by Christ to accomplish.

The more things change? Perhaps. Certainly *sperabamus* is what we can easily say after these first post–Vatican II generations.

It is probably safe to say that no Catholic prelate, no Catholic diocese, ever took that Latin word as motto. It is a glum word. But how much a part of our lives it is!

It is the genius of Kathleen Hughes' book that she can put that word on the front page, acknowledge all the complexities and the discouragements, the failures and the animosities—and then get on with the work. Get on with the work she does, and under the rubrics of mystagogia and attention. She has gone to listen to the church. She has sought out the sense of the faithful. She has opened up again the too quickly forgotten rites themselves and their introductions. She herself pays attention. She herself becomes mystagogue.

And what happens? *Spes* happens. Hope happens. *Speramus!* We are hoping!

Where attention is paid to the rites and to the assembly, faithful people are formed and they form others in gospel living. Where the hard work of catechesis is done, where the assembly of the baptized is respected, where all ministers of liturgy are schooled in service, where the documents implementing Vatican II's renewal are heeded, there is hope and there are articulate people who can be mystagogues for us, who can unfold the mysteries we celebrate.

This book is a report on the way. It is the overview we have not had in these years. It is a textbook that gathers so much of what has been intended and what has happened in the sacramental life of Catholic parishes. There is no hand-wringing here, no fear and no anger. Rather there is good news: When pastors and assemblies make and are made by the breadth of our Catholic rites, there is gospel joy and open-eyed hope.

Amen!

Amen

Be careful of simple words said often.

"Amen" makes demands
like an unrelenting schoolmaster:
fierce attention to all that is said;
no apathy, no preoccupation, no prejudice permitted.
"Amen": We are present. We are open.
We are of one mind. We understand.
Here we are; we are listening to your word.

"Amen" makes demands
like a signature on a dotted line:
sober bond to all that goes before;
no hesitation, no half-heartedness,
no mental reservations allowed.
"Amen": We support. We approve.
We are of one mind. We promise.
May this come to pass. So be it.

Be careful when you say "Amen."

Barbara Schmich Searle

Introduction

But we had hoped . . .
Luke 24:21a

I write this book because I love the liturgy and because I hope to help others understand and love the sacramental life of the church. I write in the conviction that the renewed liturgy has not been thoroughly implemented, let alone adequately experienced and explored. I write because I believe that sacraments, well prepared and celebrated, are able to transform our hearts if we learn to pay attention and to reflect more deeply about the words and gestures and symbols that constitute our worship. And — at this particular juncture — I write because some believe the new liturgy is bankrupt and they would have us return to pre –Vatican II patterns of prayer. Before calling for a "reform of the reform" I suggest that we give the conciliar reform a chance. To that end I offer these reflections.

In the last thirty years, and largely because of the impetus of the Second Vatican Council's *Constitution on the Sacred Liturgy,* Christians throughout North America — and indeed throughout the world — have been caught up in a tidal wave of liturgical reform, the first stirrings of which began late in the last century. Experimental rites were drafted, celebrated and evaluated. Consultations were conducted. Alternative services were composed. Gradually, in most mainline Christian churches and in reform Judaism as well, a new and quasi-permanent library of liturgical books was prepared, edited, approved and introduced into congregations. This happened not without some pain and division, and nearly always without sufficient preparation.

In the Roman Catholic communion, various commissions were set up to study every major rite in light of its historical, theological and pastoral development. In quick succession the rites of infant baptism, confirmation, penance, marriage, orders, funerals, anointing, eucharist and scores of lesser rites were revised, promulgated in Latin, translated into the vernacular, approved by conferences of bishops and confirmed for liturgical use. This was all accomplished by 1974, not even ten years after the close of Vatican II. The International Commission on English in the Liturgy, the body entrusted with the translation and revision of liturgical texts for the English-speaking world, is immersed in the next stage of the reform, namely, the systematic revision of each rite in light of the experience of its use these past several decades. Truly we are living in an age of astonishing and unprecedented liturgical change.

So much ferment. So much upheaval. One wonders at this juncture: to what end? Has a new liturgical library helped us to pray more deeply? Have revised rites, original texts and pastoral introductions made any difference in our lives before God and with one another? Has the transformation of our liturgy transformed us? Are we any different? More just? More loving? Have the rites become more transparent? Have they invited and achieved "full, conscious and active participation," the battle cry of the early liturgical movement and that way of taking part in worship that the liturgy constitution called the *right* and *duty* of each Christian by virtue of baptism? On the other hand, have liturgists and pastors been preoccupied with a reform of the books and a mastery of the various sacramental rites only to discover that renewal of hearts does not automatically follow the publication and implementation of the revised rites, no matter how excellent they appear on paper?

Ah, but we had hoped. . . .

Those words of the disciples on the road to Emmaus may capture for many a deep sadness at the present climate surrounding the celebration of the liturgy. Especially for those who have invested their time and talent in one or other aspect of the reform — bishops and worship office personnel, pastors and administrators, musicians and artists, writers and teachers — there is a deeply disheartening suspicion that something is very wrong. There are nagging, generally unspoken questions, too: In the process of the reform have we lost touch with the heart of the liturgy? Has the reform lost its soul?

What are we to make of the present situation? In a country as large and diverse as the United States it is difficult to generalize. But few, if any, would suggest that we have achieved that vision of liturgy as source and summit of the Christian life which so captivated the liturgical reformers in the heady days just after the Council. Granted, there are places where the renewal of worship has achieved wonderful results, where reverent and hospitable worship attracts hundreds, where the environment and the music, the proclamation and preaching are executed with great care, where the presider and all the ministers are prepared and prayerful as they invite a community to grow in God's grace week after week. And regularly, in those communities where the reform has apparently taken hold, the liturgy has further inspired a vast network of outreach beyond the community to the disadvantaged of every kind. The demands of full participation in liturgy are clear, namely, a life of justice and charity.

There also are parishes that represent the opposite extreme. Sunday after Sunday, dwindling numbers gather for lifeless, dispirited worship, eager to finish, annoyed if there are any additional rites, uncaring, detached. Too often communities are divided by issues like posture, or the naming of God, or the appropriate choreography of the communion procession or where to locate the reserved sacrament. Meanwhile worshipers are drifting away in droves, for a variety of reasons.

The vast majority of parishes find themselves somewhere between the extremes of the perfect and the lifeless. Sometimes with severely limited resources of personnel and finances, these parishes "in-between" have established catechumenates for adult initiation, promoted liturgical ministries for the laity, developed guidelines for multicultural celebrations, begun the regular celebration of communal reconciliation and the anointing of the sick, redesigned the worship space and its appointments, hired a musician or two to support assembly participation, established a liturgy committee to prepare for feasts and seasons — and discovered that the implications of implementing the renewed liturgy sometimes seem endless and that energies easily wane where response is made up of enthusiasm and resistance in about equal measure.

Pastors, particularly, are feeling the pressure of a far more demanding, better educated and mobile flock, while their duties are multiplying and their own numbers are diminishing and aging. Sizable portions of the parish budget — to say nothing of human energies — have been spent on the renovation of space, on new hymnals and liturgical vesture, and on training conferences and workshops for the burgeoning number of lay ministers in the community. But all this expenditure and all this promise has often led only to rancorous confrontations. Communities are polarized by styles of music, the absence of kneelers, the presence of women in a range of ministries, the age and focus of confirmation, and issues surrounding adoration and exposition of the blessed sacrament. These are just a few of the concerns that divide us. In general, our patterns of worship no longer seem to be those timeless rituals binding us to one another and to the God who gathers us together to worship, but rather a minefield of competing and conflicting theologies, pastoral strategies and, sometimes, simply aesthetic sensibilities.

That the celebration of the liturgy has become the battlefield of warring ideologies, ironically, was to be expected. Liturgy is the self-expression of the church. When we gather for worship we give the simplest, most immediate, most condensed statement of our beliefs. That is why the early church thought of liturgy as *first theology*—theology enacted prior to our systematic reflection upon it. Because of this quality of liturgy as enacted belief, when the church is divided about issues of authority, leadership, roles and language—as it surely is in our day—that division will come to public, visible expression when we pray. It cannot be otherwise because of the very nature of the symbolic actions we perform.

In such a climate, church leadership is rightly alarmed and possibly more weary with the calls and letters, the charges and counter-charges than most of us. It is the obligation of leadership to monitor the health of the body and to nurture its life and growth. Steps must be taken, leaders feel, to halt the steady stream of defections of the disillusioned and to attempt again to stabilize the community's life and worship. But leadership cannot provide an appropriate remedy until there has been a correct diagnosis of the disease, and diagnoses abound. Some believe that the whole liturgical reform was misguided and that it is time for a reform of the reform. Some think language is the issue, especially as linguistic changes are attributed to feminist pressures for inclusion. Some believe priesthood has been demythologized and demoted and that introducing so many new ministries has obscured the sacerdotal role. Some wonder whatever became of sin and how such a permissive climate was able to evacuate the sacrament of penance of any hold on the community's hearts. Some think too much "archeologizing" has taken place, and that much recovery of ancient patterns of prayer has led to arcane rites and a language equally abstruse to accompany them: scrutiny, exorcism, catechumenate, mystagogy and so on. Some think all experience of transcendence has been lost in casual greetings, hand-holding, an over-emphasis on meal to the exclusion of sacrifice, and too many trite additions to the once noble simplicity of the Roman rite. There is no end of diagnoses, and there is little consensus within the National Conference of Catholic Bishops about the state of the liturgy, as recent discussions and voting attest. Unfortunately, until we can adequately name the disease and its symptoms, our cures will be to no avail.

How did we get to this impasse?

Haste accounts for some of it. Never in the history of the Roman rite has so much changed so quickly. When future historians look back on this period of change they will be dumbfounded at the naiveté with which vast numbers of people were uprooted from patterns of worship, both liturgy and popular devotions, that named them and gave their lives meaning. Granted, the liturgical movement had been gaining a certain momentum throughout the twentieth century, but its adherents were a tiny proportion of the Catholic population. For vast numbers of worshipers, there was relatively little warning before the introduction of the new liturgy. And add to the massiveness of change the speed with which the revisions were accomplished. Once vernacular prayer was permitted, communities and their bishops around the world wanted liturgy in their own tongue as soon as it could humanly be achieved. The earliest products of the reform suffered from haste and lack of polish. Furthermore, these new rites were tumbling off the presses in such rapid succession that there was little time to absorb changes in one sacramental ritual before changes in another were being introduced. Such a complete ritual reorganization of the kind we have witnessed takes decades for its maturation.

We grossly underestimated the sense of dislocation the community would experience when familiar patterns of prayer were replaced, no matter how much new patterns were welcomed. History should have prepared us. History is particularly helpful in illuminating parallel periods of liturgical disorientation: the upheaval we experience, the backlash, the regression, the anger and the widespread sense of dislocation have all happened before. A period like ours has followed every major reform council. We should have been prepared.

What appears to be a preoccupation with the outward trappings of worship is just that—and at least initially it was necessary! It takes time to feel familiar with new ritual patterns. One of the first new ministries to be introduced was that of the commentator, a liturgical master or mistress of ceremonies, needed in most churches simply to direct the community from one posture to another and to introduce the various parts of the celebration. But postures and patterns of prayer were only part of the dislocation.

A rearrangement of space and furnishings was inevitable. The rites have been least successful where old wineskins are trying to accommodate new wine. But who could have anticipated the bewildering permutations of placement for the ambo, altar, tabernacle, font and chair, and the varying theological emphases to which these different placements silently attested?

Sung prayer posed its own dilemmas. A long learning curve was inescapable as congregations adapted to different musical settings and a variety of hymn styles, and in some cases, adapted to singing at all. In sacred as in secular music, there are musical judgments to be made and a vast range of taste. Thirty years is hardly ample time to produce a new vernacular repertoire of liturgical music.

A certain dislocation about terminology was equally inevitable. "Mass" became "liturgy"; "the offertory" became "the preparation rite"; "inquiry classes" became the "catechumenate"; "extreme unction" became "the pastoral care of the sick"; "reconciliation" replaced "penance" in name and in fact. Sometimes new nomenclature led to hilarious mistakes, as when a cathedral receptionist had the printer deliver the booklets for the Rite of Election to the school cafeteria in anticipation of the primaries to be held the next week. In each instance, a new language was attempting to name a new reality. But to those who were uninitiated, it all seemed like straining at gnats.

And many were uninitiated. A new caste system has developed in some places: There are those who know the *disciplina arcanae*—the sacred secrets—and there are those who do not. Even a little knowledge can be a source of great power. Many of those engaged in the pastoral implementation of the reform are fairly unbending at least some of the time. When we employ a language of *always* or *never*, when we suggest that there is only one way of doing things without room for the pastoral exception, when we quote the documents at each other but fail to give the deeper explanations upon which the documents have been framed, then we are acting like rigid pre–Vatican II rubricists. When we use language that is remote, or appoint ministers as reward, or control planning meetings, or attempt to end appropriate discussion of unresolved issues prematurely, then Spirit-driven reform falters because of personal domination of the process.

Obviously, externals had to be dealt with. Familiarity had to be achieved. The new liturgy demanded a new choreography of language and silence, of space and gesture. But when, many might have wondered at some preconscious level, would we move to the "internals"? Vestment design and color, for example, were rethought. Perhaps the purple of Advent should be more blue than red to suggest a different tone to the season, less penitential, more one of expectation. Yet such preoccupations can seem ludicrous when most Christians want to know how to make sense of a season like Advent at all in the midst of shopping for gifts and obligatory entertaining and the dreaded annual loneliness of impossible family expectations and hoping that Christ can make it into Christmas preparations just a little. That kind of emphasis on externals easily led to a conclusion about the reform in general: too many accidents; too little substance. Is that all there is?

Meanwhile, younger Catholics are sometimes puzzled by all the fuss about reform. Those born in the last thirty years hear references to the glory days of the Latin liturgy but have no memory, romantic or otherwise, of worship before the Council. They have grown up with the Easter Vigil, regular reception of the eucharist, baptism by immersion, communal reconciliation, anointing of the sick, homilies, vernacular prayer, singing, participation and so on. The renewed liturgy has shaped their religious experience completely. For them the "new" liturgy is not new at all. It is their only experience, and only a minority of young people find nostalgia for the good old days they never knew an attractive alternative.

Possibly least anticipated of all the changes we have endured has been the effect of a revision of liturgy on those who lead the assembly in prayer, bishops and priests chief among them. Whether we like it or not, the revised rites have placed new and unprecedented demands on the leader of prayer. Think about it. When one's back was to the community and the language was Latin and the gestures were relatively obscure because of the location of the altar and presider, when the ritual was governed by a set of highly stylized gestures, a presider was trained once and for all in these immutable patterns. Not so, today. It matters whether the presider is grumpy or not; we can see his face. It matters that the prayers be prepared ahead of time; we know the meaning of the words and can tell if the presider means them as the prayer is proclaimed. It matters that the readings are addressed in the homily; no longer a sermon on a topic of the presider's choice but now "a living explanation of the word proclaimed" is what is expected, a homily that will genuinely nourish the Christian life. We can tell from gestures and body language, from facial expressions and the care — or lack of it — with which objects are touched and moved whether the presider is reverent or too casual, prepared or winging it, loving what he is doing and with whom or acting by rote. Many presiders are ill-equipped to lead the community's prayer, and some will never acquire the necessary communication qualities and skills until they join communication with patterns of deep personal prayer. Presiding at prayer is no longer a role that anyone with enough practice and coaching can get down pat. Technique is not enough. The presider needs to be competent *and* believable.

Perhaps the most serious lesson to be learned from these last several decades is the almost total lack of thoughtful and sustained catechesis on the liturgy. My suspicion is that too much was presumed of a liturgy in the vernacular. Once the liturgy was in our own language we would have no more need of teaching because each of us would understand it. Just a few words of explanation would suffice, or at least that appears, in hindsight, to have been the operative wisdom.

Now we know differently. To understand the words is not necessarily to understand what we are doing when we gather to give praise and thanks, express our sorrow, pledge our lives, beg for healing or participate in any of the other sacramental moments. I have friends who will admit privately that they don't participate in the sacrament of reconciliation because they don't know what to do or say. I know others who still talk about the "last rites" — which is precisely what these rites are not. I know scores of people who do not think there is much difference between a celebration of the eucharist and a service of word and communion when a priest is not available for eucharist, yet these are two *essentially* different events of prayer.

Who is speaking and writing about these things? Where are the scores of sacramental theologians and pastoral liturgists who have been trained over the last few decades? There appears to be a widening gulf between theologians and ordinary believers. Sacramental theologians, pastoral liturgists and ritual experts speak to each other in conferences and journals. This is a fascinating conversation, but most Christians have little access to it and neither the time nor the inclination to master the specialized language and methods that are foreign to their experience but are presumed in the dialogue. We have a growing body of literature about the history of the sacraments and an even larger literature about their theology. But where is the latter-day Beauduin or Guardini or Parsch or Diekmann or Walsh who is speaking to believers and making the liturgy more accessible for those who long to find a way to worship? Where are the leaders of the liturgical movement who will help us identify what ails us?

I have a conviction that we are looking in the wrong place to try to diagnose the disease. We are looking at the liturgy and not at those who gather to celebrate it. A malaise of spirit is my diagnosis, a malaise not attributable to the reform and revision of the books or to the implementation of the rites—not attributable, in fact, to anything that was *done* in the last thirty or so years, but rather to what we have *failed to do,* namely, to invite the Christian community into an experience of worship for which they have been adequately prepared. It is my contention that we have not systematically catechized the community about the heart of our prayer. In all of the efforts at reform and all the time and energy spent on implementing the new rituals, I believe we have not yet helped people to understand and love the liturgy. But it is not too late.

The Roman Catholic communion is now moving into a second generation of post–Vatican II service books. Foremost among these revisions is the revision of the sacramentary, a book containing the prayers and pastoral directives for the celebration of the eucharist. As the sacramentary nears completion we have an unprecedented opportunity to catechize again, and this time more thoroughly and thoughtfully because of thirty years of experience of the renewed liturgy. At this juncture we can build on the good experiences of worship developed and developing across the country and from them determine the appropriate content and process for opening up the riches and the mysteries we gather to celebrate week after week.

Such an effort launched in the Roman Catholic community could have a domino effect. In the past thirty years or so, other churches and synagogues have looked to the Roman communion for inspiration and direction for their own efforts at liturgical reform and renewal. Now the reform of the liturgy could give way to the renewal of the minds and hearts of worshipers within and beyond our church.

While reformed liturgical rites do not appear to have made an appreciable difference in contemporary church life, it is my conviction that they have the capacity to transform a community. Ritual prayer is infinitely more powerful than all our talk about it. Needed is a commitment to allowing the liturgy to work its way with us. Appropriate modes of liturgical education for adult believers will not simply talk about the rites and instruct us about their history, theology and pastoral implications, but will bring us to cherish the liturgy, to understand its inner dynamic, and to commit ourselves to the vision of the reign of God which worship embodies. This kind of liturgical education describes an approach to catechesis that the early church called *mystagogia*, an opening up of the mysteries. It is an evocative form of teaching as different from instruction as poetry is from prose.

This is what I hope to convey in this book about the sacraments, a poetic reflection on the sacraments that will launch readers into their own experience of mystery. This book will explore a new way of contemplating the liturgy, based less on the history and theology of the rites than on the actual experiences of women and men at prayer. It will take seriously the adage that liturgy is *first theology* and it will explore the meaning of each sacrament from the way the church has invited us to celebrate it. In each instance, it will touch on the inner dynamic of the liturgy and the many languages of worship — the spatial, temporal, kinetic, iconic and acoustic — when and as they form part of the memorable, articulated experience of communities reflecting on their prayer. These many symbolic languages together make a claim on us, or rather, these languages have the potential to make a claim on us if we let them, if we learn how to pay attention, and if, in turn, we open ourselves to the light they shed on our own human religious experience which we bring with us to worship.

Mystagogical reflection, then, is a first theme of the book; paying attention, or contemplation, is the second. We will never learn to love the liturgy unless we enter into it in new ways, overcoming the enervating routine, the rote, the boring sameness. It will take hard work, but perhaps we need to recall that the word *liturgy* literally means *work* of the people, or, as faith refines the definition, the participation of the people in the work of God.

Chapters on mystagogy and contemplation will form the initial reflections in this book. Then we shall turn to the church's sacramental life as it is enacted in the liturgy. My selection of sacramental rites to be addressed in these pages is based on the regular parochial experience of worship. Thus infant baptism and adult initiation will be treated separately because they are distinct ritual events in the life of communities. Funerals, not strictly speaking a separate sacrament, will be included for our reflection. Orders and religious profession, the latter also a sacrament in my judgment, will be treated as parallel life choices in an addendum to the chapter on marriage.

Because I, too, am a product of the academy, with presuppositions and prejudices of my own, and a vocabulary sometimes too specialized and theoretical for the sake of clarity among a wider audience, I began this book in a series of interviews with ordinary believers. I wanted to find a way to talk about the rites that would capture experience. I wanted to use words that were true to the event and to the experience of contemporary worshipers. I decided that the only way to find this language was to pray with a variety of communities and to talk with people immediately after the liturgy about what had been celebrated and what had touched them.

The reflections in this book are the result of scores of conversations and interviews with hundreds of people. First I identified communities where, by all reports, "they prayed well there." I made no attempt in my study to visit a cross-section of communities to incorporate the lifeless with the lively. I did, in the end, visit faith communities of varying sizes and demographic situations, but what the sites had in common was a vibrant worshiping community and excellent leadership. Each is a place where great care is taken to celebrate the revised rites in a reverent and hospitable way. I made this selection because of a conviction that when we are exposed to sustained excellence in worship, the worship experience itself gives rise to a rich, symbolic language with which to describe our experience of it. In other words, I presumed that individuals who were regularly exposed to fine worship would be articulate about that experience and willing conversation partners with me.

I was not disappointed. Over and over again, young and old, cradle Catholics and those recently welcomed into the community or welcomed back after an absence, some newly involved in church life and some veteran ministers were able to speak with a certain ease and eloquence about worship, how they had prepared for it, what it touched in their lives, how it helped them name God, Christ and the Spirit, what transformation it seemed to invite. My conversation partners included a large number of teenagers recently confirmed; second-graders anticipating first communion and their parents who were helping in their preparation; couples in the first several years of their marriage; a group of friends who had each experienced the death of a loved one within the year; a community of elderly women religious, some of them chronically ill, who were anointed during their annual retreat; a group of newly initiated and others who had recently come into full communion with the Catholic church; and a few who had recently been reconciled with the church after years away.

The language I use as I explore the sacraments in this book will be the language given to me in these interviews — mostly images, stories and metaphors. I am deeply grateful to the hundreds of people who were willing to talk with me about their understanding and experience of sacraments. I came away from each interview edified by truly faith-filled worshipers. I am also greatly heartened that in nearly every instance, those with whom I met found the conversation about their experience of worship to be personally enriching. So many remarked that there are no structures for the kind of faith-sharing on sacramental experience which we enjoyed together. This suggests to me that there is a hunger and a need for the kind of reflection I will propose in the following chapters.

I also am grateful to those who welcomed me into their communities and helped with the logistics of the interviews, particularly Diane Boutet, Vincent Rizzotta, Stephen Sloper, Leticia Gillespie, Edward Hislop, Mary Jo Quinn, Dale Fushek, Joan Inglis, Judy Brown, John R. Page, Pat Kruska and Fred DeLuca.

I am indebted to the Louisville Institute for Faith and Culture for the research grant they gave me that made interviews all over the United States possible and for their additional funding of my semester of writing. I found the Institute for Ecumenical and Cultural Research in Collegeville, Minnesota, to be a contemplative situation in which to draw these reflections together into a manuscript. The experience of contemplative scholarship the Ecumenical Institute affords taught me a great lesson: One can only speak contemplatively when one lives contemplatively. I owe special thanks to the director of the Institute, Patrick Henry, and to his associate, Dolores Schuh, for their editorial suggestions.

This is not the first time such research has been conducted. I have taken advantage of previous interviews and written materials, chief among them: the Notre

Dame Study of Catholic Parish Life; "Liturgical Renewal: 1963–1988," sponsored by the Georgetown Center for Liturgy, Spirituality and the Arts on the twenty-fifth anniversary of the *Constitution on the Sacred Liturgy*; and the transcriptions of interviews conducted for the Liturgy Training Publications (LTP) *The Roman Catholic Mass* video series on the various parts of the Sunday eucharistic celebration and the video *This Is the Night* on the Easter Vigil. In addition, I have made extensive use of the LTP video on infant baptism, *New Life: A Parish Celebrates Infant Baptism*, produced in conjunction with Tabor Publishing.

Three consultants acted as a sounding board for my ideas, helped to shape the project, reviewed the kinds of questions I was asking and the locales I was visiting, and were extremely helpful in critiquing the manuscript. I thank Gilbert Ostdiek, OFM, Sheila McLaughlin and Mark Francis, CSV, for their willingness to help shape this project and for their patience in seeing it unfold. They have worked with me from the initial stages, the specification of rites to be studied and the identification of worship sites where it is reported that "they do the liturgy well," through the critique of a first draft of this manuscript.

Others were of great assistance at various stages of the project: Gabe Huck and Victoria Tufano welcomed the idea of this book and encouraged its development. Maria Leonard suggested important sites and contacts. Judy Gross made the results of her research among new Christians available to me. Ronald Lewinski gave me access to his research on parish life and worship. Eileen Crowley-Horak, video producer of the LTP series on the Mass, mentioned above, gave me copies of the video scripts. Anthony Gittins, CSSP, a colleague at Catholic Theological Union, helped me shape my interview procedures. John J. Begley, SJ, was a font of wisdom, as always, and a ready reference.

Two student research assistants were of special help to me. Bryan Cones reviewed the material of the Georgetown study and drew my attention to significant insights. Meriel Owen completed the monumental task of transcribing all the interviews in addition to the countless editorial chores she performed. I owe them both my gratitude.

Finally, I have been privileged to be part of a variety of life-giving communities of faith and prayer, especially my religious community, the Religious of the Sacred

Heart of Jesus. These women have taught me most of what I really believe about the sacraments as a way of life.

This manuscript has taken its final form during the season of Advent, a time of rekindled hope in the presence of God with us and a time of longing and expectation for God who is to come. Those of us who love the liturgy and long for the renewal of hearts it makes possible can take courage from the presence and promises of God which this season celebrates.

Kathleen Hughes, RSCJ

Chapter One
Mystagogy as Method

Listen, I will tell you a mystery!
1 Corinthians 15:51

The goal of this book is simple: to assist worshipers and those who minister among them to understand and love the liturgy more, to participate more thoughtfully in its celebration and to embrace the commitments they make to a way of life and to a vision of the reign of God each time they say "Amen." In liturgy, as in life, one thing regularly leads to another: understanding leads to loving, loving to participation, participation to commitment and commitment to a transformed way of living. It seems so elementary. Believers simply need to understand what they are doing when they gather for prayer and the rest will follow.

But the crucial question remains: How is such a goal to be achieved? How do we come to a new and deeper understanding of something so familiar and yet such a mystery? Many of us have been celebrating the liturgy for as long as we can remember. We are accustomed to its rhythms and used to its words and ways. We take so much for granted. The surface structure is so predictable. Yet the liturgy remains profoundly mysterious — and not just because the rites have been changed in our lifetime.

Mystery is used in common parlance to describe something unknown or not fully understood. It is a problem to be solved or an intellectual exercise to be worked through. The best mystery stories are those with the most intricate puzzles, which are eventually solved by a clever detective. The word *mystery* has a different meaning, however, when applied to religious truth because religious truth of its very nature is incomprehensible to reason and known only through faith. Paul uses *mystery* in this sense when he speaks of the mystery hidden for ages in God, revealed in Christ Jesus and entrusted to the church (see Ephesians 3:9–12). The liturgy of the church places us in contact with the mystery of God revealed in Christ. What we are doing when we gather for worship is fundamentally and tenaciously mysterious: We are participating in the work of God. Liturgy is simultaneously God's work and our work joined. It is a transcendent reality, and we shall never grasp its full significance nor measure its extent. We see, Paul reminds us, in a mirror, dimly; we know, but only in part. One day we will know fully; one day we will see God face to face (1 Corinthians 13:12).

In the following chapters we will explore the sacramental liturgies of the church, not in the hope of dispelling mystery, but to learn how to enter into it and to allow ourselves to be touched and transformed by its power. Understanding and loving the liturgy presuppose that the world of the liturgy becomes our world, that its words, gestures and objects, and the basic patterns that give it a structure become home to us, familiar, cherished, handed on from parent to child, from age to age.

How do we make the world of the sacraments accessible to both head and heart? That is the kind of total understanding we seek, an understanding that nurtures our loving and our cherishing. That is the question this chapter will explore. It is a question of method. After a brief exploration of the variety of methods available for the study of the liturgy, one method will be selected and developed for our purposes, a method judged most congenial to realizing the goal of deeper sacramental understanding which leads to loving and commitment.

Methods in Liturgical Studies

Each person has a preferred way of appropriating knowledge, a preferred approach to learning. Classroom teachers know this well. Every time a teacher assigns research on a particular topic, students gravitate in different directions. Some want to know where a thing came from and how it developed chronologically; others may wish to begin by asking what men and women down through the ages have thought and written about it. Some students want to know how a thing is like or unlike other things in its classification; others may be fascinated by isolating its root forms from later variants. Some turn to contemporary authoritative sources for their information and execution; others prefer to observe, analyze and judge for themselves whatever data are available about the phenomenon being explored. These various preferred styles of learning, these methods, have characterized the way liturgical studies has developed as a discipline in the last several decades.

HISTORICAL METHOD

Most of the approaches described above were employed more or less frequently in the introduction and implementation of the reformed liturgy at the national, diocesan and parochial levels, particularly in the first decade after the Second Vatican Council. Probably the method most frequently applied in introducing the revised rites in parishes across the country has been the historical method. That phenomenon is completely understandable given the thrust of the reform of the sacraments. In numerous instances the reform of the liturgy was accomplished by recovery of age-old patterns of prayer: initiation of adults was enhanced by recovery of ancient catechumenal patterns; penance was augmented by recovery of communal patterns of reconciliation; extreme unction was reformed by the recovery of its earlier focus, strength and healing for the sick, in tandem with rites for the comfort and support of the dying; eucharist was transformed by recovery of its earliest, two-part structure of word and table in place of the "three principal parts" of the Mass: offertory, consecration and communion. Numerous individual rites, such as the prayers of the faithful, the blessing and sprinkling of water, and the exchange of the kiss of peace, had ancient analogues, and these predecessors were noted regularly in the course of introducing the various reforms.

The historical approach to liturgical implementation was predicated on the principle that roots matter and that the new rite would be more intelligible if its origins were clear. Furthermore, speaking of the historical background of the reform provided an opportunity to explore and explain some of the features of the liturgy that had not changed but were generally opaque: the fraction rite, the commingling of water and wine, the general shape of the liturgical year, the origin of vesture and so on. It is understandable, then, that as pastors invited communities to appropriate the reformed liturgy, the historical background — sometimes enhanced with socio-cultural gleanings about the context in which rites came to be — would form a significant portion of their presentations. It also demonstrated to those disgruntled by liturgical change that the "new" liturgy was not new at all, but a radical and faithful recovery of earlier patterns of prayer. In some cases a little history could dispel or lessen the fears that the reform occasioned.

COMPARATIVE METHOD

Comparative approaches also have been employed in trying to make the liturgy more comprehensible: "This is what we used to do and this is what we do now"; "these are various options for the celebration, which have some features in common with each other and some differences." The case of the addition of many eucharistic prayers provides a good example of the comparative method's usefulness. There are now ten eucharistic prayers, where once we had only the single prayer known as the Roman Canon. Each of these ten prayers has the same basic structure: thanksgiving, acclamation, invocation of the Spirit, institution narrative, remembrance, offering, intercessions and doxology. But the prayers differ in some significant ways: the content and tone of several eucharistic prayers were crafted especially for use with children or in seasons of reconciliation; the first prayer employs more florid language and a hieratic style; the second is brief and designed for simpler weekday celebrations; the third allows for moveable prefaces, the fourth most amply develops the history of salvation, and so on. At least a rudimentary knowledge of comparative methods is essential for all who exercise liturgical leadership, especially priest presiders. This methodological approach to liturgy provides a grounded and informed rationale in making selections from among the numerous options included in the liturgical books.

PHILOLOGICAL METHOD

A focus on liturgical language, known technically as the philological method, has often preoccupied students of the liturgy and sometimes inspired poets and mystics. The reformed liturgy was filled with a new vocabulary. Where did it come from? Many of the prayer texts of the sacramentary were not modern creations. Sometimes they were cobbled together from a variety of early and medieval sources. A study of words was necessary especially for those who were responsible for translating liturgies into the vernacular. What is the base text? How has the vocabulary changed over time? Did the circumstances surrounding its early composition provide a particular nuance that might suggest a more thoughtful translation today? The philological method, however, was not confined to language specialists. After the Council, talking about liturgical reforms provided an opportunity to make the language of and about the liturgy more accessible to the community. Words like *paschal mystery, reconciliation* and *homily* joined *monstrance, chasuble* and *transubstantiation* in our vocabulary. Even the word *liturgy* called for some explanation. The language of liturgy and all the objects associated with it has spawned a cottage industry of lexicons developed to enhance liturgical literacy for scholars and believers alike.

JURIDICAL METHOD

The juridical or rubrical approach to worship was employed in a modified way in introducing the new liturgy. This method had predominated in the teaching of liturgy and sacraments before Vatican II. It was a way of talking about liturgy that concentrated almost exclusively on how a particular ceremony ought to be conducted according to the rubrics of the rite, canonical prescriptions and other legislation available to the student of liturgy, most often the presbyter. A juridical approach is characterized by proper execution. Unaccompanied by other methods, a juridical approach simply exposes what should be done and how it should be accomplished, not where it came from or why we are doing it. Perhaps some of us experienced this kind of approach if over-zealous teachers prepared us to serve the community in one of the liturgical ministries simply by quoting the documents as the final authority, stating the letter of the law while ignoring its spirit, or conveying a type of pragmatic approach to liturgy without any attention to the deeper meaning of the rites or the appropriate spirituality one must nurture in assuming a ministry in the name of the community.

DOGMATIC METHOD

Rarely is one method used exclusively. Certainly history, comparative studies and philology were generally accompanied by some teaching from the tradition about the received meaning of various elements and patterns of the liturgy. A dogmatic approach to the study of liturgy is one in which the development of dogma is given pride of place. The community has grown in its knowledge of the mystery entrusted to it by Jesus Christ. Over time we have found new ways to understand and articulate the paschal mystery of Jesus' life, death and rising, to enact it in worship and to reflect upon it. Emphases change, but the Spirit remains active in every age of the church's life, inspiring new questions and new insights — and thus, a growing body of systematic reflection on the event of liturgical prayer. Eucharist, for example, has been known as meal, as sacrifice and as sacrament. In different periods one doctrinal aspect was more pronounced in the church's reflection on its experience of worship than another. Eucharist is, in fact, all three, but emphases change.

LITURGICAL-THEOLOGICAL METHODS

A strictly dogmatic approach to sacramental theology has yielded in our day to what are called liturgical-theological methods, a cluster of approaches that together attempt to uncover the meaning of the rite, both in the past and in the contemporary church. The liturgical-theological approach pays attention to what is actually being celebrated, analyzes these various ritual moments, interprets their meaning in light of the received tradition including its doctrinal development, and sometimes advocates the development of yet newer forms of celebration in light of such study. Sometimes psychology, sociology, anthropology and contemporary communication theory are employed in dissecting ritual action in an interdisciplinary approach. Multiple disciplines that study human behavior are able to illuminate human ritual practices and help contextualize and ground the analysis of the celebration. These latter methods generally are employed by scholars in the academy and do not immediately affect the celebrations of a local community except insofar as liturgical specialists might offer certain insights about ritual performance or advocate certain modifications in the rites or their execution as a result of such study.

Choosing a Method

While choice of method is dictated in part by one's preferred learning style, it obviously is also dependent on other factors, such as the type of material to be explored, or the particular significance one assigns to authorities — ancient or modern, canonical or personal. Finally, we must choose a method in view of the end we want to accomplish. Methods are not better or worse; they are simply tools to be used in light of a larger goal. Each method has particular strengths and limitations. Often only a cluster of methods can meet one's stated goals.

The goal of this exploration, as stated at the beginning of the chapter, is to foster deeper understanding of the liturgy leading to greater personal engagement in the event of liturgy and deeper commitment to the way of life we rehearse together when we gather for corporate prayer. Because this goal is one of understanding beyond simply the accumulation of facts or information, a method that speaks *about* the liturgy is not sufficient. It may be interesting to know that the reason a piece of the host is dropped into the chalice is that this practice is a remnant of an ancient liturgical practice called the *fermentum,* in which a piece of the bread consecrated at the bishop's celebration in the urban center was sent to celebrations in outlying communities to link them spiritually to the bishop. The piece of consecrated bread, once received and placed in the cup, "fermented" the wine, joining the celebrations of the local church together as the work of one body. That kind of knowledge stands us in good stead for a game of liturgical trivial pursuit. It does not necessarily enhance our participation in worship. We may even wonder why such a remnant remains when its function has receded and new and even arbitrary typological meanings are assigned to once-simple and functional actions. The history of the rites, however intriguing and filled with such curious nuggets, does not automatically, in fact rarely, inspire the kind of *felt* knowledge that leads to loving.

Similarly, explaining what interpreters over the centuries have said about this or that element of liturgy may also be interesting, though not necessarily heartening. Different theological emphases are the product of every culture and every age. Doctrine develops over time and as a result of sustained reflection on the mysteries of faith. Its modes of expression are conditioned by the reigning philosophy, psychology, anthropology and so on. Again, such knowledge is interesting. But it gives us no more access to the heart of it, the mystery of what we do when we come together to pray. Where things came from and how we have thought about them and written about them and argued about them and gone into schism over them are all interesting, but all our knowledge of the Arian controversies surrounding the wording of the doxology does not, at the end of the day, help us to praise God. A systematic-theological approach, in itself, is no more adequate than a historical approach to helping us understand more deeply what we are doing when we gather for worship. Yet when liturgical catechesis has been offered in parishes in the last two decades, most often these two methods have been employed. Both approaches have been successful to the extent that they have imparted information about the liturgy, but mere information can leave us uninspired and disengaged. What is needed is a way to help us enter the world of the liturgy, not simply to think about it but to dwell inside it, not remaining detached students or spectators but rather allowing ourselves to be captivated and claimed by the mystery that unfolds.

The Mystagogical Method

How do we make the world of the sacraments accessible to head and heart? How do we talk about the liturgy and, in the process, impart not just a knowledge of facts and their history, nor even the relationship of one part to another, but that deep-felt knowledge of head and heart and faith, the knowledge that nurtures whole human persons and inspires a knowing from the inside out?

A method that flourished in the early church, although relatively untested in contemporary liturgical studies, is called the mystagogical method. Because it has some promising features suggesting its usefulness for the task at hand, mystagogy will be employed in the balance of this book, preceded by a few preliminary observations about the method itself, its origins, characteristics and applicability to a study of all the sacraments.

Even in talking about method we cannot avoid using theological methods. We will examine a mystagogical approach to liturgy first by exploring its roots, development, decline and recovery (historical method), explaining how it differs from other approaches (comparative method), looking at the meaning of the word *mystagogy* and what might be gleaned from terminology (philological method), exploring the range and development of its content (systematic method), and looking at authoritative statements about it (juridical method). Certain limitations of the mystagogical method in its classical form will be noted (historical-critical method). Then we will determine how we might make use of the best features of the mystagogical approach, adapting it to a contemporary study of the sacraments (theological-liturgical method) in light of our stated goal.

DEVELOPMENT AND DECLINE OF MYSTAGOGY

Mystagogy is a word not totally foreign to our recent liturgical experience. It is one of those words that has come into more widespread use in Christian circles since the publication of the *Rite of Christian Initiation of Adults* in 1972. The rite specifies that there are four distinct periods through which the person aspiring to baptism must pass: inquiry, catechesis, enlightenment and mystagogy. In this instance the word refers to the final span of time in the larger initiation sequence. As we shall see, it also refers to the type of teaching given the newly baptized during this final phase of their initiation.

Mystagogy initially was a word as curious to most Christians as *scrutinies, election, neophytes* and the rest of the liturgical patois that we are still learning to pronounce and spell. Is it worth it to keep such language or should we abandon it in favor of something more recognizable? In this instance, maintaining the word helps us recover a rich tradition for which there is no exact synonym in our language. *Mystagogy* is a word borrowed from Greek; it means, literally, the "interpretation of mystery" or the "teaching of mystery." To keep *mystagogy* in our word-stock allows us more faithfully to draw on the rich tradition it captures and invites us to reflect on our experience of the liturgy in new yet ancient ways—ways perhaps more attuned to understanding and loving.

In its earliest Christian usage, mystagogy was a form of post-baptismal interpretation of mystery offered to those who had just joined the community. Neophytes first had to experience the water bath, the anointing and the meal in the course of the Easter Vigil. Then they were able to talk about it—but not before. Mystagogy was a form of instruction that attempted to plumb the depths of the rites that had been experienced for their spiritual import. First the experience, then the teaching—at least most of the time. There are some exceptions of mystagogical preaching and teaching that took place during the time of preparation for the initiation sacraments, but more often this teaching followed the celebration and built on the personal religious experience of its hearers. In all cases, its function was to help its hearers enter the world of the liturgy, walk around inside it, explore their experience of its sights and sounds and smells, savor its memory, ponder the meaning of what was said and done, and live out of its vision.

There is some evidence of mystagogical reflection in the New Testament. Paul speaks, for example, about baptism and eucharist in ways that suggest he is addressing those already baptized, drawing on their sacramental memory and imagination to break open deeper levels of their experience. He asks, for example, "How can we who died to sin go on living in it?" Then he recalls explicitly the community's death to sin in baptism:

> Do you not know that all of us who have been baptized into Christ Jesus were baptized into his death? Therefore we have been buried with him by baptism into death, so that, just as Christ was raised from the dead by the glory of the Father, so we too might walk in newness of life. (Romans 6:1–4)

Paul incorporates mystagogical references throughout his teaching. He speaks in metaphoric language of matters of life and death: tombs, burial, the baths of new life, becoming new creations, entering a new age as the old order passes away. He speaks in language that is evocative, drawing on the ritual memory of his hearers, inviting always deeper understanding of their experience and what it asks of them.

The fourth century witnessed the golden age of mystagogical preaching. The most famous of the mystagogues (those who interpreted the mysteries) were the teachers Cyril of Jerusalem, Ambrose of Milan, Theodore of Mopsuestia and John Chrysostom. Augustine, too, has left us some mystagogical reflections among his voluminous writings. The mystagogical homilies of these teachers, taken together, reveal certain characteristics common to this approach to mystery: the sacramental rites are inspiration and focus; the approach to the rites is sequential; the experience of the participants is valued; memory and imagination play a key role; the language employed is one of poetry rather than prose, of metaphor and image rather than didactic exposition. The presupposition upon which these homilies are shaped is that there is a cycle of celebration followed by reflection followed by celebration, which continues to yield new insights. Learning to love the liturgy, according to this pattern, is a lifelong process.

Here are a few examples of mystagogy that illustrate some of these characteristics. The rites — the movements and gestures, the symbols and the words — are invariably the point of departure for further reflection. In this regard, Theodore is the most obvious, regularly beginning his somewhat rambling reflections with a

short synopsis of the ritual elements he is going to treat. Often, though, the mystagogue begins by posing a question about one or other of the ritual moments: What
was it we did when we gathered in the predawn hour of the Vigil? What happened
as you approached the font? Why were you asked to turn toward the west? Do you
recall the anointing of your body from head to foot when you were enveloped in
the sweet-scented oil? After asking such questions, the mystagogue describes the
ritual and its significance, bringing to mind for the hearers the patterns of this or that
rite, the sequence, the participants and ministers and their various roles, and finally
and most importantly, the deeper symbolic meanings of each word and ritual action.
Cyril, for example, in his second baptismal homily, walks through the ceremony of
baptism, the stripping, the anointing from head to toe, the approach to the font, the
confession of faith that brings salvation, and then of baptism he makes a lovely and
memorable comment: "There is a time to be born and a time to die," he says, recall-
ing the words of Ecclesiastes, "but in your case the opposite is true. A single moment
achieves both ends, and your birth was simultaneous with your death."

The experience of participants is also always in the forefront. Cyril, for example, begins his first baptismal homily by stating that he had long desired to speak
about the mysteries of initiation, but he waited until the newly baptized had had a
personal experience of what he called the visual testimony of the rites. Experience,
he concluded, made his hearers more open to his teaching. Indeed, throughout the
mystagogical homilies that have come down to us from the master teachers, memory
and imagination are everywhere engaged. Sometimes a sermon begins: "Think what
you saw; think what you said," or "Keep what you said and did in mind." Sometimes
the teacher acknowledges that elements of the ritual may have been surprising or
disappointing. A first view of the font must have been something of a shock for
some of the baptized—a font so simple, perhaps prompting last-minute hesitancy
or skepticism about the efficacy of the rite. Similarly, the appearance of ordinary
everyday bread brought from home could be a cause of stumbling. The ordinari-
ness of the signs and symbols is acknowledged in the homilies, and it is recalled
how the initial disappointment is dispelled by wonder and awe as the ordinary
becomes a vehicle for the divine. Ambrose explicitly contrasts what one sees with
bodily eyes and what one sees with the eyes of the heart. Spiritual perception reveals
the inner meaning of the ordinary—of rite and accompanying word, since ritual

words also formed part of the reflection and reinterpretation which is mystagogia. The neophytes said: "I renounce you, Satan," notes Cyril in his first sermon, and what they really meant was: "I no longer fear your power." It is hard to imagine that reflection on experience of the rites remained deadly serious. One can only conjecture about the nervous laughter when the neophytes were invited to recall their initial reactions to the opening command in the baptistry: "Take off your clothes!"

Some lovely and memorable poetic language is sprinkled generously in the mystagogical teaching. Of the kiss of peace, Cyril declares, "This kiss joins souls together in search of complete forgiveness of one another. The kiss is a mark of the fusion of souls." John Chrysostom, the teacher known as "golden-tongued," lives up to his name in the lyricism of his reflections. His second baptismal homily contains a moving description of the community gathered in Christ: all distinctions of worldly importance or conspicuous wealth are gone; differences of class, rank and ability are set aside in the life of the spirit; a grateful heart is the only requirement of membership. Perhaps most famous of all the mystagogical reflections is the aphorism attributed to Augustine about the eucharist: "Be what you see; receive what you are. It is your own mystery."

The method employed by the mystagogues generally included the explanation of the rites through a fairly uncritical (by contemporary standards) exegesis of the scriptures. Ambrose explicitly notes that his instruction is filled with what he is able to gather from the scriptures to offer his hearers. For the fourth-century mystagogues, the scriptures served as a prism through which ritual meanings were refracted. Typological and allegorical interpretations abound. Ambrose, for example, gives three reasons why water is mixed with wine in the chalice, each of them derived from a scriptural source: the rock that gave water, the living water promised by Jesus and the water that flowed from Jesus' side at the piercing of the soldier's lance. This use of the scriptures popular among the ancients has been superseded in our day by more critical interpretations of the Bible. Similarly, typology and allegory, present in mystagogical catechesis and reaching incredible heights by the high middle ages, are no longer satisfying modes of interpretation. Wisely, contemporary mystagogy does not incorporate these particular characteristics of its beginnings.

Mystagogy died out in the experience of the community by the early medieval period, when the structures that had nurtured its development began to crumble. It was a form of teaching appropriate to all the baptized, but it was reserved in practice for recent adult converts. By the early middle ages the community's baptismal ministry had shifted from adults to infants. Fewer adult converts presented themselves for Christian initiation; at the same time, the offspring of Christians were being welcomed in increasing numbers. When infant baptism became the norm, mystagogy was no longer appropriate or useful.

MYSTAGOGY REVIVED

The *Rite of Christian Initiation of Adults* (RCIA) was introduced in 1972. The RCIA has redefined the way we think about sacraments in a variety of significant ways. Because of the RCIA we no longer view sacraments as discrete ritual moments in the life of individuals. The sacraments are first of all celebrations of the church. They are larger and longer processes that nurture personal religious experience in the midst of the community of faith. Sacraments bring that experience to public ritual expression when personal readiness for sacrament has been determined. The sacramental experience continues through a period of reflection on the journey and its celebration.

In reshaping our approach to adult initiation we have identified the fifty days following the Easter sacraments as a time for such reflection on the experience of baptism, confirmation and eucharist, and we have retrieved the name by which it was called in the patristic church: mystagogy.

Some characteristics of contemporary mystagogia are the following:

It is for all the baptized, not just the neophytes. • The description of the mystagogical period contained in the pastoral notes (RCIA, 244–51) suggests that this is a period for the community and the newly baptized to grow together, all of us deepening our grasp of the paschal mystery and making it part of our lives. For example, the event of mystagogy is envisioned in the rite for everyone at Sunday eucharist, and is called "a time for renewal of inspiration and outlook." It appears, then, even in the way that the ritual book describes this period, that mystagogy is a form of catechesis appropriate to all practicing believers. Moreover, communal reflection such as this is a healthy antidote to a privatized religion and a tendency on the part of North Americans to rugged individualism, especially when it comes to communicating deeply held religious insights and convictions. In pastoral practice, however, the teaching and other events of the mystagogical period generally are limited to the newly baptized, with the community at best willing observers.

Mystagogy is lifelong. • If, as stated above, mystagogy is for all believers, then it follows that it is a lifelong commitment to learning and deepening, knowing and understanding and loving. We are not invited to be spectators as our newest members "finish" their education. Just as the RCIA (#5) invites the community to renew its own conversion as the catechumens begin their journey of faith among us, so the period of mystagogy might serve as a reminder that all of us are called to this form of reflection. The bishops of the United States may have had this in mind when they determined in their National Statutes for the Catechumenate (NSC) that the program for the neophytes should extend until the anniversary of their initiation, with at least monthly assemblies of the neophytes for their deeper Christian formation and incorporation into the full life of the Christian community. (NSC, 24)

The community's sacramental life is the primary focus of mystagogy. • Through the proclamation of the word and the experience of the sacraments of baptism, confirmation and eucharist, the newly baptized are introduced into a fuller and more effective understanding of the mysteries. The pastoral notes are lyrical in describing what liturgical participation accomplishes in the neophyte: renewal in mind and heart, tasting more deeply the sweetness of God's word, receiving the fellowship of the Holy Spirit, and growing in the knowledge of the goodness of the Lord (RCIA, 245). All of this spirit and power derives from the personal experience of the sacraments, which only increases as it is lived, opening participants to an ever-deeper understanding of the death and rising of Jesus Christ, the community of believers, the faith we cherish and the world we long to transform in God's name.

The whole of the community's sacramental life is appropriate matter for mystagogical reflection. • In practice, mystagogy has been limited to baptism, confirmation and eucharist as experienced at the Easter Vigil; in addition, those who have come into full communion in the Catholic church at the Vigil also reflect on their new corporate identity. But why do we or should we limit ourselves to these three sacraments? Surely every sacrament is a celebration of the death and rising of

Jesus and our participation in that mystery. Surely every sacrament invites us to deepen our own conversion and to commit ourselves anew to a vision of God's reign. Paren-thetically, it is important to note that the period of mystagogy is the least developed part of the RCIA process. The extension of this process to other sacraments is dependent in part on a greater attention to the practice of mystagogy in the Easter season.

Personal experience is the other indispensable focus of mystagogy. • Thus, imagination and memory are critical to the mystagogical process. The key to mystagogical reflection is that it is subjective rather than objective; it is about *my* experience and *your* experience of an encounter with God through the sacramental celebration. The mystagogical task is to enable the newly baptized to reflect on their personal experience of celebration and what it triggered in their inner world, to move from a vague awareness of the mystery dimension of their lives to a greater conceptual and affective clarity, and to find a proper way to continue to allow experience and expression to inform one another. Only through a pooling of our experiences will we have anything even approaching a full sense of the presence and power of God active in those who believe. The rites are made up of a variety of symbolic languages that can be read with multiple meanings. We enrich one another immensely when we communicate about the way we have discovered meaning in the sacraments. Mystagogy is dialogical. It relates experience and symbol and it takes both utterly seriously.

In terms of identifying personal experience, the kinds of questions I asked those I interviewed may be instructive: What did we just say and do? What was a significant moment for you? Why? What feeling was evoked? What seemed especially important? What was your experience of God, of Christ, of the Spirit, of the community? What experience did *you* bring to the rite? Did you prepare in any special way? What kind of commitment did you make when you said Amen?

The language of mystagogy is more like poetry than prose. • It is not easy for us to talk about what is most precious. We can't talk about love, for example, until we actually fall in love, and then when we fall in love, we can't find adequate words to communicate the reality of our experience. We speak of profoundly moving experiences sometimes as "too deep for words." Discovering God and enacting our relationship with God and one another through the sacramental rites is like that sometimes. The words are more poetry than prose, half-sentences, images, metaphors — all of it part of the interpretation of the mysteries, which is what mystagogy is at its heart.

The most critical element for successful mystagogy is well-celebrated rites. • Excellent, care-full, well-planned and well-executed liturgy is first-level mystagogy. It was stated above that the liturgy is first theology, that is, that liturgy is the most immediate, most condensed statement of who we are and what we believe. Good liturgy is an absolute prerequisite to rich symbolic participation and contemplation. The strong warning of the American bishops must be heeded in this regard: Good liturgy nourishes faith; poor liturgy destroys it.

In describing mystagogy with these seven characteristics I have redefined and expanded this mode of theological reflection. Its usefulness and richness will be demonstrated in the following chapters. But before we turn to the sacraments there is one more important consideration. Mystagogical reflection presumes an ability to reflect on experience. For mystagogy to be successful, we need to be able to identify and talk about our experience. That demands that we know what our experience is, that we are in touch with our own inner world and attentive to what we are doing when we gather for prayer.

Chapter Two

Paying Attention

...with the eyes of your heart enlightened...
Ephesians 1:18

In the previous chapter, we adopted the language of mystagogical reflection to describe a new way of thinking about the liturgy and entering into its celebration. This chapter will suggest that *paying attention* is an apt way to describe the process by which understanding and engagement are realized.

"Pay attention!" is a command most of us heard regularly as children. That dictate continues into adulthood, through our school years, among friends, between spouses. Paying attention must not be easy or else we would have mastered the art long ago. It is an aptitude that is critical in the process of learning and the success of human communication. More importantly, it is a proficiency without which the realization of full, conscious and active participation in the liturgy is impossible.

Active Participation

Liturgical attention is of two kinds: attending to the liturgy as it unfolds and attending to the movements of our hearts before, during and after the celebration. Both kinds of attention are essential to what we have come to call *active participation*, a phrase drawn from the *Constitution on the Sacred Liturgy* as a shorthand summary of the goal of liturgical reform. In many efforts to implement the reform these past decades, there has been perhaps no other text more often employed and less often understood than the constitution's remarks about participation. They are worth citing:

> The church earnestly desires that all the faithful be led to that full, conscious, and active participation in liturgical celebrations called for by the very nature of the liturgy. Such participation by the Christian people as "a chosen race, a royal priesthood, a holy nation, God's own people" (1 Peter 2:9; see 2:4 – 5) is their right and duty by reason of their baptism. In the reform and promotion of the liturgy, this full and active participation by all the people is the aim to be considered before all else. For it is the primary and indispensable source from which the faithful are to derive the true Christian spirit and therefore pastors must zealously strive in all their pastoral work to achieve such participation by means of the necessary instruction. (#14)

Necessary instruction — in what? How is active participation fostered? Too often participation has been equated with externals. Too often it has been gauged by the size of the crowd, where people choose to sit, how warm and friendly are their greetings of peace, how enthusiastic the responses, how participatory the singing, how promptly volunteers come forward to fill the various ministries.

Active participation in the liturgy is primarily internal, no matter how much such external manifestations may be concrete indications of what is happening within. Active participation has to do with a kind of mindful engagement in the rites, an attending to the words and gestures, the symbols, the choreography, the space, the season. Without interior participation the rites are empty formalism.

Active participation, we are told in the liturgy constitution, is called for by the very nature of the liturgy. That should give us a clue, and perhaps even some sense of relief. In a mysterious and grace-filled way active participation is easier than it seems, for according to the very nature of the liturgy, it is first of all God's work. Active participation describes first what God does, and only then what we do.

Liturgy is God's action, God's initiative, God's gift. "Our desire to thank you," states the Weekdays IV preface, "is itself your gift. Our prayer of thanksgiving adds nothing to your greatness but makes us grow in your grace, through Jesus Christ, our Lord." Liturgy is God's participation in the life of the world and in the midst of this community. Liturgy is God's gift and God's work in us and among us. Liturgy is God's initiative, drawing us together with the whole of the human race and the whole of creation to form one body in Christ. Liturgy is the action of God inviting our participation in the perfect sacrifice of Christ, and transforming us in a single hymn of praise, surrender and thanksgiving. It requires our response.

How do we respond? We respond by paying attention.

Two kinds of attending are critical. The first is the more obvious. We need to be reflective about what we are doing at the liturgy. We need to pay attention to the many languages of our prayer—the words, the movements, the objects, even the languages of space and time. So first we need to attend to the experience of liturgical prayer as it unfolds. But we also need a second kind of attending, and that is to the experience we bring to liturgical prayer, the daily dyings and risings, which we join to the death and rising of Jesus. This second kind of attending in everyday life is what Karl Rahner described as the "liturgy of the world." We need to be mindful of the griefs and the joys of our daily lives, the longings, the half-met expectations, the dreams that are dying and being born in us, the angers and fears, the lethargy or the frenetic pace, for all of it—all of human experience, no exceptions—is who we are and what we bring to worship. The liturgy is a celebration of our experience, helping us to make sense of it, to purify it, to face the truth of it, to live through it and to surrender to God, who is disclosed in its depths.

We use the language of experience rather facilely of the liturgy and do not recognize the inherent difficulty of such claims. The problem with talking about the liturgy as reflecting and celebrating experience is that we have no real awareness of what our experience is. The liturgy may have the potential to celebrate experience, but too often we are not really aware of what is happening in our lives and thus the liturgy cannot speak to it either. It may well be the case that much of the alienation people experience toward the liturgy is rather a deep reflection of the alienation we experience from our deepest selves.

Obstacles and Longings

Liturgy, then, has a double demand: attention to itself and attention to ourselves so that the experience of each informs and illuminates the other. But there is great difficulty, in our culture and in this age, in meeting this double demand. Attention is in short supply. There are so many obstacles to paying attention. At least some suggest that paying attention is a lost art and that the conditions for the possibility of its recovery are not favorable.

Noise, for one thing, is everywhere. Urban noise has to be controlled by ordinances about acceptable decibel levels. Music fills the void on elevators, in offices and on "hold." It is irresistible — and generally mindless — to flip on the radio in the car, audio headphones in the woods, the stereo in the living room and the compact disc player in the office. These devices even come in waterproof varieties so they can accompany us to the shower. Not so long ago the *Wall Street Journal* ran a short article about the lost art of conversation: Apparently, no one is listening anymore. We hear barely twenty percent of a conversation, mostly distracted by formulating our next response, our clever *bon mot*.

Speed is another obstacle to paying attention. We read and try to implement *The Seven Habits of Highly Effective People* or the countless other self-help time management books like it, hoping for results, wanting to be efficient with the use of our precious time. Our calendars are called day *timers*, possibly because they track our velocity in the fast lane. We have learned to accomplish two and sometimes three things at the same time. We dine on the run, for example, and are able to read the paper, watch TV and talk on the phone simultaneously. A recent survey indicated that the one modern appliance people would not give up is the microwave oven, that ultimate labor-saving symbol of freedom and efficiency, especially for families on different schedules who individually and sequentially "nuke" what passes for dinner but is, in fact, only fast food.

Our lives are filled with gadgets. Our children's lives are glutted with toys and games of every kind, and so are our own, but we call them by other names. We want better and faster computers, more ROM, more RAM, and we are annoyed when booting up the system takes all of twenty seconds. We can keep our phone within easy reach, in the car, under a tree in the back yard, at the symphony, even in church! We call whatever comes through the mail slot "snail mail" because we are used to the instant communication of e-mail and faxes.

Our gadgets sometimes collide with one another in claiming our attention, and information spills across our consciousness with all the speed that our search engines and hot buttons and channel surfing can support. We are surrounded by things that are supposed to make our lives simpler, and we wonder why we continue to search for a greater degree of simplicity in these complicated times. One advertiser has even used that very desire — simplicity — to sell us cars. Simplify life, not by divesting ourselves of excess baggage but by acquiring yet more! Selling simplicity, it would seem, is the ultimate consumer fraud.

The desire for these material goods breeds covetousness. And covetousness breeds violence, and violence breeds fear and insecurity, and fear and insecurity breed more desire for things to assuage our desires — but not for long. It is a vicious cycle, and none of it is conducive to awareness or an undivided heart. Surrounded by noise, cluttered with things, hurrying through life "distracted by distraction from distraction," as T. S. Eliot described it. And gradually we become like the idols we have crafted by hand — gods of silver and gold, according to the psalmist:

. . . with mouths that are mute
and eyes that are blind,
with ears that are deaf
and noses that cannot smell.
Their hands cannot feel,
their feet cannot walk,
their throats are silent.
Their makers, their worshipers
will be just like them.
   (Psalm 115:5–8)

Others, to be sure, do not have a life cluttered with the latest gadgets. Indeed, they have few material goods, barely what is needed to survive. They struggle to make ends meet, work two and sometimes three jobs, their spirits brutalized by poverty, their life a daily survival. They sometimes find themselves prisoners in their own homes, especially after dark, and the noise and dirt of the streets seep into the cracks of their homes and their hearts. These are other kinds of obstacles, even more daunting, to contemplation.

On the one hand, then, are numerous obstacles to living attentively, numerous false idols claiming our spurious worship. But on the other is another longing for other kinds of values. There is a longing for more than mere survival. For beauty. For solitude. For living an uncluttered life. For freedom from poverty's bonds. For simplicity — if it is possible to rescue the word from the world of advertising — real simplicity and making do with less so that others have more. There is a new reverence for the earth, a new awareness of the fragility of our planet and all of created reality. There is a longing for relationships that have depth and stability. There are various movements that seem to be meeting other kinds of needs. Miscellaneous workshops attract people who want to cultivate a way of paying attention even if they cannot find words to name the longing they experience. Think of the numbers drawn to journaling and dream work, to spiritual direction and centering prayer. Self-awareness motivates personality-profile testing, such as the Enneagram and Myers-Briggs evaluation and analysis. Some look for a different kind of awareness in drugs, others in physical fitness and forms of self-discipline. Some search the Eastern religions for a new connection to reality and to mystery.

So many obstacles to paying attention, yet so much evidence of a longing for the wholeness toward which attention moves. Is it not at root a longing for God in the midst of the maelstrom of our individual lives and of the world around us? Is it not a restlessness we each experience until we rest in God? Is it not a deeply felt need for union with God?

What we are experiencing is the desire for God, the desire that is the beginning and the end of paying attention. The process also is known as *contemplation*.

Contemplation: A Pattern of Paying Attention

Contemplation is just another word for the art of paying attention—to God and to oneself in God. We can learn much for our task at hand, the task of sacramental awareness, by exploring contemplation, its etymology and its classical patterns, and then making application to liturgical participation.

At the outset, it seems important to address and to dispel the myth that contemplation is for religious specialists—ascetics, saints, mystics, religious professionals. Contemplation, on the contrary, is the most egalitarian of endeavors because it is essentially the art of loving, of which we are all capable, and the awareness of, and presence to, and union with that which is loved. Nor is contemplation usually accompanied by apparitions or other miraculous events. We are rightly suspicious of such claims.

The etymology of the word *contemplation* is interesting and instructive. It comes from the Latin word *templum*, a space in the dome of the sky or, more generally, a sacred space where the omens were read. *Templum* came to mean that place where appointed people read the insides of things. Gradually, as the word *contemplation* evolved, it meant looking at the insides of reality or reading reality from the inside out. There is a nice association of *templum* and *tempus* — suggesting, perhaps, that contemplation also has something to do with sacred time as well as space and awareness. It can take important nuances from all three. What is important is awareness: awareness, in time, of place and space, of presence and of The Presence. Union with God is key, a union achieved not by reasoning but by love, a union described by spiritual writers as free, penetrating, simple, a union that proceeds from love and leads to love. It is, in the end, a matter of the heart.

This may sound esoteric, but it is important to reiterate that everyone has a contemplative vocation. Contemplation has to do with a kind of inner consciousness; it is the *templum* or sacred space of our own hearts and on what we fix them; it is the cultivated awareness of what we treasure, for where our treasure is, there, too, is our heart (Matthew 6:21).

The spiritual masters through the ages have thought and taught a lot about contemplation. One common feature of their teaching is that contemplation is a progressive experience, not achieved overnight. Furthermore, it has some predictable patterns. Origen, for example, in the third century, spoke of the successive movement in contemplation from moral illumination through the stage of natural contemplation to the contemplation of God as its highest form. For Origen, illumination was the metaphor he found most helpful in describing contemplation. For others, for example, the Cappadocian Fathers of the fourth century, just the opposite was true. Among them contemplation moved through a progression from light to darkness, from the known to the unknown and unknowable, from distance to union with the absolute unknown who is God. Their metaphor was one of negation.

Some have found it helpful to speak of the path of contemplation as a spiritual ascent, a movement up a mountain or a ladder. A spiritual classic of the twelfth century used the ladder image in its title, *The Ladder of Monks*. Its author, Guigo II, suggested that contemplation was achieved through a series of acts: First there was attentive reading of the scriptures, then meditation to probe them for their hidden truth, then prayer that turned the heart from the scriptures to God, and finally contemplation as the transcending of self in union with God. Something like this progression is captured in a thirteenth-century bas-relief carving on the north portal of the cathedral of Chartres where a very beautiful *via contemplativa*, or way of contemplation, is depicted. A woman is portrayed in a series of postures: First, she recollects herself, then she opens her book, she reads, she meditates on what she has read, she teaches others, and finally she is in ecstasy — in union with God. Modern spiritual writers sometimes speak of contemplation as the last stage of prayer; one achieves it by moving from the habit of recited prayers to meditation, to affective prayer or the prayer of the heart.

The point of this too-brief excursion in Christian spirituality is to suggest that contemplation is usually understood as a progressive enlightenment, a progressive stripping of the self, or a progressive deepening of awareness — in each case, to shorten the distance between oneself and God. It may begin with rational thought or discursive reasoning, but it moves by means of a long, loving look or a savoring of mystery to a deep awareness of and union with the object of contemplation who is God. Contemplation is a gradual process and a lifelong search.

What does all this have to do with the liturgy? The liturgy rightly could be called "contemplation in common." In the liturgy we gradually cultivate an awareness of God at the very heart of the touches, sights, sounds and smells, of the word, gestures and objects, even of the faces of those with whom we have gathered. All of this is the stuff of our contemplation. A provocative passage in the United States bishops' document *Environment and Art in Catholic Worship* makes this point clear:

> The experience of mystery which liturgy offers is found in its God-conscious-ness and God-centeredness. This involves a certain beneficial tension with the demands of hospitality, requiring a manner and an environment which invite contemplation (seeing beyond the face of the person or the thing, a sense of the holy, the numinous, mystery). A simple and attractive beauty in everything that is used or done in the liturgy is the most effective invitation to this kind of experience. One should be able to sense something special (and nothing triv-ial) in everything that is seen and heard, touched and smelled, and tasted in liturgy. (#12)

All of it, then, has the capability of leading us progressively to meet and be embraced by the One whose mystery shines through all we do and say when we are joined together in praise. It does not happen overnight. It does not happen without some effort on our part, some asceticism, some practice, some desire and some great open-ness to the work of God's Spirit who alone enlightens the eyes of our hearts.

Liturgy and Contemplation

The classical contemplative tradition gives us a provocative language and an under-lying pattern for learning attentiveness. Borrowing from that tradition and adapting the language for our purposes, we can identify the stages of paying attention, especially as these stages apply to our liturgical participation. Specific obstacles to contemplative liturgy also will be noted. Then we shall proceed to an attentive exploration of the various sacraments.

Drawing on the wisdom of the ancients, it seems possible to describe the pro-gressive stages of liturgical contemplation as these: awareness, reflection, reception and transformation. For the sake of clarity it is necessary to speak of these stages discretely and sequentially, but often they are neither as easily isolated nor as pre-dictable as these individual categories would suggest. Let us look at each of these in turn, illustrating them with a simple example, that of posture at prayer. This is an element of the liturgy to which we may rarely allude, but which is a rich symbolic language of presence, attitude, relationship and promise.

AWARENESS

While paying attention describes the whole cyclic process of contemplative engage-ment in the liturgy, *awareness* is a good designation for the first phase of this process. Awareness suggests watchfulness. It is akin to the Buddhist practice of mindfulness. Awareness describes a sensory experience in which we open our whole being to the sights and sounds around us, and specifically to the liturgy as it unfolds. Too often, participation in the liturgy is reduced to a cerebral exercise. Awareness takes us to other levels of experience. We try to watch as if for the first time, to listen as if we had never before heard the words, to experience the gestures and the movements mindful of our bodies and their responses—willing or reluctant, agile or a bit creaky.

During the awareness phase we become alert, focused, even fascinated by what unfolds before us. Awareness draws our attention to the physical choreography of prayer: Our bodies speak a language all their own. We pause as we enter, dip our hand in water, sign a cross upon our head and heart and shoulders, taking in the whole of us, genuflect or bow our head and find a space in the assembly. Then we move through a series of postures: standing, sitting, kneeling, signing, kissing and processing. As we do so we may start to identify clusters of postures that repeat themselves in a ritual pattern. There is a different kind of awareness instilled in us by each posture. As this kind of awareness begins to surface, we are already moving to a more analytic phase. But there need be no haste. Becoming mindful, in itself, is of great worth. In many ways, it is enough. Over time, the rest will follow.

REFLECTION

Eventually, awareness may yield to *reflection*, the second phase of contemplative engagement. We let the many symbolic languages of the liturgy speak to us. We probe our experience. We have noticed already that sitting, kneeling and standing are fundamentally different postures, and that we feel differently and act differently as we assume them one after the other. Perhaps we notice that we are not simply moving from one posture to another but from one fundamental attitude before God to another, being called in turn to listen, to watch, to wait, to respond. What is behind this? We begin to question and to reflect more deeply.

Why do we move from one to another? Why do we sometimes sit and sometimes stand during the readings, or sometimes stand and sometimes kneel during the prayers? Why do we feel differently in one as opposed to another? Why do we sometimes make ourselves small as in kneeling, or let ourselves relax as in sitting, but at other times stand alert, watchful, ready for action? What does this have to do with what is happening as the liturgy itself unfolds? Perhaps we notice that the liturgy is a process of listening and responding, of attentiveness and action, of welcoming God's word and speaking a reply. Perhaps we become aware that what we do, we do together, and that the postures we assume in common join us in a communion with each other, for each posture places us in a different relationship with one another and with our God.

Perhaps we notice that we do different things with our bodies in different seasons of the year and we realize that we enact facets of the one mystery as we move through the yearly cycle of the mysteries of faith. We may, as we reflect on our body at prayer, become more attentive to ways in which the words of the liturgy speak of posture. Eucharistic Prayer II, for example, contains a rich image in its line: "We thank you for counting us worthy to stand in your presence and serve you," a metaphoric statement of readiness and willingness that expresses gratitude for a fundamental relationship of acceptance and mutuality and makes a claim upon us.

It is said that the one who sings prays twice; so, too, the one who moves with attention, for the prayer of the body is an eloquent language of praise and penitence, of listening and response, of adoration and recollection, of alertness and readiness. Reflection is the stage of considering and meditating on these realities as they present themselves to us. Reflection is the phase of our contemplative engagement that moves beneath the surface of things. It naturally leads to the phase of reception.

RECEPTION

Reception describes the shift that happens when we move from more rational reflection and meditation to the prayer of the heart. Reception describes the attitude of Mary of Nazareth, who pondered many things in her heart (Luke 2:19). We now more deliberately let our hearts be tutored by the Spirit. We move, for example, from feeling the sign of the cross we trace upon our bodies (awareness), to meditating on the meaning of the cross (reflection), to giving ourselves over to the power of the cross (reception), pondering it, treasuring it, letting its power touch and transform us. The attitude of reception allows our experience to work its way into our hearts.

Contemplative engagement doesn't happen all at once. It takes time. We dwell with our experience, we ponder our reflections. In the phase of reception we receive, we appreciate, we come to cherish what is revealed to us, and even more, we experience the action of the revealer. Reception refers not so much to the welcoming of insight but of the One who inspired it. Paying attention is not a preoccupation with the elements of the liturgy but a movement from that which is seen and heard and felt to the God who, through them, opens us more to divine encounter, using the whole of our experience to draw us closer if we are open, hospitable, receptive.

TRANSFORMATION

There is a remarkable verse in the Second Letter to the Corinthians that evokes the receptive phase of paying attention and its gradual, even imperceptible progression to the last phase, *transformation:*

> All of us, with unveiled faces, seeing the glory of the Lord as though reflected in a mirror, are being transformed into the same image from one degree of glory to another, for this comes from the Lord, the Spirit. (3:18)

27

That is what happens during the liturgy. All of it is God's initiative; all of it is the action of the Spirit. Yet we must respond, be receptive, unveil our minds and hearts — our faces — before God. Then transformation happens. It is inevitable. The celebration of the liturgy with attention will change us. Gradually our conscious-ness of what we are doing — and before whom — begins to work a transformation. As we become aware, reflective, receptive, we recognize that there are consequences to taking the liturgy seriously.

Amen is a simple word uttered — or muttered, for that matter — more times in the liturgy than we can count. It is deceptive, that little word, because it bears a large promise. "So be it," is its Hebrew meaning. And when we welcome the invita-tion and recognize that it must change us, and when we are willing to let this happen, we have come full circle. We are in some measure transformed from one degree of glory to another, transformed into the image of the One before whom and because of whom we gather. It happens in every sacramental encounter — if we let it.

Daily Life and Contemplation

Proficiency in paying attention during the liturgy does not happen without practice. We do not bring our experience of life to the liturgy unless we have claimed it through this practice. The stages of awareness, reflection, reception and transforma-tion are also important in becoming aware of the deeper movements of our heart in our daily experience. Paying attention is as important in life as it is in liturgy, and practice in one will inform and enrich the other. A parallel example of contemplation in daily life may help to clarify how contemplative living can enrich liturgical participation. Eucharist and reconciliation are particularly dependent on the atten-tiveness and attunement to experience of those who celebrate them. Again, it is important to remember that while it is convenient to discuss these stages sequen-tially, experience is not nearly as tidy or predictable.

AWARENESS

Let us take, as a simple example of daily living, a conversation that leaves us dis-quieted at some deep level. Perhaps a friend draws our attention to some pattern of behavior that we would prefer to leave unexamined. It is possible in daily life to throw up every obstacle at this moment — distraction, resentment and anger, denial.

It is possible to bury disquieting experiences. It is possible to slay the messenger. Thus ends awareness. On the other hand, it is possible to let these words touch us through deliberate awareness. Becoming mindful of interior movements is a first step in contemplation. As soon as we are willing to pause, become aware and focus on the feeling a conversation occasions in us, we move to the stage of reflection.

REFLECTION

During reflection we may replay the conversation and notice the agitation it causes. We probe our experience. We begin to question and to reflect more deeply. We start to recognize patterns of behavior which we may have buried deeply. We let the words of the conversation touch us again, and we test them for the truth they name. We consider what is behind our actions, why we do what we do, what the occasions are or who the companions are that trigger the behavior. We notice our own lack of freedom — perhaps becoming aware of anxiety that awareness and reflection might demand a change. At the same time we experience in some deep layer of our being a longing to be free of whatever it is that binds us. We experience an invitation to a new way of being. We have moved beneath the surface. We are ready for reception.

RECEPTION

Just as in liturgical awareness, so in life, reception describes that shift from more rational analysis and reflection to the actions of the heart. Once we become open to change, to a new invitation of grace, to the action of God's Spirit in our heart, to a discernment of God's choice for us in the here and now, then the attitude of openness allows a simple conversation to change our imagination and our behavior. In the phase of reception we live with the revelation that we have received and with the One who reveals it. Here, our paying attention moves us from the conversation to the feeling of disquiet, to the recognition of a new truth, to the Spirit of God alive in us and inviting us to a different future. Our experience of need draws us to God's own self. We are open to being transformed.

TRANSFORMATION

Attentiveness, openness, willingness — and then God's action takes over. Choice and changes follow when one is willing to pay attention and to live out of the fruits of contemplative engagement. Amen is a word every bit as important and sometimes every bit as difficult to utter in life as in the liturgy. We can do it because of God's action and God's grace.

Obstacles to Liturgical Engagement

As we return to the liturgy, note that everything in the following paragraphs about obstacles to liturgical engagement can apply equally to contemplative living. Some years ago in *Meditations before Mass* Romano Guardini identified three obstacles to contemplative engagement: habit, sentimentality and human nature.

Habit makes us suspicious of the kind of reflection on the liturgy begun above. It is so easy to become inured to the celebration. One definition of ritual is *repeated, patterned activity*. The very quality that makes it ritual makes it also predictable, and the predictable can make us indifferent. Ritual can easily become monotonous. A boring sameness sets in, inducing liturgical torpor. Attentiveness is next to impossible in a state of enervation.

Similarly, sentimentality can undermine contemplative engagement, for we are paying attention to the wrong things. Sentimentality, in Guardini's categories, is a desire to be moved, to get something out of it, to feel good or to feel bad — but certainly to feel! Sometimes? Yes, of course. Always? Hardly. It is not possible, either in life or in liturgy, to be moved consistently by our experience.

Human nature is another enemy of contemplative engagement. As suggested earlier, the reformed liturgy has placed enormous expectations on those who preside. We may not like their style or their mannerisms, their predictable homiletic patterns or their proclamation of the prayers. Or we may find ourselves amid an indifferent congregation, which gradually saps our sensibilities. Human nature drags us down. Attentiveness is trapped in personalities and moods.

To Guardini's three obstacles to liturgical engagement we can add two more: lack of silence and the hoarding of leisure. Lack of silence refers to that mode of liturgical prayer in which we barely pause between elements of the celebration. Rather, we move with haste from one posture to another, one prayer to another, one rite to another. We are invited to call to mind our sins, but then, with not a breath in between, the litany or the confession of sins is begun. Let us pray, we hear, but the assembly is allowed no time to pray; we move immediately to the collect, the prayer that was meant to collect the prayers of those assembled and bring them to a fitting conclusion. Yet there is an essential relationship between silence and speech. The many languages of the liturgy, spoken in word or ritual action, will be far more powerful and achieve their full effect if they emerge out of silence and lead to silence. We need a careful balance between speech and silence, action and stillness. The pause allows for contemplative engagement; a frenetic pace of liturgy prohibits it. And the quality of silence is more important than its duration. A deep, momentary silence is more powerful than a longer fidgety and fretful silence.

The hoarding of leisure is first cousin to the loss of silence. The *Constitution on the Sacred Liturgy* has spoken in glowing terms of the Lord's day as the original feast day. It offers us a lovely theology of Sunday, but for many of us this seems totally out of touch with the contemporary experience of time and especially of "weekend." There is little sense of sacred time. We often experience the weekend as "my time" as opposed to "work time." The weekend belongs to me, we assert, and I will dictate how I will spend my time. Spending time, in fact, is a good metaphor for the increasingly miserly way we dole out minutes for the celebration of liturgy: Don't go over an hour! Don't insert an extra rite, for example, the rite to welcome candidates and catechumens, without warning us so we can make a decision about how welcoming we are willing to be. Many choose the Saturday evening celebration because Sunday morning is really my time. Many parishes are adding Masses on Christmas Eve for those who resist "breaking up Christmas Day." Yet contemplative engagement demands some stillness and a sense of leisure. Until we can slow our pace and willingly spend time at liturgy, we will find contemplative engagement next to impossible.

Amen

In these reflections, we have been probing how to understand and love the liturgy more, to participate more thoughtfully in its celebration and to embrace the commitments we make to a way of life and a vision of the reign of God each time we say Amen. Contemplative engagement seems to offer a way to begin the process of understanding, loving, participating and embracing. Contemplative engagement invites a way of seeing and hearing, of listening and loving. It helps us engage in liturgy as if for the first time and from the inside out. It helps us experience, however fleetingly, a new wonder and awe in God's presence.

Does all this sound romantic? Is it an example of the desire for feeling, the obstacle of sentimentality as named by Guardini? I do not think so. Contemplative engagement does not rely on feeling alone. It is a process that moves from sense to intellect to heart to feet — yes, feet. Transformation inevitably is translated into action. Liturgy, attentively celebrated, leads to mission and to more faithful and truthful discipleship. The mission of the perfect disciple whom we follow led to the cross. Not a very romantic end.

Does this process sound unrealistic? Impossible? What, we must ask ourselves, is the alternative? To continue with the all too often lifeless patterns of prayer we tolerate Sunday after Sunday? To allow the malaise that has sometimes made captive the Catholic sacramental imagination to continue to sap our energies? Is not a new mystagogical reflection supported by real contemplative engagement at least a possible hope for the future of the church's sacramental life?

Before concluding these reflections, a caveat must be offered. None of us lives on that high plane where contemplation is always the order of the day. We are, in liturgy and in life itself, sometimes attentive and sometimes engaged. We have moments of insight, moments of receptivity, moments of conversion and transformation. These moments break into ordinary time with extraordinary grace.

One of the many benefits of being members of the Body of Christ is that we can lean on one another, trusting that the engagement and transformation that happen in our sacramental life happen over time, that the Spirit moves within us and among us and that this work of a lifetime plays itself out in the midst of the whole body supporting and sustaining its members on the journey.

One of the beauties of the church's liturgical life is that it is a seemingly endless opportunity to become engaged, to pay attention, to be drawn into the life of prayer and thus, ultimately, into the life of God. There is no complex of rites more richly symbolic than that which goes under the umbrella of Christian initiation. We will begin our mystagogical reflections with the initiation sacraments.

Chapter Three

Christian Initiation
of Adults

How great the sign of God's love for us, Jesus Christ our Lord
promised before all time began, revealed in these last days.
He lived and suffered and died for us, but the Spirit raised him to life.
People everywhere have heard his message and placed their faith in him.
RCIA, 596; see 1 Timothy 3:16

PRELUDE

It may seem a bit odd to start this exploration of the sacraments with a relative new-comer in the sacramental treasury of the church, at least in the form in use today. Why not begin, as does the sacramental life for most Christians, with infant baptism? The Christian initiation of adults has been chosen to launch these reflections for two reasons.

First, most liturgical scholars would agree that the new *Rite of Christian Initiation of Adults* (RCIA) has, in a variety of ways, redefined the way each of the sacraments may be conceptualized. Thus adult initiation provides a model for the exploration and interpretation of every other sacrament. This complex of initiation rites conceives of entry into the Christian community as a process that occurs over a substantial span of time of no fixed duration, and it takes place visibly, in the midst of the community. Baptism is conceptually redefined by the RCIA, its emphasis shifting from the washing away of original sin to incorporation into Christ and entrance into the community bearing his name. In the process of adult initiation, human experience is taken seriously: the experience of coming to faith, of needing the ministry of others, of finding consolation and challenge in the rituals that mark various movements in this larger journey of conversion. In other words, the RCIA publicly celebrates the process of conversion lived out in the community and marked by significant rites along the way. Finally, the RCIA envisions a period of post-sacramental pastoral and liturgical care. Once one has experienced the rites of initiation at font and table during the Easter Vigil, the sacramental experience continues to be nurtured in a formal way throughout the Easter season and even, according to the *National Statutes for the Catechumenate in the United States* (NSC), for a full year after the celebration of the sacraments of initiation. Thus a mystagogical, cyclic rhythm of celebration-reflection-celebration is envisioned as a constant feature of parochial life (NSC, 24).

We rarely have thought of sacraments other than initiation in such terms, but all of this is true, *mutatis mutandis*, of each of them. Each sacrament is a public, ritual celebration of a personal, internal experience. Each sacrament celebrates an experience of conversion — whether of sorrow for sin, need for healing in the face of grave illness, self-donation to another in love, desire to dedicate one's life to God in service to the community, and so on. Each sacrament begins with and in human experience. But before we are prepared for sacramental celebration, that initial experience must become conscious, deliberate, purified and readied for public expression. Otherwise, the poignant line from T. S. Eliot will be true of us, too: "We had the experience but missed the meaning." It is all too easy to celebrate sacraments prematurely.

First stirrings of love for another, initial glimmerings of vocation, incipient sorrow over ruptured relationships . . . these nascent experiences must come to some maturity prior to sacramental celebration. Sacraments take time, and they each invite us to a process of conversion before their celebration. That is what readiness for sacraments involves. Discerning sacramental readiness is not a juridical measure; even less is it a punitive measure. Readiness implies a genuine reverence for the unique relationship of each of us with God. Readiness is a question of the maturity of one's conversion. Normally it is a process that takes time.

The second presupposition, in beginning these reflections on sacraments with the Rite of Christian Initiation of Adults, is that the RCIA redefines the way the whole of the Christian life is conceived, namely, as a never-ending journey of conversion. The RCIA process is not just a barometer of change among those candidates and catechumens who are so publicly transformed before our eyes. The introduction to the RCIA states that this gradual process of initiation is an opportunity for the whole community to join the candidates and catechumens in reflecting on the meaning of the paschal mystery — the redemptive power of Jesus' life, death and resurrection — as that core reality touches and transforms all of our lives.

The RCIA introduction also states that because of the presence of seekers in our midst we are literally face to face with the need to renew our own conversion (RCIA, 4). The company of catechumens in our communities is a stunning reminder that conversion is not a once-for-all-time event. Rather, conversion is that experience of putting on Christ over a lifetime, appropriating his vision and values, thinking and feeling with him, recognizing his pierced heart in the pierced heart of humanity — in a word, transformation. If we pay attention to the dynamic of grace operating in the lives of the candidates and catechumens who stand before us week after week, our own lives are mirrored back to us, God's word may be heard in new ways and their journey into God becomes our own. It is a question of paying attention.

Those who become more closely involved with inquirers and catechumens regularly find their own world turned upside down. The narrative of one sponsor illustrates what can happen:

I was the sponsor (and later godparent) to a wonderfully vibrant, intelligent young woman who was a student at the University of Chicago. Our initial meetings quickly grew into wide-ranging conversations about scripture, ethics, doctrine, current events, history, even bread-making. I needed to run pretty fast at times to keep up. I had expected that watching and listening to her process of conversion would be interesting and absorbing. What I did not expect was the effect it had on me. I found that being a sponsor uncovered my own middle-age hunger for spiritual enrichment. It challenged me to re-examine, question and ultimately recommit myself as an adult to the beliefs that are at the core of my being. It was very awkward at first to get over some shyness in speaking deeply about God and matters of the soul. But once over that hurdle, I found many kindred spirits in the other sponsors, catechumens and the other team members. The experience still reverberates. I probably have more questions now than I did a year ago. But being a sponsor has opened up avenues of further growth and study, brought new friendships and immeasurably enriched my appreciation of my faith. When I signed on I knew I was committing myself to her conversion. What I never anticipated was the challenge her journey posed to my own.

Sponsors, by necessity, pay attention. Yet this same experience of being challenged and changed by the presence of others embarking on their public pilgrimage could totally renew the church. It requires only our contemplative engagement. It requires only openness on the part of the community and perhaps some encouragement on the part of parochial leadership to help us learn to pay attention to the sacramental experiences of one another. And when we do pay close attention, we will learn to draw the parallels and make the connections between the conversion processes of the catechumens and candidates, the penitents, the gravely ill, the engaged couple, the newly professed and the recently ordained, and the struggles and hungers and longings that fill each of our hearts.

Until recently we have not thought much about conversion as a lifelong reality. Before the publication and implementation of the RCIA, conversion was what happened after someone received instructions. One converted from unbelief to belief, or from one religion to another. New members were referred to as "converts," suggesting that their conversion, now marked and proclaimed by the church definitively in baptism, was complete, finished. But not so any longer, or rather, if candidates and catechumens are "converts," so too should all in the community be called "converts" because all are engaged in the process of realizing that reality to which each member has been called — an ever-deepening relationship with God.

The RCIA provides a framework for the discovery and deepening of religious experience. It allows, even invites, each of us to become more conscious of each new invitation of grace. For just as our newest members have become more conscious, deliberate, purified and readied for their public celebration, so, too, that same dynamic is possible for every person. That is why we have an annual retreat called Lent, not a time of narcissistic mortification nor a time of self-adulation for our own goodness and generosity, but a span of the year when we live in the tension between dying and birth and try to learn the difference. Lent leads inexorably to the Vigil, enlightening, purifying and preparing us like athletes in training. That is why all of us renew baptismal commitments at the Easter Vigil. And that is what every eucharist celebrates, a mystery of grace to which we return again and again. The holy life is like a spiral. It plays itself out over time, yet always deeper. Just when we come to terms with one invitation to new and deeper life, one invitation to obey the Spirit more generously in the daily details of our lives, along comes another, asking more, yet offering deeper relationship with God through Christ and in the power of the Holy Spirit.

There is an enigmatic passage in the Book of Revelation that refers to the white stone on which is written "the new name that no one knows except the one who receives it" (2:17). The name on the stone is a perfect metaphor for the mysterious relationship God forges with each one, and for the grace-filled person God invites us to become. Deciphering and then assuming the identity of that name on the stone is the work of a lifetime.

The RCIA, then, presents a pattern that may be applied to all the sacraments, and it presents a mirror of the Christian life. In both instances, the process of conversion is critical. A brief reflection on the classical patterns of conversion will provide the particular framework we shall apply then to each sacrament.

Conversion

Few concepts in contemporary spirituality have attracted more attention than conversion. The basic meaning of conversion, elements or features typically associated with it and some of the classic patterns it assumes are the topic of a growing body of literature. Similarly, lives of individuals who exemplify the dynamics of conversion are regularly the subject of biographies, and their writings are frequently collected in anthologies.

Conversion has been a feature of the holy life from ancient times, and its meaning is illumined in Old and New Testament passages as an experience of turning, return, reversal, restoration and change of one's orientation. In the scriptures, particularly in the New Testament, conversion or *metanoia* includes an internal process and the inevitable and radical change in one's existence and way of life that are its external effects.

It is possible, thanks to the insight of Bernard Lonergan, to distinguish several levels of the phenomenon of conversion: the intellectual, the moral and the religious. The person in the process of conversion begins to apprehend differently, value differently and relate differently because the person *is* different. The words of the Second Letter to the Corinthians are apt: "If anyone is in Christ, there is a new creation; everything old has passed away; see, everything has become new!" (5:17) As a person engages in the process of conversion, everything changes, both in one's interior experience and in one's way of being in the world. The metaphor of journey or pilgrimage communicates that conversion is a lifelong striving for holiness in the midst of others. Conversion plays out at the levels of intellect and affection, it implies particular ethical choices, and it issues in a commitment to mission, broadly conceived — to living no longer for oneself.

PATTERNS OF CONVERSION

What are the classic patterns of conversion? What starts any one of us on an inner journey? What makes any of us sensitive to the inner movements in our hearts and to God's longing for our happiness? Generally, we do not identify these first movements as conversion. Initially, at least, we do not name them anything at all. The experience of the journey into God is begun often without fanfare. We are in the midst of our daily lives with their multiplicity of commitments and pressures. We move from thing to thing, responding to the needs of our family and friends, keeping up with the demands of our profession, eking out a bit of leisure as possible and mostly just living as best we can from day to day, relatively content with our lot. We live our lives, for the most part, in ordinary time.

Then our world starts to change, but barely perceptibly. Conversion, despite some classic hagiography to the contrary, is rarely instantaneous or dramatic, and it is hardly ever convenient. Sometimes the first stirrings of conversion surface in our consciousness as a vague awareness that something is missing or something is wrong or something just does not make sense. It can be a vague feeling of dissatisfaction or restlessness, of being bogged down, of being unsettled.

Then something happens to break into our awareness, to precipitate a crisis of meaning for us, not just at mid-life but at any time at all. Sometimes we are made to examine the meaning and direction of our existence because of another person who has come into our lives, a spouse, a friend, a colleague at work — someone whose vision and values seem to have a depth or a meaning that we wish we, too, could possess. Sometimes the conversion journey starts with a word that we hear, a word of hope or forgiveness. Or perhaps it is a word of challenge to us that, unlike other potentially disturbing words, we are unable to brush off. Something starts to niggle away at us. Our vague restlessness and dissatisfaction become more acute.

Major life moments, of course, are often the occasion for some soul movement. The birth of a child, for example, stirs up a myriad of feelings that leave us vulnerable to the action of God. Falling in love can precipitate a conversion crossroads. Joy, gratitude, a sense of peace, self-worth, knowing we are loved unconditionally — all of it can be the start of a movement toward God. So, too, a lingering or a sudden death of one we love. A new job or its loss, a move from one place to another, some public recognition, the completion of a project, a false accusation, the unexpected gratitude of another, a struggle with addiction, a grudge we finally admit is eating away at our hearts — the possibilities of some new in-breaking experience of God are endless.

Whatever it is — a large or small happening, a person, word or event that precipitates a crisis of meaning and brings a vague uneasiness to conscious awareness — such a critical incident is a turning point. "Turning" appears to be the heart of conversion. Sometimes turning means a movement away from sin and the company of sinners, from evil of every kind, from idols of one's own creation, and turning to the living God, desiring a change of heart, choosing life and embracing friendship with God. Sometimes the turning of conversion involves a choice between two relative goods as one tries to discern God's desires in the here and now.

Jesus' life provides a perfect model. Others discovered in his life and ministry a continuous invitation to repentance, to friendship — even intimacy — with God and to the acceptance of whatever changes such friendship might entail. In the gospels, acceptance of Jesus' invitation invariably leads to faith and to a life of discipleship. Implied in many encounters is a turning or a return to relationship, together with embracing its inevitable consequences — the latter described quite starkly as, for example, "leaving everything" or "taking up one's cross" or "falling into the ground and dying" for the sake of new life.

Conversion is a matter of life and death. Often, the inevitable consequences of one's decisions are experienced as a form of death, a giving up of something, a letting go, a surrender, a dying for the sake of new life. Often such decisions are very costly; rarely are they made either quickly or lightly. That is why it is helpful to recognize that the stages of death and dying identified by Elisabeth Kübler-Ross apply equally well to these inner deaths. Some or all of the stages of denial, anger, bargaining, depression and acceptance are routinely part of the journey one must negotiate in choosing to live a life faithful to God's invitations.

A typical pattern of conversion, then, includes hearing the voice of God or a mediated word of life, initial openness and acceptance, some active personal engagement in the process of transformation and the living out of that decision over a lifetime of gradual transformation. The shorthand for this process is vague dissatisfaction, a critical incident, choice — and, if we accept the grace of the moment, this choice involves changes and new beginnings. The lifetime journey that conversion launches is nothing less than transformation into the image of the divine as shown to us in Jesus. It involves an ever-deepening friendship with God and disentangling oneself from everything that is not of God in one's life. It is that simple!

Conversion is thus a process that entails a gradual reorientation of one's mind and heart. As lifelong pilgrimage, conversion has a few critical moments of choice, a few radical decisions that must be made in negotiating crossroads. For the most part, however, there is a dailyness about the journey, daily dying and rising in the ordinary events, a daily need for faithful living that is undramatic but no less demanding over a lifetime of small choices. As we shall see, the sacramental life of the church celebrates both the dramatic and critical moments of choice and the dailyness of the journey.

Method of Examining the Sacraments

This dynamic of conversion will dictate, in large part, the way we shall proceed as we examine each of the sacraments. Drawing on the memories and insights of the interviewees, we will examine the initial experience that impels one on a sacramental journey. We will look at the conversion involved in the process. We shall explore what readiness for sacrament might mean in each instance and what facet of Jesus' life, death and rising is played out in the lives of those who join themselves to him in sacramental life. Finally, immediate preparation for the sacraments will be noted, especially where the church has provided a variety of ritual and other forms of preparation.

Once these dynamics are laid out, we shall turn to the ritual structure of the sacrament in question. First we shall look at its overall structure and then comment on the pattern undergirding each of our celebrations, a pattern of listening and response. A final reflection, after looking at the liturgical celebration of the sacraments, is the Amen question: What is it, in and through this sacrament, to which we commit ourselves? What is it to which we say "Amen"? Thus, experience, celebration and commitment form the general outline for this and each of the following chapters.

Experience: Coming to Faith

The Rite of Acceptance into the Order of Catechumens marks the formal beginning of an adult's journey toward the Easter sacraments of initiation. But that journey actually begins weeks, months, even years earlier. In the course of the Rite of Acceptance there is a deceptively simple question posed by the celebrant. After welcoming those who have presented themselves, he inquires about their motives. "Why have you come?" he might ask, or "What do you desire?" or "What do you ask of God's church?" Often the answers given are equally simple and straightforward: "Relationship with Jesus." "Faith." "Community." "Salvation." Whatever the answer, it is an inadequate and fragile shorthand for a world of experience and desire, of fear and hope. How does one give a simple answer to an experience that has been growing over time, sometimes despite one's best efforts to stifle God's invitation?

INITIAL ATTRACTION

The experience of each one coming to faith is unique, but it is possible to discern some common patterns.

Relationships. • Many adults begin to consider joining the Catholic Christian community because they are married or engaged to a Catholic. It takes time for some. They may start to attend Catholic liturgy, but only with the intention of being a companion to their spouse or betrothed: "Don't think I'm going to change!" they say — and they mean it, at least for a while. Then the example of their partner's obvious love for the faith, or the mysterious yet fascinating ceremonies that they have never seen before, or the desire that their children have a common tradition and the example of believing parents takes hold and their journey begins.

For others, too, it is example, perhaps a friend or a member of the family who becomes a Catholic and is eager to talk about the experience. First there is interest, a certain amount of curiosity, the possibility of participating in Catholic life or worship anonymously with another. Some have gone on retreats with their Catholic friends and are attracted by the experience and the rich tradition of spirituality, conversation about religious and spiritual pursuits, or a perception that the Catholics they are with have a certain serenity and confidence about matters of faith. Some have been given books, articles or tapes, and "a light goes on." In these instances, the possibility of sharing that same faith begins to have some appeal.

Emptiness. • The experience of emptiness for some becomes the compelling reason to search for religious meaning. Some speak of searching for purpose, others of looking for something more in life — a spirituality, a form of commitment, a special relationship with God or Jesus. A woman reported being asked one day by her daughter: "Mommy, what are we?" and she didn't have an answer. That made her start looking for a tradition where they would feel at home and have an identity. A man said simply: "I just did not want to be a person without a church any more. I didn't like the feeling."

Community. • Experience of community is a powerful attraction for many. An individual and quasi-private spiritual quest to know Jesus broadens in time to a need to belong to the community of Jesus' disciples. Most inquirers are genuinely overcome by the support they experience from Catholic friends and strangers alike when they begin their initiation journey. "The connections are endless," one reported, "and everywhere I would go there seemed to be people who knew I was going to be baptized and who promised to pray for me."

For many the strong and tender love of God was experienced tangibly, in the here and now, by flesh and blood believers. "In this community I have found such a sense of acceptance and warmth and a place of true healing," one reported; another said: "Joining the church? It's all about community for me." One woman who had emigrated from China some years earlier spoke of the family values of the culture she left behind and which she had not found in the United States — had not found, that is, until she could say of the church: "There is family here." And one young man summed up his experience: "It's a 'we' thing."

Sacramental life. • For some, the attraction is the church's sacramental life. Growing up without religious ritual or in a church in which formal, structured liturgy is rare, some find the Catholic ceremonial to be profoundly powerful and appealing, particularly the centrality of the eucharist. As one reported: "I felt like I could do without the music, I could do without the homily, I could do without a lot of things, but eucharist was the one thing I didn't think I could do without." Others noted the experience of mystery and transcendence that Catholic liturgy inspired in them.

Ritualizing transformation. • Some of those who present themselves to the church have already negotiated an experience of conversion — of being rescued and set free. There are some who are in recovery from alcoholism or drugs or other forms of addiction. They have experienced redemption, acceptance and love, and they feel compelled to do something public to ritualize their new world. They are drawn to a community where they can give deeper meaning to the change that is taking place within them. The journey through the various periods and stages on the way to initiation is, in part, a symbolic reenactment of that other transformation they now know and name as God's grace.

Urgency • For some there is a sense of urgency. Once they have come to some decision to explore the stirrings within their hearts they need to act. But for many others, approaching the church takes a long time. Some choose to be "closet" Catholics for years and report that their public step comes after a long and arduous journey, a struggle with the meaning of commitment and a period of fence-straddling that has worn them out. Finally, God wins. "I knew finally that this was exactly the right time for me spiritually and that it was going to be a good process. Having said that, I'm glad that I hesitated a little bit and thought about it more, because it meant a lot more to me than rushing in and not giving it my all." Or, as another reported: "Several life-changing experiences created within me a loud and persistent calling that I found ultimately irresistible."

Hesitation. • There is, however, despite the compelling grace of God, much that makes people hesitate. Some have old histories they need to let go or preconceptions about the church they must slowly relinquish. Some have family or friends who will find their entry into the Catholic community a source of deep pain or anger, or who will experience it as outright rejection. Some grapple with the teachings of the church and struggle to figure out how to live with integrity within the Catholic Christian dogmatic and disciplinary world. For some there is a very specific stumbling block — the church's treatment of women, for example — with which they need to come to terms. Often they are able to do so by finding an "equally ambivalent" member of the church to act as their sponsor and to help them interpret the church's teaching and live it with integrity. Some men and women who begin the process of inquiry are plagued by self-doubt, a sense of unworthiness, an unwillingness to become public about their intentions. Some are afraid they cannot live up to the community's expectations.

ACCEPTANCE

All of this experience is brought to the Rite of Acceptance into the Order of Catechumens and gathered up in a single word or phrase in response to the celebrant's inquiry about motive. All of this experience and ultimately the choice it entails is enacted ritually as inquirers cross the threshold of the church, let their names be known and state their intentions. All of this experience will be celebrated, deepened and purified over the next weeks and months. Having crossed the threshold of the church both physically and symbolically, inquirers — now known as catechumens — continue to follow the way of Christ inside the household of the faith.

The most powerful experience of the Rite of Acceptance into the Order of Catechumens, as reported nearly universally by participants, is not that they have now "gone public" about God's action in their lives, nor is it crossing the threshold into the church and speaking a public word about why they are there. It is what happens next, the tracing of the cross on each of the candidates. First a cross is signed on their foreheads, "the sign of your new way of life," and then, accompanied by prayer and acclamation, a cross is traced on the catechumen's ears, eyes, lips, heart, shoulders, hands and feet. The community prays with them that as their whole being is opened to the cross of Christ and the power of his life, death and resurrection, that these inquirers may hear God's voice, see the glory of God, respond to the word of God, invite Christ to dwell in them by faith, bear Christ's gentle yoke, make Christ known in the work of their hands and always walk in Christ's way.

Thus begins the public and formal preparation of the catechumens and candidates for initiation. They experience the presence and power of God in a tangible way with the signing. They experience the community in the person of catechists and sponsors who stand with them at the Rite of Acceptance and continue beside them through the various stages of their catechumenate. They have traveled a long road. The community prays that they will press onward "until they come to share fully in our way of life."

CATECHUMENATE

The catechumenate has begun. During their period of inquiry their faith had been awakened. Now the faith of catechumens is formed and deepened through prayer, reading and reflection on the word of God, appropriation of the tradition and participation in the community's life. What was formerly called "instruction" in "convert classes" has been given a broader focus. While presenting Catholic teaching, the focus of instruction is more than the handing over of a body of doctrine. Its goal is to "enlighten faith, direct the heart toward God, foster participation in the liturgy, inspire apostolic activity, and nurture a life completely in accord with the spirit of Christ" (RCIA, 78). It is less a question of mastering material than of meeting and forming a relationship with Jesus Christ. The material is not insignificant, but it must be seen as part of a broader and deeper process.

Throughout the catechumenate, rituals help the catechumens name what is happening to them. There are blessings and prayers that have a twofold purpose: helping these seekers identify and praise God for all the good that is building in them on the one hand, and on the other, helping them become free of whatever remains that is sinful and not of God in their lives. We call these prayers "exorcisms," and we do so deliberately. There is evil within us and all around us. Ritual gives us permission to tell the truth about our world and our own lives and to beg God's help in rendering us free.

The catechumenate also includes sessions in which old, perhaps skewed, attitudes to things Catholic can be identified, demythologized and let go. There are opportunities to meet other members of the community, to explore the church building, to consider participation in its concrete service to the poor. There is ample time to investigate the doubts that remain and the hopes that have not been realized. The catechumens each take whatever time is needed, moving at their own pace on the journey. A stunning line of the RCIA text acknowledges that everything depends on the grace of God and "nothing can be determined a priori" when one recognizes that conversion is ultimately God's action and God's gift (#76).

Throughout the catechumenal period, the community blesses and dismisses catechumens after the liturgy of the word that they might go apart to reflect more deeply on God's word. At the time of each dismissal the community pledges its support and prayers, and tells these men and women that we look forward to the day when they will join us in communion at the table. One catechumen mentioned that those words of anticipation formed a deeper hunger in her. They kept her going when she started to wonder and waver.

The multifaceted nature of "coming to faith," the conversion nurtured during the catechumenate, is summarized in the rite as it delineates the specific aims of the spiritual formation and guidance of the catechumenal period. Catechumens are formed in the Christian life in several ways: by instilling in them, through suitable teaching, a profound sense of the mystery of salvation in which they desire to participate; by giving them familiarity with the Christian way of life and inspiring a progressive change of outlook and conduct; by gradually introducing them to the community's liturgical heritage of rites and prayers; and by enjoining them to work actively with others in continuing Christ's saving mission (#75). The community, through its pastoral staff and the catechumens' sponsors, determines when individuals are ready for the sacraments of initiation by a process of discernment with each catechumen, using these four specific areas as a framework for coming to a decision. The question is not whether the catechumens are finished, perfectly converted products, but whether they give evidence that they have committed themselves to the process: a lifelong journey of faith formation in the context of the community, its worship and its mission.

ELECTION

Once a mutual discernment has determined that catechumens are ready for full initiation in the church, their names are enrolled for initiation in a liturgy called the Rite of Election, the second major threshold rite. This liturgy, generally celebrated at the beginning of Lent under the presidency of the local bishop or his representative, makes an important ecclesial statement. The presence and ministry of the bishop reminds the catechumens that they are joining the church universal, not simply a local parish, and thus it is the church that ratifies the catechumens' readiness for initiation. For the remainder of their formation catechumens are called "the elect," not because we have voted for them but because we see in them God's election — God's choice. Especially when the number of people preparing for initiation in a particular parish is small, the cathedral celebration is an amazing experience for the elect as they see sometimes hundreds of people called to the Easter sacraments.

PURIFICATION AND ENLIGHTENMENT

Corresponding with Lent, a final and special time of preparation takes place. This is called the period of "purification" or "enlightenment." Both titles capture the thrust of this final intensified preparation for incorporation into the church. Catechesis gives way to the process of assimilating all that has happened. During this time of interior reflection and heightened prayer, the elect, with the help of spiritual guides, deepen their experience of conversion. The bishop sends them into this period of retreat with such words as these: "God is always faithful. Now it is your duty, as it is ours, both to be faithful to God in return and to strive courageously to reach the fullness of truth, which your election opens up before you" (#133). During this period the community stands by the elect and expresses their acceptance and support by formally presenting the Lord's Prayer and the Creed, symbols of our willingness to share with the elect all that is most precious to us about our faith.

The gospels of these lenten days include the great conversion stories of John's Gospel. The proclamation of God's action in the woman at the well, the man born blind and the raising of Lazarus help the elect become more conscious of God's action in their own lives, satisfying their thirst with living water, giving them new sight through eyes of faith, raising them from death to life through the waters of baptism. Accompanying these powerful stories are equally powerful rites of scrutiny and exorcism: the mysteries of sin and salvation, human need and divine redemption, death and life are gathered up in these prayers which beg God for freedom and deliverance for the elect. And the point is not lost on an attentive community, caught up in the same struggles, knowing they need continued purification and enlightenment, and need to beg the same grace.

Final preparations for the Easter sacraments take place on the morning of Holy Saturday. Catechumens and candidates are encouraged to fast, especially during the Triduum, to take time for silence and meditation on the gospel and to pray to be opened by the Holy Spirit. Where possible, they come together with others to share their anticipation, read the scriptures and pray together, and celebrate the rite of ephphetha (see Mark 7:31–37), a perfect symbolic climax of their time of preparation. On the day they were accepted as catechumens, the sign of the cross was traced on their bodies, opening them to the action of God. On this day when they shall approach the font, the sign of the cross is traced again on ears and lips with the words: "Ephphetha: that is, be opened, that you may profess the faith you hear, to the praise and glory of God."

Now there is only the waiting.

Celebration: Initiation of Adults at the Easter Vigil

OUTLINE OF THE RITE
Service of Light
Liturgy of the Word
- *Celebration of Baptism*
- *Renewal of Baptismal Promises*
- *Celebration of Reception into Full Communion*
- *Celebration of Confirmation*
Liturgy of the Eucharist

The Easter Vigil is the most appropriate day of the year to initiate new members into the community. We are constituted as church in the paschal mystery of Jesus. This reality is made explicit in one of the alternative prayers of blessing over baptismal water:

> Praise to you, Lord Jesus Christ, the Father's only Son,
>
> for you offered yourself on the cross,
>
> that in the blood and water flowing from your side
>
> and through your death and resurrection
>
> the Church might be born. (#389)

Only the Easter Vigil, Aidan Kavanagh has reminded us, yields up an ecclesiology that is worthy of baptism. And we might add, only the Vigil yields up an ecclesiology that makes a life of discipleship not easy but full of meaning. The paschal Vigil is decidedly not easy to negotiate. Unlike other feasts on the calendar, there is nothing gentle or romantic about the realities we gather to ritualize and there is no way we can remain unscathed if we let it work its way with us. To borrow a phrase from Emily Dickinson, "It stuns us by degrees."

SERVICE OF LIGHT

First there is the waiting and the darkness. The church of antiquity recognized the power of a night watch extending from after sundown until the breaking dawn of the following morning. Night was a time of waiting and watching, tension and terror, darkness and dreams and death. Indeed, according to the wisdom of the early church, the quiet and solitude of the night made it a favorable time for prayer, a time to put aside worldly occupations, to stand with attention undivided in the presence of the Holy One, there to be transformed in encounter with the divine.

If such was true of night generally, how much more true of the Night of Nights, the night of the pascha, the night of transformation par excellence? We confess to the Easter Vigil's pre-eminence in the language of our prayers, referring to the Vigil as the "Passover Feast," "night of God's passing," "Feast of the Spirit," "Pasch of the Lord," "most blessed of nights," "night when heaven is wedded to earth." We know it to be true and even hymn the power of this holy night in the words of the Exsultet, testifying that this blessed night dispels all evil, washes away guilt, restores lost innocence, brings mourners joy; it casts out hatred, brings us peace and humbles earthly pride.

In the darkness of the paschal night watch we come face to face with evil and death. The darkness surrounding us invites us to confront the darkness within—the corruption, unbelief, violence, falsehood, idolatry, jealousy and anger, pettiness, greed and indifference of which we are capable. Darkness renders us blind and powerless—and best of all, darkness makes us know our need for light, especially for that light who is Christ. It has been dark for all of us in turn. The Christians who will most welcome the darkness of the Vigil are those who need and desire the presence and power of the Risen One in their lives.

We come because we need to acknowledge the power of him whose cross has redeemed us and whose rising renews our hope. We come together to keep vigil because we need to be supported and sustained by believing others who, with us, remain vigilant and hope-filled when face to face with the terrors of the night. We come to stand in awe of God's power at work in our newest members, drawn to our company not because of anything we have done but because of God's initiative and their fidelity.

Now each action—the lighting of the new fire; the carving of the candle; the proclamation of Christ's dominion over seasons and ages, over day and night; the bearing of the candle through the assembly; the spreading of fire from one to another—all of this makes the radiance of the Risen One tangible and real among us. We pray that God will make this fire holy and, even more urgently, that God will inflame us with hope. And then we light the candle from the new fire and we say: "May the light of Christ, rising in glory, dispel the darkness of our hearts and minds." And we long to mean the words we say because we know our continual need for Light.

Darkness was a metaphor not lost on one candidate who said: "Waiting in darkness was very meaningful for me. I had lived in darkness and uncertainty. I was waiting for this thing that I had also been dreading. I remember the edginess of everyone, the coughing and the shifting in the darkness. It was an incredible moment of expectation. It had been dark for me! Now the light was what I hoped for. It was amazing." And another remembered the time of darkness as something that might recur: "Beginning in darkness helped me to remember what someone had said to me which really reassured me: 'You can always have doubts about your religion. When you do you say: I believe, I want to believe. Help my unbelief.'"

Liturgy of the Word

Storytelling follows, words around the fire, prophecies, meditations, visions, tales, harshly realistic tales of suffering and slavery and sin and—hope against hope—of deliverance and reconciliation. Like all good stories, the ones we tell at the Vigil express the kernel of ourselves. But unlike other kinds of narrative, these stories are not just "once upon a time," nor told merely to remind us of our origins. They are repeated because the very telling of them moves us always more deeply into their reality, into their realization.

"It's like you are there," one of the neophytes said afterward of the creation story as the light came up in her church and the stars in the dome were visible. We are there! That is the whole point. The stories about our ancestors in the faith are about us, too, sinner and saved, weak and strong, bound and free. And, simultaneously, as we laud the mighty acts of God throughout the ages and culminating in Jesus, we discover who we are and are called to be. We tell stories of beginnings and the delight of so much goodness. We hear narratives of sacrifice and rescue, of redemption, everlasting love and covenant longing. But we also listen to words about humiliation unto death, the mystery of love that knows no limit, obedience that liberates from servitude, life that ultimately triumphs over death. Our storytelling reawakens in the elect and in each one of us the promises of God.

"Somewhere around the third reading," one of the newly baptized recalled, "the readings picked me up and funneled me into the water." What a striking insight about the power of the word to draw out and focus sacramental response.

Celebration of Baptism

We come to the heart of the Vigil, the celebration of bath and meal. Such common actions to effect an uncommon end—forging ourselves anew as God's people through bathing and anointing, embracing and dining together as a family. We rely now on the power of ritual actions to plunge us deeply into the paschal mystery that frees us from darkness, joins us to Christ dead and risen, makes of us one body giving glory to God, a new creation in water and the Spirit.

After the presentation of the candidates, the community prays once more that they have the light and strength to follow Christ with resolute hearts. Not content with the efficacy of its prayer, the community joins itself to the great chorus of witnesses, the saints of God. One of the newly baptized reported the litany of the saints as one of the high points of the celebration, bringing forth a sense of church not simply local or even universal but of all times and ages. "I felt like all the saints were there." Indeed.

And yet, for another, "When the priest began to bless the water, all of a sudden nobody else was there. Everything disappeared except for me and Father John and the words of the prayer and the sound of his hand in the water. I was totally floating. It was like an experience I had once of surgery and I was about to go under and I felt like I was hearing the first sounds of the instruments. I remember him putting his hand in the water and making the sign of the cross, and the sound of the moving water." That prompted another neophyte to recall: "I remember kneeling in the font and I had a similar feeling — that there was no one there. All I saw in the water was the shadow of the presider and then it wasn't Father John at all. It became spiritually the presence of the Lord."

The blessing over the baptismal waters is a completion of the Scripture proclamations that tell of divine action in creation and human history. One after another the mighty images of water are recalled: the waters of creation as wellspring of holiness, the waters of the flood which delivered from evil and caused a new beginning, the waters of the Red Sea through which God's people were freed, the waters of the Jordan which testified to God's election of his Beloved, the completeness of Christ's gift in blood and water that gave birth to the church, the command to the church to baptize with water and word. One image after another, stirring history that gives foundation to our sure and certain hope that God will be faithful again, will unseal the waters of the font to cleanse from sin and give new birth in innocence: "May all who are buried with Christ in the death of baptism rise also with him to newness of life." In the end, a single hope — that these candidates for baptism will be joined in death and new life to Christ through the power of the Spirit.

The power of the symbol evoked a variety of responses: "I remember watching them one after another really getting doused and knowing I was coming up soon and thinking more, more, like Peter, 'Not just my feet but my whole self.' Drown me in the water. Make it real." "Maybe it was the shock of all that water being poured but there was initial nervous laughter, and then it died down and the water and the singing and all that joy was so palpable." "I stepped out of those waters and I left so much in the pool. I was brand new." "I remember being very nervous before going into the water and then I went into the water and there was such a serenity. I felt: well, here you are! Be at peace." "Going into those waters at midnight I left the old self behind. I've changed so much in the past year and a half. I've changed in so many ways and when I look back and think how I used to be, it is just miraculous—the change." "I left behind a lot, and I think and I feel as a different person."

A bystander also was deeply moved: "I remember watching them one after the other. I loved the repetition and the increasing sense of the power of the water, and the power of what we were doing there together. As they came up out of the water I wanted to take each one of them and wrap them in myself." And another, commenting on the use of lavish amounts of water in her community, remarked: "These people were doused with water; when they came up every one of them was glowing with new life."

After the water bath the neophytes were clothed, and one spoke about the alb he was given: "I loved the baptismal garment. We were given albs. I wanted to wear mine longer. I didn't want to take that thing off. I wanted to be a neophyte for a longer time. The garment told me I was set apart. I felt that in putting on the garment I was putting on something new, but in another way it wasn't new, but a symbol of what had already happened in my life."

For another neophyte, the other explanatory rite, the giving of a lighted candle, sent her in imagination back to the darkness at the beginning of the celebration, a mirror of the darkness she had experienced for several years as she was fascinated by and fearful of faith's demands.

RENEWAL OF BAPTISMAL PROMISES

It is interesting and probably typical that the neophytes who were interviewed recalled the symbolic actions of their initiation rather than the words they spoke. As they described the experience of being baptized they described an enactment of the renunciation of sin and the profession of faith they made verbally before entering the pool. These baptismal promises may be more significant for the gathered assembly, who observe the symbolic actions and, while less engaged in the mechanics of the rite, are more intentional with the words they say as mirror to the action they observe. The community's renewal could not be less at this moment than renunciation and profession, a promise to be faithful to the same dying and rising that had just been pledged by their brothers and sisters.

CELEBRATION OF RECEPTION INTO FULL COMMUNION
Frequently at the Easter Vigil there are baptized Christians whose faith has been nurtured in other Christian denominations and who now seek to join themselves to the Catholic Christian community. At the Vigil they renew their baptismal promises with the rest of the assembly and then come forward to make profession of the Catholic faith. The question of life history is an important one. One of those who joined the Catholic community was assured by the priest who received her that she would always be a "Protestant Catholic," an assurance that she found comforting. "You are not going to leave that outside the door. You're going to bring it in here with you. That's who you are when you join us. You don't leave that behind but bring it with you. You bring all of your history."

The same celebrant formulated a prayer of thanksgiving which deeply moved all of those joining the community from other Christian denominations. "You have come to us from the Baptists, the Lutherans, the Presbyterians and the Methodists. They have nurtured your life with God. We join you tonight in giving thanks for these communities which gave you roots and first taught you about God." It was a very strong and beautiful bonding, especially for those who had Protestant family members present in the assembly. No triumphalism, just a sense of continuity and roots in the midst of a certain experience of displacement.

After the power of the baptismal ritual, the reception into full communion requires its own integrity. The act of transferring from one communion to another, often from inactive membership to active commitment, is, for the one going through it, as much a kind of death and new life experience as for the candidate for baptism. And yet the formula is so simple. Invited forward with sponsors, candidates declare: "I believe and profess all that the holy Catholic Church believes, teaches, and proclaims to be revealed by God" (#585). For one man, a former minister who was coming into communion, the formula was reminiscent of another rite: "It was actually a very profound experience for me, because the last time I took those kinds of vows in the church I was being ordained. It was very reminiscent of that and yet it was a total change of my life." For a woman who had been inactive in her community for a number of years and yet had struggled with God "as much as Jacob and the angel" about some of the ethical demands of her new commitment, an addendum to her profession was essential. To the formula "I believe and profess all that the holy Catholic Church believes, teaches, and proclaims to be revealed by God," she added, under her breath, "and by God I intend to practice it!"

CELEBRATION OF CONFIRMATION

To her delight, the next words of the presider encouraged just that. Introducing the celebration of confirmation, he included a promise that the outpouring of the Spirit would strengthen the candidates for active membership in the church. Then presider and community together, in silence and with outstretched hands, prayed for the gift of the Spirit.

More and more frequently, the community is invited to join the presider in calling down the Spirit, using the gesture of outstretched hands. For sacramental candidates and for community members alike, this is a very rich and moving experience, as their recollections illustrate. One parishioner spoke of her initial awkwardness which had given way to the "rightness" of this act: "When I raised my hands the first time I felt a little strange. What am I doing, I thought. But now I believe that with these hands God is coming in and God is with us." A neophyte recalled being the recipient of this ministry: "The whole community extended their hands in calling down the Spirit. That's when I felt like I'm connected with the church and they are praying for me. There are six hundred people out there at my disposal and I have a responsibility to be at their disposal and to live up to these promises. I could feel the Spirit moving among all of us."

Another member of the assembly said he found that raising his hands over those to be confirmed helped him hear the prayer that was said, the prayer for the seven-fold gift of the Spirit. It was his experience that his physical participation through this gesture made him more attentive to the prayer of blessing, made him make it his prayer, too, for the candidates.

When oil is used lavishly in the anointing of confirmation, the power of this ritual nearly rivals that of the water bath for those who are being sealed with the gift of the Holy Spirit. "It was incredibly fragrant; I remember smelling it long before it was my turn. It drew me to it." "With the chrism on my head I felt like a mantle was covering me from top to bottom and I felt like I was reborn, like I was brand-new, a new creature." "I loved the signing and being addressed again by name. It was like being singled out and being bathed in love."

That it was oil was one thing; that it was traced in the form of a cross also mattered enormously: "Any time the sign of the cross is given you are saying that you see life through the cross. And you view life through the lens of the cross. So having the anointing with the cross on my forehead was very powerful. It was like an embedding of the cross on my body. Later in the evening, driving home, I touched my forehead and the oil was still there and it said to me this was not a dream; this was real."

Then "one sealing was completed by another," or at least that's how one person perceived the welcome given to the neophytes and those who had come into full communion by a round of applause. What lingered in the memories of these men and women was the sound of it, the length of it, the obvious delight of the assembly, the sense of being loved and welcomed warmly and "of being proud of the choices and changes that had been made to bring us to this moment." "What amazed me was that we were three hours into the service. You would think people would be prepared to leave, but no, here they were giving a five-minute ovation."

LITURGY OF THE EUCHARIST

The initiation sacraments are completed at the table of Christ's body and blood. It is impossible to convey the depth of this experience for those who approach the table for the first time, or who receive the bread and cup as Catholic Christians for the first time. For one neophyte, the whole ceremony culminated with communion: "I felt so deeply the love of God. I realized it has been present my whole life but just in different ways. That night I really knew it." For another: "What stood out for me was eucharist. It's something I've waited for and longed for." For a third: "I had so much love and energy at that moment that I just wanted to be able to give some back."

One woman found herself reflecting on the meaning of it: "That bread; it's good bread, and it's such a bittersweet thing because it is his body and he gave up his life for me. It becomes so visible at communion. Here I am eating him. I remember hearing once, 'Those who eat of him must change.' I thought of that again. I accepted it. Then I went to the table."

For a man who came into full communion, it was less the formula of profession than the act of communion itself that helped bring his experience to expression that night: "The power of the liturgy really brought me in. I remember the words just before the sacrament: 'Lord, I am not worthy to receive you but only say the word and I shall be healed.' That has swept over me with unbelievable power. Ironically, though, the highlight of the whole service for me was after we had gone forward to take the sacrament. I was kneeling and watching everybody go by and feeling like I was now a part of these people. I was in communion."

Amen

The paschal mystery frees us from darkness, joins us to Christ, makes us one body giving glory to God, indeed makes us a totally new creation in water and the spirit. The initiation rituals of water, oil and table-sharing—when done lavishly in our presence—stir our own baptismal consciousness, invite us to embrace ordinary, everyday dying and rising with Christ, urge us to live no longer for ourselves, summon us to live in deed what we proclaim in word and ritual action, what we seal with "Amen."

The words of the neophytes need no interpretation. They were unbelievably articulate about the commitment they made with their Amen. What is striking in reviewing their comments is the recognition that the fourfold focus of catechumenal formation is reflected in the variety of commitments that sum up their experience, namely, a faith-filled relationship with Jesus Christ, a commitment to the community of his disciples, a love of the community's patterns of prayer and worship, and a commitment with others to service.

"This building, this church, is nothing if it isn't about Jesus. It's all about who he was, what he taught us. It's just overwhelming. The covenant he gave us, the difference between the old covenant and the new—it's a life thing. It just keeps meaning more and more and more to me."

"Going through the RCIA as an adult is an opportunity to affirm putting on Christ. That changed me even though I am already a part of this great body of Christ."

"I feel like I've made a commitment to somebody I always knew was there but this is just the beginning. This is a great new friend and this is just the start."

"There is a burden of saying you are a Christian, right? People can expect something of you. Every day I'm on a teeter-totter there between living a life of integrity and being a hypocrite."

"For me the commitment is to search out the truth, to take the wisdom of the ages and what the scripture has to say and then search out the truth in each situation. In order to love you must love beyond what is asked for."

"I said yes to being Catholic. I think of the word *Catholic* as meaning everybody, and this wasn't for me an intellectual process at that point. I saw our kids out there, and our friends, and all those people that you know and that you don't know. And I think that the Catholic church, beyond the theology and the truth claims, is about accepting all of humanity. It's like all of us people are in here together and we're going to struggle through it somehow, and that is really what any of those words mean."

"RCIA has helped build an awareness of where God is. God is everywhere . . . there, and there, and there. Now I am able to focus and to discover this presence. God is in the bread and part of every single person."

"I love the transubstantiation. I go to morning Mass, and we have the same people who come every morning. There is a man who is deaf. There is a woman who is mentally ill. There is a man who has some major physical problems, another who is gay. There are old people, young people. But we are all there around the eucharist. His body is the thing that ties us all together. I love being in the line. I'm just another person going to get my food for the day. I'm glad that the church protects that so vehemently. That is the thing that appears to me that has enabled this church to live for two thousand years. We have not compromised the eucharist. This is the center and it's going to stay the center. It's his body."

"Me? I've committed myself to service. Having gone through a pretty powerful conversion experience myself, I'd be happy to be present when someone else goes through one or say something that might help somebody else, or help shape the environment where this kind of stuff can happen, where the light can go on for somebody else. That means that I have to wash people's feet and there are ways of doing that . . . service within the church, the local shelter . . . the thing that enables me to do that is my own prayer life. My ability to be present to others and be of service will spring from my prayer life. And in turn going and doing the service will give me things to bring back to my prayer life, building it. It's a lifestyle. For me, now, it's a totally different lifestyle."

"I treat my job as a case worker as if I'm bringing the presence of Christ with me when I go into these homes. There is a power in that. I try to do my work now as my place of ministry."

"For me it's about that awareness. Once you are aware, you don't have a grace period anymore. You have to act. It's about giving and overcoming fears of opening yourself to Christ and to other people, to service."

Christ, community, liturgy, mission. What an amazing collection of commitments. What an amazing process and ritual that is able to help a wildly disparate collection of inquirers begin the journey of conversion, gradually come to faith and then throw in their lot with the rest of us.

And what of the rest of us? How do we keep our initiation commitments alive, especially when they were made for us by parents and godparents? How do we grow in our knowledge and love of God, our presence to community, our participation in worship and our commitment to live the vision of the reign of God we enact in the liturgy? The liturgy itself can teach us. One first-time participant at the Easter Vigil proclaimed: "I am always going to come to the Easter Vigil because I want to hear these new people say that what I take for granted sometimes is really important and that helps me to say yes again and again. How does this change me? Hopefully it makes me live life more reflectively. New people say to me: 'You've got something precious to hold onto.'"

Truly, the initiation rituals of water, oil and table-sharing—when done carefully and lavishly in our presence, and when we are attentive—stir up our own baptismal consciousness, help us embrace daily dying and burial with Christ, prompt us to promise to live no longer for ourselves, and urge us to live, in deed, what we proclaim in word and ritual action.

So Be It

What do we do when we say Amen?
Do we not know:

The waters wash us
and draw us out of death
into Life
and into Love that melts
the fiber of our being?

The oil anoints us
for healing
for service
for the grave?

The bread feeds us
for the journey
for the hunger, soul-deep
that cannot be filled
except by bread and cup
of sacrifice?

The words heal us
whole us
join us together
in bonds stronger than death?

Know we not that we are baptized
into death
into Life?

When we take this cup do we not say, "Amen,
Come, Lord Jesus"?

Kathleen Spears Hopkins

Chapter Four
Infant Baptism

In those days Jesus came from Nazareth of Galilee and was baptized by John in the Jordan. And just as he was coming up out of the water, he saw the heavens torn apart and the Spirit descending like a dove on him. And a voice came from heaven, "You are my Son, the Beloved. With you I am well pleased."
Mark 1:9 – 11

PRELUDE

In light of everything said about the initiation of adults in the previous chapter, infant baptism poses some interesting theological and pastoral questions. If the *Rite of Christian Initiation of Adults* celebrates the conversion experience of adult initiation as "coming to faith," then how are we to identify and interpret the issues of experience, conversion and process when the candidate for admission to the Christian community may be just days or weeks old?

The RCIA, with its emphasis on process and rites in the midst of the community, was proposed as the model for the celebration of all sacraments. Furthermore, initiation was presented as the sacrament that redefines the way we think about the Christian life, namely, as a never-ending journey of conversion. Both claims suggest that there is something normative about Christian initiation as described by the RCIA: a process, in community, over time, reflecting and celebrating human response to God's initiative, human acceptance of a new or deeper invitation to conversion and life in God.

What does any of this have to do with babies and with the celebration of their baptism in the *Rite of Baptism for Children* (RBC)? Are we to regard infant baptism as a harmless anomaly, a slight deviation from correct contemporary sacramental theology? Or, in light of the RCIA and because of its normative status, should we consider postponing the baptism of infants, waiting until children are at least of catechetical age, able to give evidence in their lives of their allegiance to Jesus Christ and able to make a personal choice to be initiated of their own free will when and as they are ready?

The Constitution on the Sacred Liturgy, in an important, foundational passage about the life of the sacraments, poses another kind of dilemma for understanding infant baptism. The constitution explicitly declares that faith is a precondition for sacramental participation:

> The purpose of the sacraments is to make people holy, to build up the Body of Christ, and finally, to give worship to God; but being signs they also have a teaching function. They not only presuppose faith, but by words and objects they also nourish, strengthen, and express it; that is why they are called "sacraments of faith." (#59)

If sacraments presuppose faith, as the constitution states, is it possible to baptize infants not yet capable of a faith-filled response?

How can we identify the experience of faith in relation to this sacrament? Whose experience is being celebrated? Is there some appropriate way to speak about the faith experience of the child, only weeks old, as part of what is brought to the sacrament and nurtured in its celebration?

Is the faith that is presupposed actually the faith experience of the parents and family, the domestic church, who present their child for baptism and who place their own faith at the disposal of their infant child? In this case, it would be possible to speak of an experience of conversion on the part of the parents, an invitation received, a choice made and celebrated, a commitment pledged.

Or is the faith presupposed in this sacrament actually broader than that of the domestic church? Is it, perhaps, the experience of the church at large, not simply the parochial experience of this child, but the experience of a community that needs both rites of initiation, for infants and adults, in order to have anything like a whole view of baptism, faith, salvation and the life of God with us? In this case, we need to pay very careful attention to infant baptism in order to identify the conversion and faith required of us as a community that welcomes infant members and, in the process, makes commitments to them about their future and ours.

Infant initiation, far from being a harmless anomaly in our sacramental system, is actually an important corrective. The emphases of adult initiation on maturity, adult religious experience, conversion and coming to faith provide only a partial glimpse of the divine-human communion which the sacraments celebrate. The metaphors used in the scriptures and the language of the adult initiation rites include exodus from bondage, salvation from the flood, washing from sin, enlightenment and re-clothing in Christ, renewal by the power of the Spirit, and particularly, participation in Christ's death, burial and resurrection. These metaphors provide a rich tapestry for the interpretation of adult passage from unbelief to faith and from sin to grace and holiness of life. The voluntary choice made by an adult, the change of heart that it reflects and the break with the past in the passage from unbelief to faith and to commitment to a life of discipleship are the heart of the process of conversion. Adult choice and change, and the lifelong journey they precipitate, have been developed previously and at length. Burial with Christ, paschal mystery, tomb imagery and an emphasis on regeneration all capture the meaning of adult sacramental initiation, whose dominant concern is the development of a living faith in the person of Christ and initiation into the priesthood of all believers who offer themselves through, with and in him. Emphasis is on human action and human response to the gift and grace of God, human acceptance of God's own trinitarian life and the living out, over a lifetime of choices, of all the commitments entailed in the ritual engagement of bathing, anointing and dining together.

But there is another side to divine-human communion that infant baptism highlights, and that is the utter gratuity of God's action in human lives — God's election, God's choice, God's complete acceptance of us as daughters and sons, acceptance prior to anything that we are or do, choose or shun. God's faithfulness to humankind is expressed in infant baptism, where womb imagery replaces tomb imagery and God's gifts and grace are showered on infants, adopted into the family of God not because of their choice, their conversion, their change of heart — indeed, none are possible — but because infants are so beloved of God that divine pleasure knows no bounds: The heavens open, the Spirit descends, and a voice names and claims them for God's reign. This beloved child is a gift to the community, on loan to us from God, to be cherished as much by us as the child already is by God, to be nurtured and set on the path of faith and love, the path of return to God.

In looking at the celebration of infant baptism, we will discover that the metaphors used in the lectionary and in the language of the baptismal rites for infants present a different pattern than those used in adult initiation, reflecting the age and condition of the infant or young child. The passion of Christ yields to Jesus' baptism in the Jordan, the opening of the heavens, the gift of the Spirit, the experience and expression of divine vocation and the faithfulness of God who offers, instills and nurtures a life of graced relationship.

Experience: Newborn and Beloved of God

Still, the question remains: What faith experience is presupposed in infant baptism? The *Rite of Baptism for Children* addresses the question of faith directly. It acknowledges that since this sacrament is for those who have not yet reached "the age of discernment," they cannot have or profess personal faith. Nevertheless:

> From the earliest times, the Church, to which the mission of preaching the gospel and of baptizing was entrusted, has baptized children as well as adults. Our Lord said: "Unless a man is reborn in water and the Holy Spirit, he cannot enter the kingdom of God." (John 3:5) The Church has always understood these words to mean that children should not be deprived of baptism, because they are baptized in the faith of the Church. This faith is proclaimed for them by their parents and godparents, who represent both the local Church and the whole society of saints and believers: "The Church is at once the mother of all and the mother of each" (Augustine, *Epistle* 98, 5). (RBC, 2)

We shall explore this question further by looking at the experience of the parents, the experience of the church, and, insofar as this is possible to imagine, the experience of the infant who is presented for baptism.

EXPERIENCE OF PARENTS AND FAMILY

Why do new parents decide to present their child for baptism? For a good number, at least, the testimony of one faith-filled couple captures their sentiments: "We think it is important for her to follow in our faith, and we wanted her to be able to share in the community; we feel it's an important part of her life." For such parents, faith is a central part of their own experience. It is something they treasure and want to pass on to their children, a precious gift, an inheritance to be shared.

For these same parents the faith community appears already to occupy a significant place in their lives. Perhaps the community sustained them in their first years of marriage. Perhaps it supported them with wisdom and prayer through a difficult pregnancy. Perhaps the community provided the nurturing environment in which their own adult faith had broadened and deepened as they gradually assumed other adult responsibilities. For these active Catholic parents, as one said who was surprised by the query: "There was never any question" but that the birth of their child would be followed shortly by its baptism into the faith they hold dear. In other words, for active, faith-filled couples, the baptism of their baby is not a decision so much as an inevitable consequence of their own experience and convictions. Furthermore, the baptism will function, when there are older children in the family, as an opportune moment to explore with siblings how each of them was welcomed by the church and reborn in its baptismal waters—to make it, as far as possible, a living reality in their developing sacramental imaginations.

Other new parents are faced with a different situation and a difficult choice. For a significant number of couples, faith and religion have been less central or even absent from their lives. They may have drifted from the church during or after their college years. They may have found the demands of their careers consuming most of their time. Perhaps now concern about original sin is the major reason they consider baptism, a kind of spiritual vaccination to ward off evil.

Other couples did not drift from the church but chose to leave it because of some hurt or misunderstanding. Still other couples have never talked about the religious dimension of their baby's life or, for example, in a mixed marriage, have never been faced with a decision about church affiliation.

Now all of these couples find themselves with a newborn who convention or grandparents say should be brought to the church and christened. Are all of these parents in a position to proclaim the faith for their children? Are all of these couples apt representatives of what the RBC called "the whole society of saints and believers," or should we exercise caution about what some commentators have called "indiscriminate infant baptism"? Will baptism for babies of those with little faith be simply pro forma naming ceremonies and rites of socialization having little to do with Christianity? Possibly, but the alternative of denying or delaying baptism may further alienate men and women from the church at the very moment when their own faith life might be rekindled by the miracle of new life and the tender ministry of the faith community and its ministers.

For a hundred different reasons, the birth of a child is nearly always one of those threshold moments of conversion discussed in the previous chapter. But in this instance, there is nothing subtle about the in-breaking event inviting conversion or about the life-transforming impact it will have on new parents. First pregnancies and births, especially, involve a physical, mental and spiritual stretching and straining, like labor, and the choices and changes of one's whole identity and experience are beyond counting. At times joy and fear mingle in about equal measure, delight and inadequacy, love and frustration, exhilaration and fatigue. All of it makes couples utterly vulnerable, and all of it can be the stuff of conversion.

Convention and the urgings of grandparents may be themselves occasions of grace, opportunities to shore up the depleted faith of the parents with that of the larger Christian community, moments when God can break into parents' lives and instill in them a longing—for themselves and their child—for new or deeper life with God and with the community called together in God's name. Parents of fragile faith need not have the baptism of their infants postponed until they are somehow deemed up to standard. Rather, they need to be able to lean on the faith of others, that larger life of faith that belongs to the church as a whole, across all continents and ages.

The time of formal preparation for the sacrament can be a graced time of mutual support within a local church, especially when the preparation is provided by other parents of young children whose personal experience of grappling with faith and unbelief can be placed at the service of new parents, and whose experience of sorting out their own relationship to God and the church is fresh and able to be put into words. Said one: "It was really nice to be able to share with other new parents some of the frustrations we felt, some of the joys we felt. It's often hard to find people who are in the same position you are, with small children, bringing them forth for baptism, in your same level of spirituality." Said another: "I'm surprised by the number of people who have been away from the church and are coming back specifically for baptism. It's a good opportunity for us to show them how the church may have changed since they left, to welcome them back, to help them heal some past hurts that they may have experienced."

Perhaps the most effective of all forms of immediate preparation for infant baptism is to take the rite that will be used and, possibly in the company of other couples also preparing themselves for this sacrament, reflect on the numerous instances when their involvement will be required and their own beliefs will be celebrated. Parents publicly ask that the child be baptized; they sign their child with the sign of the cross after the celebrant; they renounce Satan and profess their faith; they carry the child to the font; they hold the lighted candle; and at the end, they are blessed with special prayers, begging God to help them carry out the responsibilities each of these actions has symbolically pledged. Parents invited to reflect about these many ritual actions they will perform before the community cannot but be moved by the gravity and grace of the moment. One father acknowledged as much: "It really made me think about what we are asking; it made me start to pray again."

For all new parents, whatever their previous faith history, preparation for the birth of their child and a decision about his or her baptism is a wonderful opportunity to recover or deepen their own life with God and with their spouse. For one young couple, virtually absent from the church since their marriage, it was a way of coming home, no questions asked, and for another, it was a time to make some new decisions about how they wanted to live. Both couples were right. The decision about infant baptism is simultaneously a decision for adults about their own membership and participation. They may take comfort in the discovery that they are not alone in this new experience.

EXPERIENCE OF THE CHURCH'S FAITH

It takes a village to raise a child, as we have been reminded recently, according to African wisdom. And so, too, in the church. It takes a whole church—the strong and the weak, the committed and those hanging on by a thread, the suffering and the victorious, the frightened and the confident, the young and the old—adequately to represent the society of saints and believers, and to live out Augustine's image of church: parent of all and parent of each. It takes a whole church, furthermore, to provide a corrective to any notion that baptism and faith are part of some private preserve. The rite calls us to such largeness of heart: "The faith in which children are baptized is not the private possession of the individual family, but it is the common treasure of the whole Church of Christ." (#4)

Moreover, according to the introduction to the rite, our village obligations are not voluntary: "[B]efore and after the celebration of the sacrament, the child has a *right* to the love and help of the community." (#4) What a strong word to use—a *right*—to name the prerogative of the child and his or her claims on the whole of the community. What could it mean? What does it ask of us? This is one testimony to village upbringing: "When we celebrate a sacrament within the community, it's not just a magic action that is done to someone by the priest; it is an action in which we are all participating as members of the Body of Christ, as members of the Christian community. We are all joining together to welcome this child into the faith community, to support this child and this family with prayer." Prayer, then, is the primary support in the village, followed closely in importance by our living in such a way that our newest members recognize in the events of our lives God's concrete manifestations, and on our faces, the revelation of the face of God among us.

EXPERIENCE OF THE CANDIDATE FOR BAPTISM

We would not deny that infants are incapable of having or professing personal faith. Nevertheless, it is important to name the experience infants do bring to the sacrament, an experience upon which the sacrament builds.

We can speak about the incipient faith of the infant, of course, that seed of faith planted in every human heart to be opened, nurtured and tended until it comes into its own full flowering. But there is another experience that many, though sadly not all, infants bring to the font, and that is the experience of being loved, of being held and caressed and cared for, of being bathed and stroked, powdered and oiled, cuddled and cradled, rocked and walked. While we cannot speak of personal faith as part of the infant's cognitive and affective experience, there is still that sensory and tactile experience on which the sacrament may be constructed: the infant's experiential world of care, which communicates the place this child holds in the domestic church of family, the total acceptance, the naming of the child as beloved in every word and action, the embrace of the child as daughter or son, brother or sister. The child's experience is one of absolute surrender, complete vulnerability and need, acceptance of the ministrations of all and openness to the numinous revealed in these holy experiences of everyday life.

Surely these qualities of the infant's experience make him or her a perfect subject for the community's symbolic actions. It was clear in looking at adult initiation that words mattered less than actions and that the power of the symbols remained the abiding experience of the neophytes. How much more is it possible for the sacrament of infant baptism to draw on the baby's immediate experience of being cherished and cared for—to take advantage of the very elements familiar to the world of the child in the act of welcoming the child as one cherished and cared for equally by God? Warm water, scented oil, touch of parents and sponsors, the signings and anointings and embrace of peace. All of it, in some inchoate way, builds on the experience of the child and deepens an innate, though inarticulate, knowledge of being beloved of God and of beholding the divine.

For those infants who have the good fortune to receive the love and care of their families, the symbolic actions of their initiation will mirror and deepen their daily experience. For those who have received a less warm welcome, the tenderness of the church's sacramental ministry and the care with which it is exercised may awaken for the first time in the pre-conscious child an experience of being beloved of God, an experience denied through the neglect of some, yet available within the village and its sacramental ministry.

Celebration: Rite of Baptism for Children

The context of the baptismal event described in this section is the regular Sunday eucharistic assembly. While most of us are now familiar with initiation at the Easter Vigil as the normative celebration for adults, few communities regularly celebrate infant baptism during the Sunday eucharist for reasons having to do with time, logistics, the particular needs of the parents and the expectations of members of the Sunday assembly. Yet consider this: We baptize adults at the Easter Vigil, not alone with only their families present, not any day chosen indiscriminately, but at the Vigil. We initiate new members at the Easter Vigil because we can think of no better context than the celebration of the life, death and rising of Jesus, writ large in the annual paschal feast, for adult incorporation into Christ. The *General Introduction to Christian Initiation* (GI) makes the case strongly:

Those who are baptized are united to Christ in a death like his; buried with him in death, they are given life again with him, and with him they rise again. For baptism recalls and makes present the paschal mystery itself… the celebration of baptism should therefore reflect the joy of the resurrection. (#6)

Context matters. The celebration of infant baptism on a Sunday afternoon with a handful of relatives gathered, while representing certainly the most frequent pattern for infant baptism, is not the ideal context, nor for that matter the context envisioned in the rite. Celebration of infant baptism within the Sunday eucharist brings out, again, the paschal character of baptism and the necessary relationship between baptism and eucharist is maintained (RBC, 9). More importantly, the community into which the child is ritually welcomed is present — hardly insignificant in a sacrament that celebrates ecclesial incorporation.

As we examine the experience of the rite of infant baptism, let the question of ritual context surface. How would these faith-filled insights differ if parents and members of the assembly were recounting quasi-private, sometimes abbreviated, celebrations of the rite? How would the rest of us experience God's gift of each child to the community, make the commitments to the child as expressed in the rite, or have our own journey into God renewed because of the witness of these newest of Christians if we were not present at least some of the time, paying attention to the words and the gestures and the symbols of water and oil that we lavish on these beloved children of God?

OUTLINE OF THE RITE

Reception of the Children

Liturgy of the Word

Celebration of Baptism

(Liturgy of the Eucharist)

Concluding Rite

It is interesting to note at the outset that the several distinct parts of the rite of infant baptism parallel, in a collapsed fashion, the whole process of coming to faith which an adult celebrates over many months, even years. The reception and welcome of the infant functions as a parallel to the Rite of Acceptance into the Order of Catechumens, complete with questions of intent addressed to the parents and the signing of the child with the sign of the cross. The reading of the word of God and homily are akin to the period of the catechumenate when the word of God in all its fullness — the word of scripture and tradition, and the word lived and celebrated by the community — is heard and appropriated over the period of at least a year. The sacrament of baptism with a post-baptismal anointing is parallel to the Easter sacraments of initiation. And finally the conclusion of the rite of infant baptism in front of the altar anticipates completion of initiation at the table of the Lord when the child will be welcomed to the eucharist.

These several rituals are envisioned as, when pastorally feasible, a stational liturgy, as of a people on pilgrimage, with some representative group of those gathered making a ritual procession from the door of welcome, to the ambo for the proclamation of the word, to the font for the water bath and anointing, and finally to the altar for the concluding blessing and sending. The movement is yet another way to spell out ritually that the journey of faith upon which this infant embarks at the doorway will in time be regularly nourished by word and sacrament, and will conclude at the great end-time banquet. The parallel processions during the opening and closing rituals of the *Order of Christian Funerals* — the reception of the body and the final commendation and farewell — will be developed in the chapter on funerals but here the comparison can be noted. Life begins and ends in procession negotiated only with the assistance of others and the prayer of the whole church.

RECEPTION

Too often, opening rituals, whether of baptism or other rites, are treated as peripheral and insignificant. They can be minimized, it is sometimes thought, without prejudice to the central action. The testimonies that follow suggest, however, that the reception at the door, the naming of the infant, the request of the parents on behalf of the child and the signing of the infant have all functioned as powerful symbolic language for parents, sponsors and the community at large.

"When I stood at the front, at the door," one parent remembered, "I felt, walking through the door, I was being accepted by a group of people who were very committed to the community and to God, and I felt very warm and very accepted and I knew that my baby was going through the best type of baptism she could go through." Another parent concurred: "When we brought our son to be baptized five years ago it was the most wonderful experience that we've ever had. To stand at the door and see all those people there to support us, they were watching us, we knew that they were there for us, we could see the love in their eyes and in the way they respond to the children." And finally, in commenting on the importance of having a community gathered, one godparent found it reminiscent of the crowd that had gathered when John baptized in the Jordan: "It brings you back to the way it used to be when Jesus was there being baptized and all the people around him, and the crowd. It almost gives you the same feeling."

Just as adults who are asked to state their reasons for requesting admission to the catechumenate find that a word or a phrase is a delicate and imperfect vessel to contain all their hopes and longings, the same is true of parents asked to state their hopes for their child at this threshold moment. One mother commented about formulating the request for baptism: "When we were asked what we wanted for our child, the words caught in my throat. I wanted to say 'life and joy, faith, love, good health.' I wanted to say 'a community as loving as this one for the rest of her life.' I wanted to say 'happiness for ever and ever.' What I said was 'the grace of Christ' — and that said everything."

The signing is particularly powerful for the parents who, up to that moment, may never have signed their baby with the sign of the cross, and for onlookers at the rite, one of whom interpreted it: "When the parents and godparents sign the child, it is a very beautiful sign. Through this sign the child is claimed for God." Some see in the act of signing a kind of concelebration or co-presiding of parents and godparents with the priest celebrant, joining them together as ministers of the sacrament: "It's important that the parents sign the child. Baptism is not just something that the priest does." One parent recognized how the future was caught up in this action: "When I made the sign of the cross it meant to me that I have a lot to do with her growing up in the Catholic environment, and it means a lot, that God is coming through all of us." Another parent was overwhelmed with the significance: "When I make the sign of the cross I am actually blessing my child."

LITURGY OF THE WORD

The readings, homily and intercessions follow the reception and signing. They take place at the ambo, the same place the readings are proclaimed at every celebration. Besides the story of Jesus' baptism, optional gospel passages include the great commandment to love God and neighbor, the mandate to go forth and baptize all nations, the invitation to children to come to Jesus, the conversation with Nicodemus about being born again of water and the Spirit, the stories of the woman at the well and the man born blind and the great Johannine passage about union with Christ as intimate and life-sustaining as vine and branches. These are all passages that depict God's action in the lives of individuals and the community and the community's obligations of life and mission. When baptism takes place at the Sunday eucharist, the readings of the day are also possible and generally preferred. In all cases, the point of the readings, homily and intercessions is to stir up faith in parents and assembly alike and to pray that this baptism will be effective in the life of the child or children being baptized and in the life of the whole community. The sacramental rhythm, true of every sacrament, is one of listening and response, of listening and then loving in return.

Two powerful rites, the second of them optional, conclude the liturgy of the word and form a bridge to the sacrament of baptism. These rites are a prayer of exorcism and a pre-baptismal anointing.

What is the place of an exorcism in the celebration of a child, beloved of God? It has been quipped that the doctrine of original sin is closed for repair. Certainly it is now recognized that the faith of the parents would suffice as a baptism of desire should a child die before baptism. But original sin is an important reality with which to be reckoned, however joyous this day of baptism, however pure and innocent this child. Original sin is a doctrine that recognizes that the environment into which we are all born is one in which the power of evil is overwhelming and will color the way we think, the choices we make, the desires of our hearts, even the warring factions within us as well as all around us. The point of the prayer of exorcism is precisely to ask God to free this beautiful child from all that is evil in the world, to spare the child from temptation and the cunning of the evil one — or at least to empower the child to face temptations squarely and to fight everything demonic by the power of the Spirit and through the victory of Christ.

Just as the darkness of the Easter Vigil helps us know our own darkness and our need for light, so the prayer of exorcism can jar us into an awareness that we must daily struggle to live in reversal of the sinful human condition. The prayer interjects into this celebration of grace the reality of sin and the dangers these infants will face from without and from within. One mother said she actually felt a shudder go through her body and she held her baby more tightly during the prayer, begging God that the baby be spared from all that is evil and sinful.

The anointing that follows the exorcism is accompanied by a brief prayer for strength, a simple and fitting sealing to the exorcism. One participant saw in this action of anointing an act of the laying on of hands: "The most sacred rites in our religion involve the laying on of hands. What better time to do it than when you are initiating a newborn or recently-born child into the community. What better time to lay on hands." While not technically a sacramental laying on of hands, the anointing involves touch and the communication of strength and blessing typical of the imposition of hands in prayer.

Celebration of Baptism

After the procession from ambo to font, the rite of baptism begins with the prayer of blessing over the water and the same renunciations and profession of faith as at the Easter Vigil. Many prayers in the rite are identical to optional formularies used at the Vigil. The power of the symbol itself again outstrips all our language about what we are doing: "Water is a primary symbol of baptism. Water signifies life, and water is also able to produce death, in the case of drowning, for example. That whole paschal mystery of Christ, that dying and rising of Christ, that walk of the cross of Christ to new life is symbolized and embodied in that water, and as a child is brought to the church in baptism the child is immersed in that water to rise to new life in the Catholic Christian community." One would have to conclude, on hearing that reflection, that the Easter sacraments, including the blessing of water and the immersion of new members at the Vigil, has had a profound, catechetical effect in shaping such religious sensitivity. Another commented on the water, saying: "Water is life. It's a life-giving element and it is a very powerful symbol that we believe in, and the idea of full immersion into the baptismal font and being surrounded by the life-giving element of water is very powerful."

A distinct difference from most adult baptisms, and one that has given rise to profound reflection, is the fact that more and more infant baptisms are celebrated by the full immersion of the infant in preference to just a sprinkling with water or the pouring of water over head and shoulders. In the case of immersion, the child is naked — and nakedness has given rise to mystagogical reflections. A priest remarked: "I think it makes an extraordinary difference when you have a naked child at a baptism. Once I thought: So what. What's the difference between holding the baby up with a dress or a little diaper. It's only when I did it that I knew the difference." More explicitly: "The baby is present in all its honesty, all its reality. Just as it was birthed into the world, it is being birthed into the Catholic community, as it is, as a gift from God; it is immersed in its nakedness into the water and presented to the community." The nakedness of the child also suggested to some our own stance before God: "The nakedness is its vulnerability, and it says that we are approaching our faith naked, so to speak. It's very, very important. I wouldn't change it for anything." And finally, "That's how she came into the world and that's how she should join the church as well. It's like joining God, and that's how we feel. I mean that's your own self, it's nothing fake, nothing phony. It's most pure."

After the triple immersion and baptism in the trinitarian name, the anointing with chrism follows. As with water, the use of a lavish amount of oil at the Easter Vigil may have given rise to these reflections about the oil, some of them suggestive of confirmation images as well: "In the baptism they are using the oil to seal the babies with Jesus." "We're using oil as a very precious thing." "When the oil is placed on the child the smell is overwhelming. It's like a perfumed oil, and it reminds you of some of those scripture passages about perfumed oil." "The oil is a kind of sealing; it's a protection and strengthening for all her life ahead of her."

The clothing in a white garment, "a beautiful adornment," the giving of a lighted candle "which means to us that Jesus will always light the way," and the prayer over ears and mouth (the ephphetha rite) conclude the baptismal rituals at the font. It is interesting to reflect on the significance of the ephphetha at this point in the celebration. In an adult initiation, the ephphetha rite is part of the preparatory rituals of Holy Saturday morning—a rite of opening the ears and the mouth of the elect that they might hear and proclaim the mighty acts of God and profess the faith that has been built up in them by God's grace. For an infant, the blessing of ears and mouth anticipates that the child is just beginning a catechesis that will extend over time. Parents and godparents, ministers, teachers, faith community—all will have a role to play in nourishing the faith awakened in this child through baptism and bringing this initiation to completion at the table. One godparent was profoundly moved simply by being present throughout the rite in the midst of the community: "Watching the baptism from behind the font as a godparent, you feel like the whole community is there to welcome the child. The love of the place comes and grabs you in." In a way, the entire celebration of baptism is a prayer that the same experience of love as celebrated on the day of baptism—God's, the parent's, the community's—will "grab" these infants, take hold of them, surround them, protect them, bless them, strengthen and sustain them, and nurture their life of holiness to the praise and glory of God.

Concluding Rite

When infant baptism does not take place within the eucharist, the Lord's Prayer, blessings and dismissal conclude the celebration. These take place in front of the altar so that the connection of baptism and eucharist is forged in people's minds and hearts. "Our celebration of the eucharist is very strongly connected to baptism because the mere fact that we were baptized calls us to the table, and calls us to be one with each other." Not a bad way to summarize how we hope this child will experience the Christian life—a call to the table and a call to service.

Amen

To what do we say "Amen" when we celebrate an infant baptism? There are distinct commitments made by the parents and made by the church.

Parents of newborns enact a web of promises when they present their child to the church for its christening—that celebration of its being joined to Jesus Christ and the community of disciples who bear his name. Parents speak many words on behalf of their child, words of hope and promise, words of renunciation and faith. They speak even more eloquently without words in the gestures they perform:

crossing the threshold, signing the child, carrying their child from place to place in the church, receiving God's word, presenting the child at the waters of the font and ending their journey before the altar where they themselves will be nourished at the table of God's body and blood to remain faithful to their own journey even as they continue to provide for all the needs of this beloved child. In the course of the celebration, parents proclaim by word and deed that they will hold the child, clothe it, care for its bodily needs, give it light and warmth, defend and protect it in the face of evil and teach it gradually about the ways of God and the person and work of Christ the sign of whose victory they have traced on its body. Faith, trinitarian life, adoption into God's household, participation in the paschal mystery of Jesus, and incorporation into the community of church are the gifts the church bestows on their child. The parents turn, at the end, to the church and ask for the church's blessing that they may keep faith with their child and with the church in cherishing and preserving these gifts for the one designated God's beloved.

The assembly, too, receives a blessing at the conclusion of an infant baptism, underscoring that it has also enacted commitments during the rite. Living as faithful members of God's holy people, being present to each other, participating as far as is possible in the life and growth of the child and its gradual assimilation of all that the community hold's dear — these are the kinds of commitments articulated by members of the community, truly representing that whole society of saints and believers we call the church. These words of testimony illustrate that some members of the community take their commitment very seriously: "To feel such a part of that family and that child's life, to see them immersed and then brought out of the water and then Father usually walks them around so that we can all witness that child and that family. I think for us it makes us feel more like a community. It gives us more of a stake in each other's lives, to be there for all the times, good or bad, that happen in our lives." Another person concurred: "Once I've seen a baby baptized I feel like I have an obligation to stay connected because we are connected." Said another: "I feel we're part of baptizing the baby. You watch all those babies, how they grow up, become teenagers, adults, and you remember the time when they were baptized, and you were there. You were part of that."

"It's wonderful to see people sitting forward and craning their necks to see, and we just feel part of it every time. It's really kind of a miracle." A miracle, yes, and more than that. It is a remembering and a recommitment on the part of those who pay attention: "It showed me that baptism wasn't an isolated event. Baptism was the beginning of a journey and it was the beginning of the journey that everyone in the room has gone through and everyone in that room has shared." And another parishioner summed it up: "Baptism is kind of like our vows into this community. And when we see baptism on a Sunday, it's a redefining of our vows, it's a remembrance of our vows, it's a promise. Baptism at Sunday Mass? It enriches the whole parish."

It takes the blessings of God for the parents to live up to their baptismal obligations. It takes the village of God's people and the sacramental rites as they have evolved in the tradition to welcome and incorporate God's beloved children, to enlighten their minds, to clothe them with Christ, to empower them with the Spirit and to revel in the utter gratuity of it all and in the overwhelming sense of God's delight as we name and claim these infants in the name of the Father and of the Son and of the Holy Spirit. Amen.

Chapter Five

Confirmation

Those whom [God] foreknew he also predestined to be conformed to the image of his Son, in order that he might be the firstborn within a large family.
Romans 8:29

PRELUDE

In chapter three, which dealt with the Christian initiation of adults, we explored the sacraments of baptism, confirmation and eucharist celebrated as a single event at the Easter Vigil. How do we make sense of confirmation apart from the full celebration of Christian initiation? Does it change in any fundamental way when it is celebrated separately, and if so, how? Does it change its focus when candidates are neither infants nor adults but adolescents, who are subject to different pressures than their adult counterparts are and thus are vulnerable to very particular ways of being converted by God to the holy life?

When confirmation is celebrated as a separate sacrament, it poses a number of interlocking questions. What is its meaning? What is the best age for its reception? How do we prepare candidates for confirmation, and what evidence do we look for when we discern their readiness? We begin this reflection on confirmation with a brief historical survey of its origins and development in order to understand why there is such a variety of pastoral choices and strategies today.

Origins and Development of Confirmation

Making sense of confirmation today is a challenge in light of the fluidity of its historical and theological evolution. The origins of confirmation are intimately linked with baptism and eucharist as a unified rite of initiation into the Christian community. In the post-apostolic church, the water bath was followed by a post-baptismal anointing or the imposition of hands with prayer. Then the candidates were led to the table, where they symbolized their full communion with God and with their brothers and sisters by reception of the bread of life and the cup of salvation.

The early Christian community performed these several rituals in a variety of ways, and as they reflected on their sacramental activity, the full meaning of these mysteries began to unfold. Christian initiation claimed one for Christ in the power of the Holy Spirit. Sin was washed away and the neophyte became a participant in the very life of God as well as a member of the community that lived in the memory and hope of God's Beloved One. These men and women who were baptized in water, sealed in the power of the Spirit and fed at the table of the Lord pledged themselves to a shared faith and a way of life with particular ethical demands. Such was the developing theology of initiation in its earliest stages.

Minister of the Sacrament

Gradually, several developments complicated the historical and theological unfolding of Christian initiation. The churches of the East and the West made different decisions about the normative minister of this sacrament, with important theological and liturgical consequences. In the West, it was the local bishop who presided over initiation rituals, assisted by his deacons and presbyters. The ritual of full immersion in the waters of baptism necessitated relative privacy because candidates went naked into the waters. The baptismal immersion was overseen by presbyters and deacons, and in some instances also by deaconesses, while the bishop usually remained with the assembly, keeping vigil with readings and prayer. When they were again clothed, candidates were led into the assembly of the faithful for the post-baptismal anointing and prayer under the ministry of the bishop, who then presided at the table and gave communion to the neophytes for the first time.

As the number of communities increased and the exigencies of travel made it impossible for the bishop to be present always and everywhere for initiation, presbyters and deacons presided at these rites in the bishop's absence. Candidates were welcomed into the community through baptism and then invited to the eucharistic table. The post-baptismal anointing, reserved to the bishop, was postponed until he could be present, sometimes days or weeks later.

In the Eastern church, the bishop exercised pastoral oversight of the initiation of new members not by being the regular minister of the sacrament but by blessing the oil used by his presbyters in the post-baptismal anointing. For that reason, even as numbers expanded and members widely dispersed geographically, the Eastern church has been able to maintain the custom to this day of keeping the unity of the three sacraments of initiation, usually celebrated with infants and through the ministry of presbyters.

Meanwhile, through the Middle Ages, the post-baptismal anointing in the Western church continued to drift further from its baptismal origins. Eventually this anointing was understood and executed as a separate sacrament, quite distinct from baptism and celebrated after a good number of years had elapsed. The separation of anointing from its baptismal context was further complicated by the reordering of the initiation sacraments that the deferred anointing had occasioned. What had once been an initiation through baptism, anointing or laying on of hands and eucharistic communion in a single celebration became baptism and eucharist followed after a lengthy interval by anointing and prayer.

MEANINGS AND EFFECTS

The Western church was faced with the dilemma of making sense of the anointing as a delayed and separate sacrament, especially in identifying sacramental effects distinct from baptism and appropriate to one who had already received the eucharist. Not only was a theological rationale needed for what had gradually come to be called *confirmation*, but the community also had to decide who should be confirmed, how readiness was to be determined and what age was optimal for its celebration.

Over the centuries, the sacrament of confirmation has attracted to itself a variety of theologies, most of them having to do with "strengthening." One such theology understood that confirmation would strengthen a candidate with the grace to fight internal battles against temptation and sin. In another, confirmation was interpreted as strengthening a candidate against hostile external forces with the grace to become a soldier for Christ and to work actively for the reign of God against this world's ungodly powers.

This latter understanding of confirmation as preparation for witness and mission caused an elaboration of the particular role and gifts of the Holy Spirit. Just as there was an outpouring of the Spirit on the apostles at Pentecost for the service of church and world, so too, in confirmation, there is a fresh outpouring of the Spirit to take up the church's mission. However, just how the role and gifts of the Spirit differ in baptism and confirmation is not a little confusing, especially if there has been any implication that the candidate for confirmation, already baptized into the triune life of God, is receiving the Spirit for the first time.

The Present Situation

These discussions continue to this day. They have been further tangled in recent years by the recovery of the catechumenate for adults and the resulting restoration both of the unity of the three sacraments of initiation and of their ancient order at the Easter Vigil. The clarity and simplicity of the pattern of adult initiation suggest that confirmation now must be seen and celebrated in relation to baptism and to initiation as a whole. Indeed, it was an articulated goal of the *Constitution on the Sacred Liturgy* (#71) that confirmation be revised so that the intimate connection of this sacrament with the whole of Christian initiation might stand out more clearly. Confirmation thus understood is a completion of the baptism one received in infancy. Consequently, the same godparents and the use of the baptismal name are encouraged in the celebration of confirmation, and baptismal promises are renewed immediately before reception of the sacrament. The anointing with chrism and the words "Be sealed with the gift of the Holy Spirit" thus form a modest ritual moment in the larger journey of conversion, the work of a lifetime. Furthermore, some dioceses now encourage, or at least permit, confirmation prior to or in conjunction with first eucharist, thus restoring the order of the initiation sacraments and particularly the symbolism of the eucharist as the sacrament of full membership in the church. Thus candidates for confirmation may be seven or eight years old. Indeed, canon law (canon 891) suggests that the age of discretion is the normative age for confirmation unless another age is determined by the conference of bishops or there is danger of death or another grave cause.

Nevertheless, the pre–Vatican II tradition of interpreting confirmation as the sacrament of Catholic Action, the sacrament that created "soldiers for Christ," did not thereby fall by the wayside. This interpretation emphasizes that confirmation does not simply confirm and complete baptism but rather confirms and strengthens the baptized and enables them, now that they can speak for themselves, to embrace the commitments and the mission that were chosen for them when they were infants. These ideas still color the thinking about confirmation today. Strengthening for mission is accomplished in the power of the Spirit, whose sevenfold gifts of wisdom and understanding, right judgment and courage, knowledge and reverence and a spirit of wonder and awe in God's presence enable — even deputize — the candidate as a witness of the gospel, filled with the Spirit, to proclaim fearlessly the mighty works of God. When mission, witness and adult responsibility for the church are emphasized as elements of the theology of confirmation, the maturity of candidates and their ability to make and keep commitments become important considerations in determining optimal age and readiness. In this case, older teens or young adults would seem to be candidates for the sacrament.

Both interpretations, confirmation as a modest completion of initiation at a younger age versus confirmation as strengthening candidates for adult mission, are supported by the current *Rite of Confirmation*. Clearly the gift of the Pentecost Spirit, empowering a Christian for witness and mission, has a prominent place in the rite. The Pentecost event is the overarching theme of the introduction, the subject of one of the suggested readings, the focus of a petition of the penitential rite, the opening image of the instruction, the central point of the concluding prayer in the model intercessions and a strong strain of the theological underpinnings of the rite spelled out in the apostolic constitution with which the rite was promulgated. The same constitution distinguishes the effects of baptism and confirmation thus:

> In baptism, the newly baptized receive forgiveness of sins, adoption as children of God, and the character of Christ by which they are made members of the Church and for the first time become sharers in the priesthood of their Savior (see 1 Peter 2:5, 9). Through the sacrament of confirmation those who have been born anew in baptism receive the inexpressible Gift, the Holy Spirit himself, by whom they are endowed with special strength. Moreover, having been signed with the character of this sacrament, they are more closely bound

to the Church and they are more strictly obliged to spread and defend the faith, both by word and by deed, as true witnesses of Christ.

Despite this strong emphasis on the giving of the Spirit for mission and witness, the introduction to the rite also supports an understanding of confirmation as a completion of initiation. Even the use of the comparative form in the paragraph just cited suggests the intimate connection of the two: "more closely bound," "more strictly obliged." Confirmation is thus a continuing and deepening of baptismal life.

"Conformation"

These several historical and theological developments have strongly influenced the understanding and celebration of confirmation today. Moreover, as young people attempt to name the experience they are celebrating in confirmation, both emphases—confirming one's baptism and strengthening the baptized for mission and witness—find resonance in their language. Some teens experience confirmation as continuous with baptism; others experience the sacrament as a radically new moment of fire and passion and the in-breaking Spirit.

Moreover, a third and startlingly apt understanding of confirmation emerged in the material of my interviews with newly confirmed adolescents as well as in more than a hundred letters written by teens to their pastor, asking to be confirmed. The sacrament was called "conformation." What at first seemed to me to be a misspelling and a "misspeaking" was so frequent that it raises some interesting possibilities for us to ponder together with the deeper question: Why is it that a good number of young people have found that the meaning of this sacrament is captured in the word *conformation* and the idea of conformity to Christ?

Confirmation does *conform* one to Jesus Christ. Certainly all the traditional theological themes of confirmation—sealing, strengthening, gift of the Spirit—are enacted in the words and gestures of the rite. But at the same time the rite's emphasis on becoming more like Christ is as prominent as the theme of the Spirit's empowerment. The model homily describes the role of the Spirit as making candidates more like Christ and more perfect members of the church; the prayer immediately before the anointing begs that the Spirit will be poured out to "anoint them to be more like Christ the Son of God." And the introduction to the rite rehearses the meaning and potency of the sacrament precisely in these terms: "This giving of the Holy Spirit conforms believers more fully to Christ and strengthens them so that they may bear witness to Christ for the building up of his body in faith and love" (RC, 2). While church professionals debate the meaning of confirmation, teens seem to have found a way to make sense of it — *conformation* — and, as will become clear in the following pages, they are able to talk about conformity, not to the crowd, but to Christ, with a simplicity and clarity that is quite astonishing.

Throughout the rest of this chapter, as I cite material from conversations or letters I will retain the use of "conformation" and its derivative forms if that is what was said or written.

THE AGE OF CONFIRMATION

Finally, regarding the age of confirmation, sustained debate about the best age for reception of the sacrament has not yet resolved the question to anyone's satisfaction. The bishops of the United States, after several times tabling a decision on appropriate age, voted that the normal age of confirmation is from 7 to 18, a range that manages, for the time being, to endorse the variety of patterns across the country until more persuasive evidence narrows the span. While there is some discussion of adopting the Eastern practice of full initiation of infants, and also some experimentation with restoring the ancient order of the sacraments by celebrating confirmation before first eucharist and thus at about the age of seven, by far the most prevalent sacramental pattern in the United States remains the confirmation of adolescents, often in the later years of high school.

The balance of this chapter is limited to an exploration of adolescent confirmation. It presents an amazing picture of adolescent religious experience. You may wonder who these young people are, how they became so articulate about their faith and when and how they became so responsible in their moral choices. You may wonder also what kind of process and support structure were provided to nurture their life with God. These are remarkable young people by any measure. They have obviously been the recipients of extraordinary pastoral care and support from numerous adult volunteers.

In the end, these reflections may also present a persuasive case for the candidacy of young adults for confirmation. While some wonder whether teenagers are able to commit to anything for the long haul given the volatility of their experience, it may be that their experience is uniquely suited to this sacramental experience.

Experience: Conformity to Christ

The experience of adolescents is one of enormous upheaval. The teen years typify Arnold Van Gennep's category of "betwixt and between" in his classic *Rites of Passage*. Young people are no longer children, nor are they yet adults. They long for autonomy and independence yet are enormously influenced by the opinions of others — peers and respected adults in their world. Even as they are engaged in the mighty upheavals that accompany individuation, they are deeply caught up in conforming in hairstyle, clothing, leisure pursuits and so on, often becoming virtual clones of one another. They sometimes rebel under the demands of others, yet they crave a sense of clarity about expectations and positively thrive in situations where boundaries are established and maintained. They want to be held accountable even as they chafe against its demands. They seemingly change daily — physically, emotionally, mentally — and they sometimes can't make sense of the volatility of their own experience and mood swings, let alone their own behavior. They regularly experience what Paul has described in Romans: "I do not understand my own actions. For I do not do what I want, but I do the very thing I hate" (7:15). Or, as a latter-day Paul declared, "I was into some bad things and had no idea how to get out." They are pulled by school work, part-time jobs, sports and other leisure activities, family expectations and the endless testing and sustaining of friendships. They are preoccupied by questions of meaning and purpose in the present moment, and by the concrete need to think about the future — finding a job or making college applications, for example — even as they wonder whether they have a future at all.

Young adults today are subject to pressures that many of their elders can hardly imagine. Drugs, alcohol, sexual experimentation, physical and sexual abuse, loneliness, depression, suicidal thoughts, serious illness in the home, dysfunctional families, broken homes, absentee parents, gangs, violence, death, hanging out with the wrong kind of people — all these are regularly part of their experience, either personally or through their network of siblings, friends and acquaintances. This is the experience that forms the backdrop of the sacrament of confirmation when celebrated with teens.

Negotiating these pressures is the stuff of their growing up and it is the material out of which they may be drawn to conversion and deeper life with God during their adolescent years. In terms of the classic patterns of conversion discussed earlier, teenagers are remarkably vulnerable to such invitations. Because of their betwixt-and-between situation, they are susceptible to forces for good or ill. As will become evident, they are ripe for the action of God.

COMING TO CONFIRMATION

The reasons young people become involved in the confirmation process are many. Not surprisingly, family expectation and parental pressure are responsible, at least initially, for bringing some teens into the process, just as convention and expectation were factors in the presentation of some infants for baptism. "To be very honest I didn't want to be here and had a very bad attitude toward everything, even life itself." "I never allowed God to be in my life until now, and I was really resentful of my mother for making me do this." "Looking back on these months, I can't even imagine what I was thinking when I didn't acknowledge God's presence in my life — but I didn't, and I didn't want to be here." "I thought I didn't have time for it and that I didn't need to prove my faith to anyone." "I came here because my parents told me I was going to be confirmed and I said, 'Okay, whatever.'" "In the beginning of the year I was doing this for my mom and my family. I felt that it was kind of expected of me. But now I realize that I did it for myself as well." "I totally had no clue I was Catholic."

Some are willing to turn up without too much outside pressure, but in the beginning they reserve judgment about the whole process: "When I signed up for conformation it was of my own will, but I really just figured, what the heck, let's get it over with." "I never thought it would affect my life very much." "I'm not sure why I came to confirmation, but I'm glad I did." "I knew it was another sacrament I had to make, but I didn't know it would hit me like this."

For some, it was a sense of emptiness or absence that made them vulnerable to the sacramental moment: "I was away from the church for such a long time and I started to realize recently, last year or the year before, that I needed something else in my life. There was something missing." "I realized how empty my life was without Jesus." "There was some conversion that took place. It's hard to describe, actually it was a healing in answer to prayer, and it brought me back to attending Mass on a regular basis and then I saw how really alive these teens were, and not afraid to say the name of Jesus. That was my calling and how I got involved."

The positive influence of others is not infrequently the beginning of the process: "Last year when I saw my brother and all of his friends get confirmed I wanted to be confirmed because I saw how much God worked in their lives and I hungered for that. Little did I know that I already had it. I just had to let God work in my life and then I was able to recognize him everywhere."

The process of confirmation, then, begins in a variety of ways; participants arrive with an assortment of mindsets and certainly with different degrees of willingness to engage in the conversion that the sacramental process invites. Yet there is a remarkable correspondence in the articulation of what goes on within them and among them once they give themselves over to preparing for the sacrament. What they name as the highlights of their year of preparation corresponds in large measure to the content of the catechumenate for adults, but reordered to reflect more clearly their adolescent vulnerabilities.

CONVERSION

Three distinct elements stand out in the experience of conversion among teens: development of a personal relationship with God and Jesus, especially through establishing patterns of prayer; discernment of personal choices in light of the teachings of Christ and the church; and taking adult responsibility for the mission of the church in light of the gospel. These three elements are dimensions of a single process: falling in love with a person, wanting to please and be like that person, and needing to do something as well as be something for the sake of that person. Such is the personal experience they bring to be transformed in the course of the process of sacramental preparation. Remarkably, they also gather up the several strands of the theological tradition of confirmation into a single whole: the continuation and deepening of divine life that has consequences for one's own life and impels to mission. We shall return to this synthesis later, but first we need to hear from teens how they articulate the conversion journey celebrated in their confirmation/conformation.

A personal relationship with Christ • Friendship is central to teen experience, the desire for it, the development of it, the hurts associated with it, the need for acceptance and love that is reciprocal and unconditional. The great-hearted longing of teens for relationships that are deep and trustworthy appears to be satisfied in discovery of Jesus or God as Friend. "This year I have fallen in love—pure and full of passion. Jesus is the most wonderful friend I could ever have and he has exceeded all earthly expectations." "Conformation is accepting Christ into your heart and living out the gospel as much as possible." "Confirmation is about feeling, breathing, and living him. What Jesus has done for me this year is confirmation. It is the change of heart and life that I have been waiting for Jesus to work in me." "I realized that there really is no purpose but death if you don't believe in God." "Every night I try to pray and I feel like I am being cradled by God." "I always used to pray every night to God. Now as an added bonus . . . I listen to God. I love God so much." "I learned to have an intimate relationship with God and not to think of him as a character in a book." "I decided to become a better disciple and closer to God and Jesus."

Discernment of personal choices • Teens are engaged daily in the process of differentiation, of trying to make choices, of being caught in conflicting demands. Discernment of personal choices is exercised often in face of overwhelming peer pressure. It can also be assisted by the support of one's friends. Developing friendship with Jesus and the support of others in the confirmation process are important for such discernment to be sustained and for one's choices to be tested and challenged against the judgments of discerning others. One person seemed to capture the process quite simply when he said, "A lot of it is parallelism: how Christ dealt with issues in his life and how we need to deal with them."

Clearly the young adults in this confirmation process have found that scripture, personal prayer and the process of small group teaching and faith-sharing all played a role in conforming them more and more to the mind and heart of Christ: "I try to live my life so that it reflects my faith and others see Jesus in me." "I have expanded my knowledge about the Bible and the ways of Jesus." "I try to ask myself if God would be pleased with my decisions." "I have chosen to walk with Jesus when it is convenient and inconvenient." "I can feel his presence and I can hear him telling me what he expects and wants from me." "Now I pray more often and think about what Jesus would do when I need to make a decision." "Confirmation has shown me that God is there for me and working in my life. I have thought about what Jesus would want me to do and have tried to carry out those wishes. I am not ashamed or embarrassed to say that." "The faith-sharing process made me look at what I was doing. . . . The gossiping, arguing with my parents and friends, choices about time . . . the question is whether it is building up the kingdom of Christ." "My greatest desire is to be a Catholic woman able to teach my children the truth which is so often absent in our world."

The struggles are enormous. "A lot of my friends are the types that get drunk and do drugs and things like that. And they are really good friends, but they do stupid things. But there's always this voice in my head that says 'don't do it.'" Sometimes bad choices are made. Then discernment and decision-making have another focus, namely, acceptance of the consequences of one's actions: "I got in a lot of trouble on the weekend before confirmation . . . but I learned confirmation is about courage, having the courage to come forward and admit it when you screw up."

Adult witness and mission • Membership has its privileges; membership also has its obligations. For these candidates for confirmation, mission and witness do not remain abstractions. Community service at nursing homes, soup kitchens, homeless shelters and other kinds of volunteer work have taken the energies of these teens and channeled them, making concrete the issues of mission, service, witness, and "living no longer for yourself," a biblical phrase proclaimed as part of a eucharistic prayer and cited by one teen to describe his present motivation. Remarkable is the commitment of these confirmandi to the works of mercy: "Among us we have fed the poor, welcomed strangers, clothed the naked, comforted those in prison, visited the lonely, given example to those in despair from drugs and alcohol, brought hope to those contemplating abortion and in every way we have tried to spread the good news of Jesus to our peers."

Besides this strong and concrete service component, an even more immediate issue of adult witness and mission is the eloquent testimony of all the tiny daily choices for good or ill. "I learned to be aware of God's love for me, to be a disciple of God and to spread God's love and teachings with the people I meet every day." "I want to be seen as an adult in the eyes of the church, an active member of the

Catholic community." "I want to be confirmed because it will make me a full-fledged member of the Catholic church." "I want to show my love for God and confirm it." "I want to become a contributing member of our Catholic community." "Confirmation has taught me to make my life a living prayer." "I want people to see Christ through me." "This year in conformation I have learned a lot, not only about my relationship with God but also my relationships with my friends, my family and myself." "My conformation family has revealed to me a deeper sense of church and community. They have convinced me that I do have gifts to share." "I learned about setting time aside for prayer. What's good is that we learned how to make our whole life a prayer. You don't just have to be on your knees to pray. Your actions can be your prayer, like taking a test, forming a relationship, anything. When we are living a prayer, things are a lot smoother."

What makes them think they are ready? "I want to be confirmed because I want to make a commitment to live my life for God." "I feel like I'm ready to be conformed because I feel very strongly in my faith and I try to show it in the way I act toward others and to be *more like Jesus*." "Without Jesus my life falls apart. All the little miracles every day reveal to me the grace and majesty of God." "I want to seal my love and faith with God." "I realize I need God in my life more and more; I want to be confirmed for I want to grow stronger in my faith and be a witness to everybody." "I've learned to love myself, others, God and the church a lot more." "Every day I try to do my best to live my life for Jesus." "I believe I should receive confirmation because this is one step more to becoming fully one with God." "I've accepted that I need God in my life to make it complete."

None was more articulate than one young woman who, in a contemporary Magnificat, described her readiness for the sacrament:

The Lord has done awesome things for me this year. I was excited about confirmation for quite a while before I was in it, but the spiritual growth I've experienced while preparing for the sacrament has far exceeded any expectations I had. I think the most important thing this preparation has done for me is to introduce me to Jesus in an intimate, personal way, a way I'd never known him before. That, in turn, released in me a desire to know God, and especially to know God's will for me, in a deep, loving relationship for the rest of my life. And it has made me realize how empty my life will be if I ever lose focus on

God. God helps me in every area of my life — in coping with stresses, in my family relationships, in my relationship with myself. I am amazed *daily* at the way God works. I can't wait for confirmation. It is my chance to publicly profess my promise to God and the Catholic church that I will live out his word for the rest of my life. It is, with no comparison, the most significant step I will take at this point in my mature life.

The experiences described above have been limited to those of the confirmandi. The scope of the interviews did not include significant others in the lives of the these young people. Nevertheless, it seems inconceivable that the growth and change undergone by these teens would be missed by those around them. Their experience in the confirmation process will have a ripple effect to the extent that those significant in their lives pay attention. Their parents, siblings, friends, classmates and co-workers will themselves be edified, in the best sense of that word, and perhaps even invited to deeper personal faith because of the great-hearted commitment of these newly mature women and men.

Celebration: Rite of Confirmation

As we move to the ritualization of this experience, several preliminary comments are in order. The first and most important is to acknowledge that the ritual of confirmation is an utterly bare-bones rite, especially when compared to the RCIA. The *Rite of Confirmation* has no provision for rituals during the process of sacramental preparation — no prayers, blessings, celebrations of the word of God, scrutinies and so on. There is nothing by way of liturgical support throughout the period of preparation. That does not mean that ritual is not possible, but that it must be developed locally.

Furthermore, the rite itself obviously suffers from its ritual history. The rite consists of laying on of hands, anointing and prayer — three modest elements of the larger initiatory ritual. There are optional intercessions and a model homily for the bishop but both are regularly developed for the concrete situation and in light of the scriptures selected for the rite. The candidate only speaks when asked to renew baptismal vows. Particularly in light of the extraordinary religious experience of the candidates, it is obvious that attention needs to be given to the development of more adequate and ample rituals throughout the process of preparation and in its sacramental climax. Teens who were exceptionally eloquent about their experience of the journey by and large had little to say about the ritual, a point to which we must pay attention.

OUTLINE OF THE RITE

Introductory Rite

Liturgy of the Word

Sacrament of Confirmation

- *Presentation*
- *Renewal of Baptismal Promises*
- *Laying on of Hands*
- *Anointing with Chrism*

Intercessions

Liturgy of the Eucharist

Concluding Rite

INTRODUCTORY RITE

After the rich and deep experience of the year of preparation, the discoveries of God and self and a community that will support and sustain their relationship with God and their daily choices, after all that growth and depth, the rite of confirmation is decidedly understated. It is a simple and brief celebration of a reality that has already taken place: "I am already confirmed in my heart and would love to take the final steps toward confirming my faith. My journey will not end here, but it is just the beginning."

One significant element of the rite for participants is the presence of the bishop, a tangible sign for them of the larger church and of the importance that the church attaches to this moment. More importantly, the presence of the bishop provides the opportunity for a human encounter with a respected leader of the community in which they now assume adult responsibilities. While most of the celebration appears to candidates to be "just like Mass," at least one noticed and commented on the bishop's unique greeting "Peace be with you" as true to the experience of the moment. "There was so much peace and so much love in that room it was incredible, and then he named it, and he said it again after the anointing."

LITURGY OF THE WORD

The homily provoked some comment: "What sparked me was in the homily; the 'love one another' came up three times in the readings. And one of the things the bishop was saying was that Christ chose us first and that's why it is our responsibility to choose Christ, really, actively. That's one of the things that really kept going through my mind."

SACRAMENT OF CONFIRMATION

After the presentation of the candidates and the homily, there is a simple renewal of baptismal vows, the one opportunity for the candidates to speak for themselves. This renewal could be enhanced with a blessing and sprinkling of baptismal water, another important symbolic and tactile element which might forge a stronger and more obvious link with baptism.

Next the bishop begins the laying on of hands and prayer. In large groups, an individual laying on of hands is regularly forgone in the interests of time. That decision virtually guarantees that the gesture will be forgettable. (Compare the power of the gesture of imposing hands over a larger group all at once and of the gesture of laying on of hands individually as described in chapter seven on reconciliation.) The communal laying on of hands also has the effect of minimizing the accompanying prayer for the gifts of the Spirit: wisdom and understanding, right judgment and courage, knowledge and reverence, wonder and awe in God's presence. One young woman remembered that there was "some prayer," but the content was lost on her as she was transported by the grace of the moment: "I just closed my eyes and prayed to Jesus that I would be set on fire."

ANOINTING WITH CHRISM

Anointing with chrism, being called by name, the closeness and support of the sponsor and the words "Be sealed with the gift of the Holy Spirit" — these are experienced together as the powerful moment of God's presence and activity. As in other sacraments, the tactile element — the touch, the scent of the oil, the feeling of the sponsor whose right hand rests on the candidate's shoulder — all of this contributes to the power of this rite. The tracing of oil and the joy of the moment are what linger in memories and continue to unfold.

Remarkably, the many layers of biblical and contemporary meaning attached to oil form part of the experience articulated by one or another of the confirmandi: abundance, joy, cleansing, limbering, healing, soothing and making its recipient radiant with health and strength. "For me the oil was this rush, and I really felt the presence of God in my heart." "I could feel the Spirit." "I could see the Spirit glowing on everybody's faces." "It was just the most amazing feeling. To truly know that the Holy Spirit is with you and the Spirit will be with you forever and that you are chosen as one of God's own people to live eternally with Jesus and all the saints." "The oil was like a sealing of my love and faith in God." "I felt healed and whole."

Then the applause began, a warm and sustained approval on the part of the community who wanted and needed to express their joy for these young men and women and their acceptance of the confirmandis' pledge of active membership in the church. The year of preparation had been a time of mutual ministry between the teens and the adults in the parish, months of preparation when teens and adults pay attention to each other and witness to one another the active presence and power of the Spirit in daily life. Indeed, one spokesperson for the teens addressed the assembly with these words:

> You have held us up as we have walked this journey of faith. You have given us example. You have shown us the face of Jesus and given us hope for tomorrow. We have pledged all that we have and all that we are to Jesus Christ and to his people, knowing that this is possible only through the power of the Holy Spirit. Thus we humbly request the gift of that Holy Spirit from this community through the sacrament of confirmation.

Liturgy of the Eucharist and Concluding Rite

Fewer teens commented on the eucharist, perhaps because it was the more predictable element of the celebration. However, there were nods of assent as one stated: "The most precious gift is the eucharist. Jesus gave himself up for us."

Finally, one parent captured the miracle of grace which had taken place over the previous year in the hearts and lives of the young adults, now confirmed/conformed:

"The glow of the faces of the teens after they are blessed and after the bishop gives the blessing. It is remarkable to see the faces and the joy and just to think about where they started from, from day one to here, and the choices they have made."

Amen

What about the Amen? Teenagers who take this "conformation" journey seriously cannot help but be touched and transformed by it. They may have been made to begin the journey by family pressure; by the end there is a personal commitment to the process and a recognition that they have only just begun. A number of those who continued throughout the year decided that they were not yet ready, perhaps because they felt like this young man: "The truth is I was scared of the commitment." Others drifted away in earlier stages. But for those who persevere, who give themselves over to the process, there is growth in relationship with God, greater confidence in moral decision-making and a recognition of responsibilities to the community and to the whole of humanity. The process as well as the rite invite commitment for the long haul. "I think the biggest responsibility is afterwards. Just because you are confirmed doesn't mean that it's over. That's just a beginning. You've made the commitment and now you have to live on that commitment."

What happened in the sacrament? What, concretely, was the "Amen"? "We made an actual commitment. We said yes." To what? "To God's call, to serve, to discipleship, to becoming like Christ, to love, to follow." "My yes was turning away from my old lifestyle, which was a struggle for me because of all the doubts and everything that held me back. I went through a phase of testing God; I went through a phase of rejecting God. And when it comes down to it I knew deep in my heart that God was real and that God was calling me. And I just kept searching for the truth and searching for God. This has meant drastic changes."

There was a sense that conversion made very real demands, "drastic changes" in the day to day. Some are still in the process and the struggle: "I haven't made all the changes yet, but I'm back in school and I've been sober for months. I've broken off all my old contacts, all my old friends."

For others, confirmation proved to be a kind of awakening: "I've made God part of the daily routine." "I am so in love with God and my faith is on fire." "I want to stand as a witness to all as a confirmed Catholic that I will live and die for Jesus.

I have a wonderful relationship with God that is constantly getting better." "I basically said I'd give my life, I'd change my life if God would help me. That's it." "Here I am happy and holy. I have learned that living for Christ is possible." "I believe I have learned to love more deeply, which to me is the purpose of life." Indeed.

Are the young people I interviewed unusual? I do not think so. They seemed to me to be pretty typical kids. What was unusual was the process that they had traversed. The experience they articulated does not happen without enormous pastoral support and a structure that made demands on their time and commitment. There were required weekly meetings in groups small enough for acceptance, trust and good dialogue in safe company. There was accountability about service. There were expectations about regular attendance at Mass, a retreat, days of renewal and the celebration of reconciliation. There was a large group of adults and recently confirmed teens willing to be part of the journey and to become faith-sharers, committed people who were actively on a personal spiritual journey and trying to live faith-fully. Capturing the hearts and imaginations of teens, harnessing their energies, drawing on all the great-hearted good will of which they are capable, providing structures and expectations and an enormous amount of trust and support make it possible for these young people to imagine themselves conformed to Christ and to attend seriously to the journey they began in baptism, their journey into God.

There are a growing number of dioceses in the United States that are adopting a different pastoral strategy for confirmation, namely, restoring the ancient order of baptism, confirmation and eucharist and placing confirmation immediately before first eucharist for children seven and eight years old. This decision has a number of implications. Age is a critical consideration in the process designed for the candidates for the sacrament. The retreats, faith-sharing, prayer and attention to moral development would all need to be modified in the sacramental preparation of younger children who have a different kind of religious awakening at what is called the age of reason. Reinserting confirmation between baptism and first eucharist has the advantage of restoring the more logical ordering of the initiation sacraments. Confirmation, in this schema, serves as a modest ritual completion of the water bath leading one to the table where full membership is most perfectly symbolized. The service component, the idea of public witness of one's faith and the assumption of adult status in the church would necessarily yield to other values in the process of preparing younger candidates.

More critical, if confirmation in the early grade-school years becomes widespread, is the need for dioceses and parishes to provide some other form of pastoral care for teenagers that will draw out the same kind of large-hearted response to faith and commitment as is evident in these pages of testimony. The tendency in many places is to write teenagers off, to think of them and treat them as church drop-outs, difficult, intractable, resistant to religion and to God. Teen programs languish in many parishes. I believe the experience described in these pages cries out for a ministry to adolescents, whether or not confirmation is involved, as thorough and thoughtful as the one detailed here.

Chapter Six

Marriage and Vocation

. . . that those who live might live no longer for themselves . . .
2 Corinthians 5:15

PRELUDE

In this chapter, we will look first at the meaning of vocation and then turn to marriage as a particular expression of Christian vocation. Once we have explored the experience, celebration and commitment of sacramental marriage, we will conclude the chapter with brief comments about the sacrament of orders and the rites of religious profession.

There is a most interesting parallel among the rites of marriage, orders and religious profession which demonstrates at a liturgical and symbolic level that each of these rituals brings to public expression a similar though clearly distinct experience — the experience of divine call and human response lived out in different states of life.

First, then, vocation.

VOCATION

Traditionally, when Catholics spoke about "having a vocation" it meant that someone was called to religious life or to the priesthood. Those "with a vocation" had received a special calling to follow Jesus more closely. Theirs was a special summons to make a gift of their lives to God. A vocation, a call from God, was something that used to be coveted. Catholic mothers, particularly, would pray that one of their children might enter religious life or be blessed with a vocation to the priesthood. Even today we persist in using the word *vocation* in this restricted sense. We speak, for example, about a "vocation shortage" and we are regularly enjoined to "pray for vocations."

But the fact is, we do not have a vocation shortage because vocations are not in short supply. Everyone has a vocation. What is in remarkably short supply is the awareness that each of us has received a unique call from God, a divine vocation. That general unawareness is the real vocation crisis today, and it is a crisis because it seems to insinuate that priesthood and religious life are the only God-oriented vocations. By extension, the implication is that as people choose a state of life and give themselves to its unfolding, those who do not embrace a "religious" calling need not take God nearly as seriously as those who do. This misapprehension plays itself out in a variety of ways, not the least of which is that we appear to ask far more of teens preparing for confirmation than we do of those preparing to enter the lifelong covenant of marriage.

The scriptures know no such limitation on the word *vocation*. The pages of the Bible are peppered with the language of call, indeed, of divine call: We are called by God to freedom (Galatians 5:13), to peace (1 Corinthians 7:15) and to hope (Ephesians 4:4). We are called in one body (Colossians 3:15), with a holy calling (2 Timothy 1:9), as children of God (1 John 3:1). We are called to eternal life (1 Timothy 6:12) and to eternal glory (1 Peter 5:10). We are called to belong to Jesus Christ (Romans 1:6) and to enter into fellowship with him (1 Corinthians 1:9). We have been called out of darkness (1 Peter 2:9) to be saints (Romans 1:7) and to be friends of God (John 15:15). Indeed, before we were born, from our mother's womb, we were called by God and given our name (Isaiah 49:1). "Thus says the Lord, who created you, O Jacob, who formed you, O Israel: Do not fear, for I have redeemed you; I have called you by your name, you are mine" (Isaiah 43:1). Thus does Isaiah describe the call of God in language of creation, redemption, vocation and possession. But God's possession of us is not coerced; it follows our free human response. One might even hear in God's calling the longing of God for each one of us to be in relationship with God, to become God's friend. The divine call is a free gift; human response must also be freely given.

Vocation, then, is not just for the chosen few; it is for each one of us whom God has made, whom God loves and longs for, whom God calls by name. God's call is dependent on our hearing it, of course. Vocation involves being attuned and attentive to the voice of God, mediated to be sure by the people and events of our lives, in order to discover and grow into the unique name God has given each one of us. Everyone, then, has a divine call to "enter the religious life," in the sense that everyone has been called to be in relationship with God.

The basic Christian vocation, celebrated in baptism, is what Vatican II described as a "universal call to holiness." What does that mean? The word *holiness*, once regularly reserved to the saints, is another word being welcomed back into general religious vocabulary. Holiness, the Christian's lifelong task, is achieved by becoming more and more fully human. That is the message of the Incarnation.

Holiness includes delighting in this world rather than fleeing it, recognizing that God, the creator and sustainer of all things, is revealed at the very heart of the world and of human experience. Holiness involves becoming the person whom God calls us to be in the midst of the world, allowing the action of God and the life of God to pervade and transform our lives. Holiness is coming to be more and more Godlike by putting on the mind and heart of Christ, for Christ is the perfect sacrament of God.

"Putting on the mind and heart of Christ." It seems that we have circled back to the theme of becoming like God by *conforming* ourselves to Jesus Christ. Jesus Christ is not only the revelation of who God is for us but also God's revelation to us of what it means to be fully human. If that is so, then Jesus' dying and rising is the law of human life, no matter which path is chosen. As Christian women and men approaching maturity begin to weigh which particular state of life will lead them most surely to becoming holy and human, conformity to Christ takes on new depth. The language of dying and rising, the language of the paschal mystery of Christ and our participation in that mysterious cycle for the life of the world — that is the only legitimate way to talk about the universal vocation. Every state of life involves death and life if it is to be our avenue to full human life modeled on that of Jesus Christ.

While we share the universal call to holiness, each of us is unique in God's eyes and each of us has a singular vocation and mission. The Book of Revelation uses an intriguing metaphor that seems to capture both the universality and the distinctiveness of our vocations: "To everyone . . . I will give a white stone, and on the white stone is written a new name that no one knows except the one who receives it" (2:17). Discovering and becoming that new name written on the stone involves a life of discipleship in order to learn daily from Jesus the way to be human and holy. At the same time, being faithful to the "white stone" takes us down different paths of discipleship.

Marriage, the single life, the religious life and the priesthood all represent ways of holiness, ways of discipleship, ways of dying and rising. We may discover, as we fall in love with another person, that we will become most fully human and holy by following Jesus in totally self-giving love to another in marriage. We may be drawn to the single life and to imitation of the solitary Jesus, rootless and restless about the reign of God, going about freely doing good. We may realize that we need to throw in our lot with others of like vision in order to follow Jesus, poor, chaste and obedient in a community of life and mission, and thus experience an attraction to religious life. We may be drawn to the imitation of Jesus whose ministry was that of word, unity and charity, and that predilection would signal a call to ordained ministry in the church.

Only two of these vocational choices are numbered among the seven sacraments. That religious life is not included among the sacraments of the Roman Catholic church today is largely an accident of history and the perhaps too-narrow medieval interpretation of institution by Christ. Single life has never been designated a sacrament, strictly speaking, because historically and culturally it was not considered a suitable choice — or a choice at all, for that matter! The single life and the religious life are obviously open to sacramentality, although only the choice of religious life is blessed by a liturgical rite. Perhaps, now that the single life is culturally acceptable and more frequently a vocation of choice, some form of religious ritual may eventually be prepared to bless this life choice and provide the prayerful support of the community for its maturation.

Marriage, single life, religious life and ordained ministry are four distinct ways of responding to God's call. Vocational choice hinges on selecting that way of life which will most clearly help us to fulfill God's longings for us. The vast majority, of course, choose marriage as their path to God. To that sacrament we now turn.

The reflections that follow are from couples who took their marriage preparation very seriously and entered into marriage precisely as a path to God. Their reflections are not the usual language with which young couples speak about their preparations for marriage or the celebration of their wedding, but the insights of these faith-filled couples provide us with a glimpse of what marriage can be when couples choose this way of life as their path to becoming human and holy in Christ.

The question these witnesses pose by their perceptive appreciation of the real meaning of a sacramental marriage is the question of how to bring other baptized Christians entering into marriage to this same realization of sacramentality. It is a challenge addressed in the introduction to the *Rite of Marriage* (RM): "Priests should first of all strengthen and nourish the faith of those about to be married, for the sacrament of matrimony presupposes and demands faith."

The sacrament of marriage plays itself out over a lifetime; couples become the sacrament they have professed in a process of lasting fidelity and mutual affection. More than any of the other sacraments, marriage is a process whose beginnings we mark with ritual care but whose full sacramentality is realized only over the life of the marriage. Perhaps this process, with Christ as its sure foundation and inspiration, is what Pope John Paul II had in mind when he spoke of marriage as that which unites the spouses and binds them "to their eventual souls" — two spirits gradually, almost imperceptibly, becoming human and holy in Christ through the ministry of the other and the grace of God. Such is the experience of Christian marriage.

Experience: Loving and Dying

What is the conversion journey that marriage celebrates? To which facet of the paschal mystery do couples who decide to have their marriage solemnized by the church join themselves? Why are we even using the language of "conversion" and "paschal mystery" for an experience as joyous, as beautiful and tender as falling in love and getting married?

Simply stated, we use language about conversion and paschal mystery because loving and dying are synonymous. Every loving is a dying — a dying to my own time, comfort, convenience, wants, needs, concerns, interests. Every loving is a dying to self-interest and self-aggrandizement in an act of generosity and self-giving. Every loving is a dying to egoism, a dying to "I" in order that two "I's" become a "we." Every loving implies acceptance of the other, single-heartedness, mutuality and giving and taking without keeping score — and all of it happens not just when one or the other feels like it but daily, and for all the days of ordinary time as well as in the high holy seasons of a marriage.

We use language about conversion and paschal mystery in speaking about the reality of married love — and about mutual and lasting fidelity as a witness to God's steadfast love — because these realities need to be spoken to a starry-eyed couple caught up in the easy springtime of relationship, where life abounds and death in its many guises seems remote. Until couples face up to and embrace the real demands of conversion, until they choose to die as well as to love — and to beg God's help and God's blessing on all their loving and all their dying — their marriage has not yet become a sacrament. A wedding does not make a marriage. A wedding simply makes a marriage possible.

Some of the dimensions of the paschal mystery that a couple faces are spelled out explicitly both in the promises and in the exchange of consent that are part of the ceremony. There are three questions asked of a couple at the beginning of the celebration, questions about freedom and faithfulness and children (RM, 44), and each of them is really an invitation to a kind of personal death for the sake of new life: "Have you come here freely and without reservation to give yourselves to each other in marriage?" The couple is invited to state before all present that they choose freely to bind themselves to each other without reserve. "Will you love and honor each other for the rest of your lives?" In pledging faithfulness, the couple accepts the death involved in choosing *one* person and the foreclosure of all other choices. "Will you accept children lovingly from God?" Couples are asked to make a public promise that the world they share is radically open to others lest the death of the ego that becomes "we" simply becomes the closed world of "ego squared."

The vows of consent also spell out a rhythm of dying and rising: better and worse, sickness and health, poverty and riches (#45). The exchange of consent names some of the ways in which the paschal mystery will touch the lives of this couple, and the metaphors of health and prosperity and their loss are just that, metaphors for the rhythm of our days, of dishes and work schedules and children to be fed and cars that need servicing and the thousand details of life, large and small, that constitute the keeping of these promises — to say nothing of the crises, the moments of grief and loss, grave illness, financial woes, that form larger challenges to promise keeping.

But how is any of this possible? Keeping promises is the way by which the old self is changed into something light and generous and good and for the other. One couple said, "I think we found a lot of our identity in the whole paschal mystery, in death and rising and that kind of rhythm of life. That's why we chose to have our marriage at a eucharist. It's where we have found our deepest identity."

MARRIAGE PREPARATION

How do couples get to this depth? One person described a Sunday eucharist that took place shortly after a young couple had become engaged. The couple were recognized at the end of the celebration of eucharist, and invited to come forward. They were given a Bible and urged to make the scriptures part of their preparation and to realize that they were inviting Christ into their lives. Then they were blessed by the whole community. "It was very moving," was the response, "and it made me think about my own vows. But that kind of attention to the engaged is the exception."

Another couple was blessed with the support and the prayer of friends of like mind: "I will say that it was really beautiful, the small faith community that we had been with every other week, mostly the same people for probably a year and a half. They were very much a part of our marriage preparation as plans went along. The week before we got married, the person who had volunteered to plan the prayer did a whole prayer time with us, nuptial blessing and that sort of thing. That was very supportive, in addition to their own individual support as friends."

While the present *Rite of Marriage* makes no provision for rituals of engagement or other forms of prayer during the time of preparation, the revised rite now in production is likely to pay more attention to the several successive stages of the process of marriage preparation. The Bishops' Conference of England and Wales, for example, has recently approved a new rite of marriage that incorporates rites for the celebration of engagement at home and in the church, prayer for the period of engagement, the blessing of food in the home, the blessing of couples at Sunday Mass, and the blessing of a son or daughter before marriage. Such rituals, modeled on other phased rites such as the *Rite of Christian Initiation of Adults*, respect the process nature of this rite of passage, the progressive stages of conversion, and the need to bring personal experience to ritual celebration along the way.

Couples regularly cite the importance of pre-Cana conferences in their formation, or alternatively, their disappointment with the marriage preparation offered by the church. Here is a positive assessment of its strengths: "The pre-Cana time was just a wonderful time for us to stop and talk and reflect and pray together, but that's because the priest was our friend and was willing to spend time with us. We met regularly for almost four months, seven times or so. It gave us a solid chunk of time to discuss things and we had a little ritual that we did, always praying together."

Marriage inventory tools bring to the surface potential issues of compatibility and values, and assist a couple in examining the viability of their living for each other. Pre-Cana discussions and prayer, when thoughtfully organized and skillfully overseen, can explore these areas and others: issues and practices of faith, ways of emotional separation from families of origin, development of a talent for friendship, ideas about sexual intimacy, expectations about children and child-rearing, and all the while, learning a ministry of forgiveness. Finances, friends, interests, problem-solving and communication patterns are also important topics to be explored. Often unspoken fears need also to be brought up, chief among them the fear of failure and insecurities about one's ability to sustain love for the long haul.

"In terms of the engagement, it was really important for us to have the time to talk and reflect and think about what it was we were doing and why we were doing it, just one more time. . . . We had blessings every time. We might just all hold hands and say something, or pray together a common prayer. It was always something a little different, but was always some prayer. We always opened with a prayer, too. And we had to tell each other at the end of every meeting why we loved the other person. Every single time. And then the priest who was with us who was our good friend told us why he loved us. It was really awesome."

That description, however, applies to only a small portion of pre-Cana preparation. Too often preparation is rushed — "The first thing the leaders said was 'Why don't we skip lunch so that we can get out of here sooner.' It was a big disappointment." Sometimes leaders are apologetic about the church and its accumulated wisdom — "This deacon couple made fun of the church, and they were very nonchalant about its teachings, especially about sexuality and children." Sometimes pre-Cana leadership presents an oddly distorted view of married life — "The couple talked a lot about the problems they had in their marriage. It seemed as though it was focused on the problems. There are not always going to be happy times in a marriage, but I think there ought to be a better balance. They focused way too much on the negative things."

Pre-Cana appears to be a mixed blessing, almost exclusively dependent on each group's leadership for its focus and direction. The other major difficulty with pre-Cana preparation is the mixture of people who come, many because it is one more requirement to be gotten out of the way—rather on the same order as finding the dress and ordering the flowers and planning the menu for the reception afterward. It is something to be checked off on a list. One pre-Cana leader said, "You see a lot of couples coming who are not churched. The common denominator is unchurched couples coming back to church for this kind of gateway experience. We certainly oftentimes fail to bring them back or to welcome them into the church or see this as a wonderful opportunity to try to rekindle baptismal faith."

Others are disappointed that they are not more stretched in their faith and in their loving and dying: "What is there for people like us who have claimed our faith and want an experience that uses that, that gets below the surface?" And one wonders how serious conversation could possibly have been expected of the following group: "We went to the one-day special pre-Cana for those who had been married before, or were old! So we were there with PhDs and with one poor young woman whose first husband was in jail and she was pregnant and trying to get married again. And this attorney couple were very concerned about all the financial things, about whose children were going to get what money. It was an interesting small group discussion!" Interesting, yes, but hardly capable of moving from the surface issues to the heart of it.

There appears to be widespread dissatisfaction with the way the church accompanies those preparing for sacramental marriage. Indeed, we may question the value of our sacramental preparation for marriage when the divorce rate among Catholics matches that of the population at large. In comparison with the preparation for other states of life, marriage preparation is minimal. Men preparing for ordained ministry regularly receive four or five years of preparation. A four-year divinity degree is often joined to a year of pastoral internship where the candidate is mentored in his ministerial experience. Along the way the candidate is tested in a variety of ways to ascertain that he is suited to this way of life, that he has the maturity and stamina to fulfill the duties, and the heart and hope to be a true icon of Jesus before the community he serves. Women and men contemplating religious life are sometimes asked to spend one or two years simply getting to know the community they wish to join before any formal candidacy is possible. Spiritual direction and personal prayer become part of a discernment of call. There follows a year of candidacy, much like a catechumenate, during which the candidate lives the life from inside and tests self for suitability. Temporary vows come next, allowing yet more time for a definitive discernment of call and aptitude for the religious life. Both of these choices are undertaken only after years of preparation, careful mentoring and some attempt to live the life and to hear one's heart in the process. How can we treat couples preparing to take similar solemn vows before God and the community with the same seriousness?

PLANNING THE WEDDING

Invariably, the planning of the wedding ceremony is an opportunity to turn the couple toward the scriptures, the promises and the prayers — and toward the One before whom all these words will be uttered. If marriage as vocation to holiness has not heretofore been brought up, this is a critical opportunity not to be lost. Three important questions may surface during the planning phase: the meaning of Christian marriage, the role of the community and the choice of eucharist as the context for the sacrament.

One couple began their preparations with the question of meaning: "We started with the larger questions: What does this mean for us? What do we want, in general, to be about? And then we turned to the readings — they were unbelievably rich and they help to give words to what we hoped to say and do." Another couple stated quite simply: "We are doing this as Christian people and we really wanted that to be clear."

Marriage as an ecclesial act was a weighty consideration for others: "I remember us discussing first that this was definitely a public thing for us, and it wasn't something we were doing alone. That was really important, that the community was there." The role of the community for another couple had to do with their presence and support at the wedding as promise of presence for the long haul: "For us it ties back to who we think we are and how we will turn outward and express God's love to these people around us. We turn outward to people who then support us in who we are, together, so we can support each other and then turn outwards again." Yet another couple concurred: "We know we can't do this alone, we don't do this alone. It's those people who were there who not only help us stay married, but invariably act in supportive roles."

Whether or not to solemnize marriage in a eucharist is another question to be explored candidly. What does it mean? What could it mean? Does it even matter? Absolutely, according to these respondents: "When we celebrate eucharist we celebrate God and that is so intimately related to what we were celebrating that day." One couple remembered that their friends had suggested skipping the eucharist and having the marriage in the midst of a short prayer service, to which suggestion they responded: "For us that made no sense because eucharist was very much the rhythm of our lives. It wasn't an add-on to do it for the wedding, it was part of our ceremony because it was part of us. Plus our gospel reading was the Emmaus story, so the table was very central — central to our thinking and central to our lives."

Celebration: The Rite of Marriage

OUTLINE OF THE RITE

Introductory Rite

Liturgy of the Word

Celebration of Marriage

- *Questions before the Consent*
- *Exchange of Consent*
- *Explanatory Rites (Exchange of Rings)*

Intercessions

Liturgy of the Eucharist (including the Nuptial Blessing)

Concluding Rite

The *Rite of Marriage* is a curious amalgam of domestic and ecclesiastical ceremony reflecting its cultural origins and Christian development. For the first few centuries of Christianity, the community simply adopted and adapted familial customs of marriage, which revolved primarily around the bride. Accompanied by her family and friends, the bride was led in procession to the groom's home for a protracted party. Promises, exchange of money, exchange of rings, meals, veiling, other celebratory attire, the joining of right hands, the first public kiss—all of these ceremonies had their origin in domestic, not ecclesial, practice. Some of them marked the period of betrothal, others that of the marriage itself. While marriage remained largely a domestic ritual, the bishop's approval was sometimes sought and gradually came to be expected before the marriage of a cleric. When the bishop or one of his presbyters was a guest at the wedding banquet, it was natural to ask for a blessing of the new couple in the course of the celebration. Gradually, the church's blessing moved from the banquet hall to the church proper, where couples might pause in procession from one home to the other to exchange consent at the door of the church and there receive a blessing. Eventually, before the end of the first millennium, many of the domestic practices of betrothal and marriage had been transformed into a single liturgical rite. The church recognized that it had a major stake in the strength and stability of marriage and that God's blessing on these rites was less an honor than an urgent requirement.

INTRODUCTORY RITE

The wedding celebration remains laden with custom, some of it under scrutiny in light of changing cultural realities—although it is interesting that sometimes even the most ardent feminist misses the anomaly in being given away by her father to her bridegroom. The couples represented in the interviews that follow all considered the flexible elements of the marriage ceremony, particularly the pattern of the procession and introductory rites, in light of their relationship to one another and to their families and friends. For all of them, the wedding was first of all a time to make a public, ecclesial statement of their growing experience of loving and dying and their intention to embrace both.

"We walked in together. That's what we had done week after week in our parish and it was also the mutuality that we wanted in our marriage. And his parents and my parents were part of the procession. It was a liturgical procession with the cross, the book and the priest."

"One of my favorite memories is that we processed in together and we sang a hymn, this wonderful text, 'O praise the gracious power' and we really tried to be sensitive because of having so many musician friends and liturgy friends."

"I remember being astonished by the people, and also by the coming together for a single purpose. It seems like everyone is there on regular Sundays for a whole lot of different reasons but everyone comes to a wedding for just one reason. And there is still a lot of it I haven't completely understood. I don't know what happened or why, exactly, but this singleness of purpose was overwhelming."

Another couple had a similar experience: "We processed in with our families. My parents and his parents. We both walked in together. And I also had the experience of all of a sudden having it hit me that all of these people were here because they loved us and delighted in our happiness."

Furthermore, the public and ecclesial import of the rite is something that often dawns on couples in the course of planning the celebration:

"At first I thought of this marriage as a private thing. I didn't expect to be married again, and my husband never expected to be married, having been in a religious community for a while. When this surprise happened, my first instinct was that this would just be a small little thing we will do. But because we lived and worked with people who care about us and are very much community-oriented, we really grew into it. They taught me along the way that this was something that a lot of people cared about and it was just going to have to be this public thing. One of the most touching things for me was that as we stood in the back of the church everybody stood up and turned around, and it just struck me to see their faces. I was so touched when suddenly I realized that these were all people I knew, and how much this whole church cared about us. That really struck me."

One couple decided to place the three questions—about freedom, fidelity and children—at the beginning of the celebration, at the door of the church, thus signifying by speaking their intention at the threshold of the church their entry into a new way of life.

"We greeted people at the door and I remember at the beginning of the ceremony the procession came to the back of the church and the priest welcomed everyone. Then the three questions, the statement of intentions, were asked of us and then we crafted a question in return. We worked it out with the presider to ask the assembly a question of support. 'Will you support this couple?' So in addition to 'Will you accept children lovingly from God?' and 'Have you come here freely?' and 'Will you love each other faithfully?' we turned to the community and asked that they would support us in this love that we were professing and in this family that we were forming. That was very important."

LITURGY OF THE WORD

There is a wide latitude in the readings suggested in the *Rite of Marriage*. Reflection on the scriptures and the selection of readings can become a rich source of grace in the course of marriage preparation. A couple will be led to reflect on a variety of passages and to decide how best to capture their experience in light of the word of God. At the same time they may find in different passages both consolation and challenge and thereby be led to deeper reflection on the meaning of this step as a specifically Christian choice and action.

"The Wisdom reading was so much about the fact that God created us in love and God would not discourage whatever God has made. And then we wanted to focus on the gathering so we read 'where two or three are gathered there is Christ in their midst.'"

"In a way the homily was somewhat written by us because the presider asked us why we chose the readings and wove in our responses. We had two readings: One was the Colossians passage 'You are God's chosen race, a royal priesthood, a people set apart' and the other was the Emmaus story. And we chose that because we believe our marriage will be a journey with Christ walking with us, and we also talked about how that relates to the eucharist and the eucharistic prayer. It all tied together."

"The homily part I remember was on commitment and paschal mystery and the challenge of committing to another person and the struggle of relationship—and that was very important and a really central theme."

CELEBRATION OF MARRIAGE

The exchange of consent is the central sacramental act of the marriage rite. Preceded by the triple declaration of intent, perhaps at the door of the church, the exchange of consent takes place in the sanctuary before the community and the altar—a place of witness and of sacrifice. "Just to stand there and say those things to each other in front of all those people who love us was really very moving." That is the nearly universal experience of the marriage rite: The heart of it is the exchange of vows.

"The highlight was the vows. Mary wanted me to memorize the vows, which I argued about at first, because I didn't think I could do it. I didn't feel comfortable. I'm not a public speaker and for me to stand in front of 150 people and recite the vows—I was just terrified by the whole idea. I didn't think I could do it. She convinced me that I should, and I'm glad I did, because the whole thing of the priest saying two words and the groom saying two words, and the priest saying two words seems kind of funny, that you're just repeating and not saying what you believe and what you feel. By me saying the vows I felt like I was really professing what I wanted to happen."

His wife added: "Exchange of consent, vows—it was definitely a highlight for me, too—that public witness. And to be able to do it in a Christian context, to stand up there before the altar and make a profession of faith, saying 'with Christ's love I choose you for my spouse.' Again, I keep going back to that meeting along the road in the Emmaus story, which is so much a part of me. To stand up there and say we will be journeying together. That was what was important. This is only the beginning."

This couple suggest by their comments an understanding that the wedding ceremony is simply marking the beginning of the sacrament, the beginning of the journey, the beginning of what will happen in a life of vowed relationship, public promise and public witness: "I publicly said these vows to Jim, but I was also saying them to these people. I really felt like that."

LITURGY OF THE EUCHARIST

"I think it culminated at communion, actually. We stood at the altar, and then also distributed communion. And for me that felt like a seal on the vows in that we were saying that we were going to love each other, and that our love is going to grow and blossom and spread out into the world in the way that God calls us to love every human being on earth, in the way that Jesus did. And we share this bread with you now. It was just the ultimate sign of love to share the bread and wine with every individual. This is what it's about. It is Jim and me, but it is so much more. And I wanted to cry at that moment. It started with this realization at the procession and then sort of culminated at communion."

SIGNING OF THE MARRIAGE RECORD
"Instead of having a guest book sort of thing, we wrote out our vows on big pieces of paper that we then were able to put into a book and have people sign the vows. It was their participation in what we were saying, sort of taking off from the Jewish tradition. It is amazing to go back and read those things, and that was one of the ways for us to draw people into the communal aspect of all of that."

A FINAL COMMENT
"What mattered to us a lot was that at the reception people weren't focused on the 'nice dress' kind of comments but said how much they were moved by the liturgy. That told us we had planned it well."

Amen
In all the rites and sacraments of vocation, as we shall see, there is a heightened awareness of commitment because that it precisely what the sacrament is all about. And Amen takes a number of different forms: the questions of intent, the exchange of consent or public vows or promises, the sacramental blessing, the music and readings and prayers carefully chosen to express faith and the aspirations for the life just beginning.

"Amen for me was to the grace of the sacrament, to the love and the strength to commit myself to another person, even to knowing the pain of a fully generous love."

"I promised to love the way God loves us, without waiting for a return."

"I hope to help transform our house into a home for ourselves and in offering a place for others—hospitality. And within the boundaries of our home I will try to meet God."

"I think the blessing of a marriage goes beyond the two of us to interaction with the world and I want to extend our love to that wider community."

"I promise to love and to cherish and to honor and to forgive, and to keep Christ a part of our lives. That's my Amen."

OTHER RITES OF VOCATION

The rite of marriage is only one of the community's rites of vocation. It has close ritual parallels with the rites of religious profession and the rites of ordination. Each of these rites brings a personal, internal response to vocation to public ritual expression. Each of these rites helps to articulate in different ways the evangelical counsels — poverty, chastity and obedience — because each of the vocations must come to terms with the goodness of the body, the wonders of material reality and the community of discernment within which men and women choose to live out their unique call.

Each of these rites of vocation has a similar pattern: questions of the candidate about intention, specific promises spoken before a faith community, reference to baptism as here enriched and strengthened, discussion of duties assumed and witness promised — and all of it a way to ask God's blessing on this person in this path of holiness, all of it a pattern of reading and prayer and promise that this man, these women, that couple might become more fully human in imitation of Christ. Each of these vocations is a way of loving and dying and joining ourselves to the paschal mystery of Jesus Christ. And, interestingly enough, orders, profession and marriage are each and all ways of ordering the church for the spiritual good of its members and for mission in the world.

Chapter Seven

Reconciliation

While the son was still far off, his father saw him and was filled with compassion; he ran and put his arms around him and kissed him.

Luke 15:20

PRELUDE

One of the best-kept secrets of the renewed liturgy is the sacrament of penance, now more often called the sacrament of reconciliation. This nomenclature comes from its central focus and the titles given to its several individual parts: Rite I, Rite for Reconciliation of Individual Penitents; Rite II, Rite for Reconciliation of Several Penitents with Individual Confession and Absolution; and Rite III, Rite for Reconciliation of Several Penitents with General Confession and Absolution.

The bishops at Vatican II said very little about penance, only that it was to be revised so that it might more clearly express both the nature and the effect of the sacrament (CSL, 72). That seemed like a relatively modest goal in light of the major revisions anticipated for the other sacraments. A committee of scholars and pastors carefully studied the liturgical, theological and pastoral variants of penance over its long and sometimes curious history. By 1974, they had recovered some of its earliest features and completed a new *Rite of Penance* (RP) made up of the three distinct ritual patterns named above and a number of penitential services.

What is particularly striking about the new rite is its ecclesial emphasis. It did not simply incorporate rites to be celebrated in common but recognized that both sin and conversion are the concern of the whole church. Elaborating on the words of

Pope Paul VI, the introduction of the *Rite of Penance* emphasizes the solidarity of the community in sin and salvation:

> "The hidden and gracious mystery of God unites us all through a supernatural bond: on this basis one person's sin harms the rest even as one person's goodness enriches them." Penance always therefore entails reconciliation with our brothers and sisters who remain harmed by our sins. In fact, people frequently join together to commit injustice. But it is also true that they help each other in doing penance; freed from sin by the grace of Christ, they become, with all persons of good will, agents of justice and peace in the world. (#5)

Other remarkable features of the new rites include a recognition of the eucharist as primary sacrament of reconciliation, a focus on continuing conversion and the holy life, a new emphasis on healing rather than on judgment, and thus on discernment of the Spirit's movements in penitents' hearts, and an identification of deepening friendship with God as the ultimate goal of the sacrament.

Nevertheless, despite these new theological and pastoral features, the reception of the sacrament of reconciliation has languished in many places for at least two reasons, both having to do with timing. The *Rite of Penance* was the last of the revised sacraments to be issued. By the time this ritual book appeared Catholics had already received—and were attempting to understand and celebrate—many other new rites, chief among them a fully renewed eucharist. Some parish communities became weary or testy with so many changes within such a short time. Pastors became defensive about asking for yet more understanding and liturgical flexibility from their communities. Often, then, little energy was devoted to introducing the *Rite of Penance*. In some of the communities where it was discussed, instead of pointing out the new features of the sacrament of reconciliation, pastors stressed its sameness with its predecessor. "Don't worry," some promised. "Nothing much has changed."

Nothing could have been further from the truth. Besides, such an assurance was hardly likely to inspire vast numbers of disenchanted penitents to embrace reconciliation once again. By the time the new rite came along, confession had already fallen into disuse. Why would Catholics be motivated to look closely at a new rite when it was widely reported to be very like something they had already abandoned?

Catholics drifted away from penance for a number of reasons. Many stay away from the sacrament because of bad childhood experiences and the overwhelmingly negative attitudes to confession that these occasionally humiliating or fearful experiences generated. Others relate a nagging memory of the sacrament's predictability and its seeming disconnectedness from their actual experience. Still others name a basic unfamiliarity with the new rites and the inaccessibility of individual reconciliation in some places. One woman noted that reconciliation is now available by appointment only in her parish and, reluctant to pick up the phone or ring a doorbell, she concludes, "You really need a whopper before you'd want to do that." Such experiences remain fairly widespread, leading to the quip: "Bless me, Father. It has been three rites since my last confession."

Memories of going to confession linger in the imagination of older Catholics: the regularity of it as a Saturday afternoon ritual; waiting in line as a family or a class; the examination of conscience using the Ten Commandments and the precepts of the church; the attempt to remember whether it was five times or six that I hit my brother — and whether the gravity of my sin was mitigated because he deserved it; the darkness and anonymity of the confessional — usually called just "the box"; the sliding window; the shadow of the priest leaning close to hear; the hand raised in blessing and absolution; the doing of penance — three Our Fathers and three Hail Marys being pretty standard fare.

There were deeper issues as well. It was not just the routine that made us drift from confession but the dawning realization that God is first of all a God of love and not of judgment, and that incidental matters once elevated by hierarchical directive to disproportionately serious moral levels have been reconsidered. As one man noted: "No longer are the faithful to believe that hellfire awaits the Friday meat-eater, the Holy Communion fast-breaker, the Sunday Mass-skipper, the Catholic attending a non-Catholic service. . . . For those who carry such memories but who experienced the freeing sense of a God of love after Vatican II, return to confession as we knew it would be somewhat akin to a prisoner voluntarily returning to a cell when he has otherwise been set free. For what purpose, the prisoner asks, am I to return to such captivity?"

Besides this changed sensitivity to what constitutes grave sin, there is also the realization that sin is not a private affair. "We sin against others. We need to reconcile ourselves with our brothers and sisters and with God. We get to God through the people that we live with. Every other sacrament involves other people. For some reason confession used to be a private thing, but now it's got a community focus."

While individual confession of sins continues to wane, many Catholics have had a communal experience of the rite and nearly all greet it with enthusiasm. Celebrations of communal reconciliation regularly occur in parishes across the country during the seasons of Advent and Lent as preparation for the community's high holy days, and they have become, for many, a seasonal expectation: "It's a given at our house that we go to communal penance. The sacrament has become part of the celebration of Christmas and Easter for us."

Probably we shall never definitively determine which came first, the communal rites or the shift in our understanding about the social nature of sin and the ecclesial context of reconciliation. What will become clear in the balance of this chapter is that a communal celebration of reconciliation can awaken a profound change in the community's consciousness of the meaning of sin. One woman attempted to articulate the shift: "I have come to realize what sin is and what it is not. I grew up in a time when sin was spots in the milk bottle—and I'm not trying to trivialize it, but it's that sort of a concept. Over the years I've come to realize that sin is a deeper and more serious sort of thing than the individual 'I swore three times today, I did this, and I did that.' My list never changed, only the number of times changed. But now what's changed is the concept of sin, and as we think about it differently we need to pray differently together."

That wonderful insight goes right to the heart of the ritual process: As we think about sin differently, we need to pray differently together. Liturgy celebrates experience. As the community's experience changes—about the meaning of sin and the holy life, about God and grace and the role of the community, about when and why and how God draws us to repentance—we do need to pray differently together. In turn, paying attention to the experience within, and to the symbols and gestures and objects of our prayer, gives rise to deeper insight.

The reflections that follow are based on recent experiences of the two communal celebrations of this sacrament, known as rites two and three. These rites differ in one important respect: In rite two, there is an opportunity for individual confession and absolution; rite three incorporates a public acknowledgment of sin but there is no individual confession of sins. Rite three is used only

if there is grave need, namely when, in view of the number of penitents, sufficient confessors are not available to hear individual confessions properly
within a suitable period of time, so that the penitents would, through no fault
of their own, have to go without sacramental grace or holy communion for a
long time. This may happen especially in mission territories but in other places
as well and also in groups of persons when the need is established. (#31)

Except in an emergency, the judgment about the need to celebrate rite three is
reserved to the bishop of the diocese. In the United States, a number of dioceses
now routinely celebrate rite three because of the shortage of clergy and the great
distances that separate some parochial communities. The majority of dioceses, however, use only rite two for communal reconciliation.

Experience: Deepening Friendship with God

What is the experience we bring to reconciliation? What conversion is called for?
Unlike the sacraments previously discussed, reconciliation is not a once-in-a-lifetime celebration but rather a way of life; not an isolated event but something that
happens on a weekly, even daily, basis between spouses, friends, colleagues, neigh-
bors and within families and communities. One man talked about the connection
this way: "It has to be part of our whole worship experience, part of our experience
with one another and as a community, as a parish, as a people within the church
itself, as Christians all together. The liturgical aspect of reconciliation is enriched by
our experience of just trying to live in harmony here on a day-to-day, year-to-year
basis. Everything flows together and you can't isolate a rite; it's all one big sphere."

How true. The rite cannot be isolated from daily life or it makes no sense. The
sacrament of reconciliation is radically continuous with the day-to-day. Communal
celebrations of reconciliation can be every bit as disconnected from life as the old
experience of "the box" if they are not the celebration of ongoing conversion. Such
conversion, described in the rite as a continuous journey, "affects a person from
within toward a progressively deeper enlightenment and an ever-closer likeness to
Christ" (#6a). Reconciliation celebrates a particular facet of the journey, the recognition of sin and grace at work in us, and the mercy of God continually drawing us
to repentance, change of heart and ever-deeper friendship with God.

PATTERNS OF SIN AND FORGIVENESS

In one sense, the experience celebrated in reconciliation is as varied as are the human persons who present themselves. Reconciliation is not just about "what I have done and what I have failed to do"; it re-establishes relationship and therefore has everything to do with the uniqueness of each one's friendship with God, diminished or damaged by sin but restored in the mystery of God's forgiving love.

At the same time, despite the uniqueness of each relationship, there are some patterns in the way the mystery of sin and forgiveness is described. Today there is an overwhelming recognition that sin is relational, that sins of omission are often as grave as those of commission, that individual sins only point to a deeper pattern of rupture, and, ultimately, that friendship with God is what is at stake. "Now sin is different," said a middle-aged woman. "Before it was just a list of 'shalt nots.' Now it has to do with what we should do, who we should help, when we should give money or pray or whatever, and it has to do with omissions like when we ignore the homeless. I don't think we ever learned that before." Another woman nodded in agreement and added: "We used to talk a lot about individual sin and its effects. Now we recognize that as members of a community we have responsibilities — what we do certainly affects the rest of the faith community. Sin has social ramifications. How we consume, or how we treat employees — it all has a social aspect which we often ignored when we focused on individual sin." Many respondents identified the same shift in their consciousness of sin, their sense of the common good, their recognition that "what I do affects others" and that "we are on this journey to God together." In the last several decades, what constitutes sin has been vastly expanded in the community's consciousness.

A second recognition about sin today is that it is a condition of life. In speaking of original sin in an earlier chapter, we recognized that the environment into which we are all born is one where the power of evil is overwhelming and will color the way we think, the choices we make, the desires of our hearts, even the warring factions within us as well as all around us. The sinful human condition is part of our struggle all our life long. One man's insights, offered to me in a letter, are worth pondering: "The post–Vatican II church has properly sensitized us to the broader reality of sin as a condition in life. No longer are people viewing sin simply as a violation of a juridical list of 'do's and don'ts' largely focused on the appetites — although it is my experience that these traditional sins are not ignored. Rather we have identified sin in all the rest of our lives — sins that no longer neatly fit a formulaic approach to reconciliation. We have identified sin which is complex and frustratingly interlaced with the good in our lives. This is the sin which, for want of better description, is the social evil, the communal fault in which individually I share but individually am incapable of completely expunging. It is subtle, it is insidious, it is sinful. And it is difficult to enumerate one's deep-felt realization of a life lived short of the beatitudes in the present rubrics of the sacrament of confession. That such does not occur is not because people fail to realize and struggle with social sin."

A third shift in our consciousness of sin and grace appears in what is said and what is not said about God. Absent from the interviews is any sense of fear. God and/or the priest are not perceived as judge. There is a consistent pattern of naming God as forgiving, loving, caring, compassionate, welcoming — and these traits are experienced personally. People spoke with confidence and even tenderness about the God they encountered in reconciliation: "It's about mystery. Okay, I am wounded, but sin's power to destroy is somehow lessened in this great mystery of forgiving love." People described God as "absolutely forgiving, no matter what." One woman gave testimony about twenty-five years of "you are not good enough" erased when she moved from a fundamentalist community to the Catholic church and knew for the first time, in this sacrament, the love of God. Others had experienced and could name "the overwhelming and overpowering love of God, the kind of love that does not let me off the hook." Rather like the hound of heaven, God was described as relentlessly in pursuit of us: "I think God is a sneaky God and I don't mean that as a negative. God just sort of sneaks in and turns your whole life upside-down right in front of you and makes those changes and brings you home." Sin, then, appears to be a painful reality in people's lives not because they are afraid of God's anger but because sin causes fractured relationships with others and especially with God whose love we want to reciprocate.

A fourth shift in our consciousness is this: A pervasive sense of unworthiness, which some associated with the previous rite, has been replaced by a different attitude toward created reality and toward the self: "Creation is good and we are good. We don't begin faulty. We are not evil at heart. It's important to hear that in our holiest gatherings. It's important to believe that God made us to be happy and made the things around us for our delight."

Many pointed to friendship — with God and with others — as something that needs to be nurtured and tended. "Friendships sometimes fail because one of the parties becomes too busy, distracted, even indifferent to the other," someone said. This insight prompted another to use the language of "remembering" to describe a reconciled life, a word she also associated with the eucharist. "In the celebration of the eucharist, we remember the mighty acts of God, especially in the gift of Jesus Christ for the life of the world. When we gather for eucharist we gather precisely to remember." Having made the connection with eucharist, she then stated that sin enters her life when she stops remembering: "Sin is forgetting, at least in my own life. It's not remembering, it's forgetting. It's getting so caught up in stuff that I just forget God. But remembering is what God and faith are all about. And when you think of the overwhelming love of God you cannot not change. You have to say, well yes, I've done this, and I won't do that. I have to make some way of getting it right. But I can go on as long as I remember."

"It's relational for me," said another. "When I prepare for reconciliation I look at my relationships, my family, the people I work with, everyone I run into, and ask myself how I am doing. What am I doing to enrich their lives, not what can I get out of them. And I ask how I am falling down. That's how I prepare. I look at all the relationships that I have and see where I am not attending as well as I could." To which a woman replied: "That's what's really helpful for me, too. Not just — what am I doing that's bad. But what can I do to strengthen relationships in all areas of my life."

PREPARING FOR THE SACRAMENT

Besides examining relationships, individuals found a variety of ways to prepare for this sacramental encounter. In one parish the Sunday bulletin supplied a series of questions, an examination of conscience, which many used alone or with spouses, children or friends: "I applied the questions to my life and we talked about some of these questions at home." Some reported that "a very good letter on reconciliation from the bishop" was a useful preparation. Some read the Bible; others reflected on the Ten Commandments; one woman prayed "for stronger faith and for peace and joy in my heart," and a man prayed for "light and help." One person said that he "thought of my life and my family and how I treat the community. I just took some time to go through what I did and what I didn't do and what I should have done"; another "did some soul-searching over the weekend when I had a little time to prepare myself mentally and spiritually for the celebration."

The people with whom I spoke did not approach this sacrament lightly. "There's a lot of accounting that you do before you get here. It's a discipline." And furthermore, some recognized that the celebration of reconciliation toward the end of Lent is really the culmination of a process begun weeks earlier: "For me part of the preparation for all of this during Lent has been the Sunday liturgy and the RCIA scrutinies and the Chrism Mass, everything." Another added: "We've been preparing for this sacrament since Ash Wednesday. We've been on this journey. That's where the homily began. Father said: 'Remember when you were signed with ashes. Remember almost forty days ago we began,' and it has been a process building to this moment of reconciliation. This is not an isolated moment."

Careful preparation was accompanied by a sense of responsibility and a feeling of need. That was what was communicated when people described why they decided to come to a communal service. "I actually wanted to be there because it's my place to be there. I have a responsibility, not just for what I get, but to be a doer too. I don't think I always understood that." Cleaning the slate, attending to brokenness, renewal of spirit, strength in the support of others — all these were reasons people chose to celebrate reconciliation, and so was the more colorful recollection that brought one woman to the sacrament: "My mom used to say, 'Honey, you can fall, but you don't have to wallow!' All my life I've remembered that. That's why I come."

Finally, one woman had an astonishing insight: "There's a different kind of power in the communal rite than what we've known in individual reconciliation. That, to me, is the same as if we were to receive communion all by ourselves in a little closet." To which another added: "I can't be Catholic and not participate in that very special part of my sacramental life!"

Celebration: Communal Reconciliation

INTRODUCTORY RITES

For many respondents, a very powerful experience occurs as they enter the church. "There were so many people here. That's what really spoke to me. We must all be feeling that we're needing something." Over and over, as respondents reflected on their experience of communal reconciliation, the first thing they needed to mention was the participation of others and how it enhanced their own participation. One remarked: "Even though you can get absolution individually in the confessionals, it is more meaningful to be getting it with everyone else at the same time." Another added: "I always felt very alone when I had to go to confession behind the door. I felt like I was the only person on the earth that ever sinned. And when you come here to communal reconciliation it's clear we're all in the same boat."

When pressed about the difference between the experiences of individual and communal reconciliation, one said: "For me it is very important that we journey together as a people, as a community. The universality of sin and the experience of sin as a societal act rather than an individual act, or people against each other, against the world, against the poor, are very important things for me—that we're together to say that out loud and to do it with the people that we like or don't like."

Solidarity in sin and in grace, solidarity on the journey: these were frequently the topic of reflection. In addition, one person noted: "Part of the gift of belonging to a community is that when you can't pray, the community prays for you. At one point I got distracted and then I was thinking, they are praying for me, carrying me. I guess it was the waves of response. The truth of that really hit me."

LITURGY OF THE WORD

The *Rite of Penance* states that one or more readings may be chosen, and if more than one is read, a psalm response should be inserted between them so that the word may be more deeply interiorized and heartfelt assent may be given. The role of the readings and the music was continually the subject of further reflection. "The beauty of singing psalm responses like 'Be merciful, O Lord, for we have sinned' is that it continues to go through your mind. They plant themselves in your heart."

The gospel of the prodigal provoked deep reflection: "The son was forgiven and welcomed home, but there was loss. He was still wounded." The gospel and homily invited people to reflect on reconciliation as homecoming, as choice, as renewed relationship. "The readings, especially the gospel, opened up an understanding of who God is and who we are—sometimes the older son, sometimes the younger son, sometimes actually we're also the parent, reaching out to other people."

The importance of the homily is underscored in the rite. "It should call to mind God's infinite mercy, the need for interior repentance, the social aspect of grace and sin and the duty of making satisfaction" (#25). In one celebration, the homily appears to have been particularly successful. "Because of that homily and how it was expressed, that opened me in the Lord. I could say yes, I did this wrong, I did this wrong, and this is what I'm guilty of—because of that homily. And I knew at the same time that I was loved and welcomed, and I thought of that psalm: 'What return can I make for all God's goodness to me?'"

INCENSE

While the *Rite of Penance* makes no mention of the use of incense, it was a thoughtful addition to one celebration of reconciliation, engaging both sight and smell and, even more, the sacramental imagination. Incense spoke to one person of forgiveness, to another of "some kind of almsgiving and praise of the Lord." The burning of the incense "engulfs the people," "helps us let go," "lets God descend upon us," "is like the sins are going away from us," and "helps us experience the Spirit."

Incense prompted one particularly lyrical insight: "Incense is almost like singing for me, seeing the incense dance. First there is nothing and then it just explodes and it circles everyone — it intertwines." The role of symbols to gather up a history and a tradition was also remarked: "Once, the other day, I walked into the church and I could smell that there had been incense, and I thought, 'I love being Catholic.' Where else can you go in and say, 'this place has been used.'"

THE EXAMINATION OF CONSCIENCE

Silence and an examination of conscience are suggested as ways of assisting the awakening of true contrition (#26). Despite the serious and sustained preparation for the sacrament which so many had reported, the litany of forgiveness chanted by one presider became another invitation to recognize sin while confidently seeking the mercy of God. Even kneeling itself was matter for attending: "Finding myself on my knees helps me express how sometimes I feel I need to come to God. The litany was like a musical examination of conscience, and we pleaded 'forgive us, forgive us,' and that's when I felt one with everybody as we were all bracing ourselves in such a humble position before God."

Continuity with the season of Lent, the community's annual retreat, was part of the reflection: "The penitential litany took me back to our scrutinies. It moved me back to where we have been coming from. And it all tied in so beautifully. The scrutinies of Lent have led me to this moment and reconciliation is like a culmination of the whole lenten journey."

The length of the litany and its concreteness were very important aspects of the experience for many: "The litany touches on every human frailty, everything we've done wrong and everything we're smug about like the older son. I thought I was prepared, but there are still things in my life I must change and places where I've failed, and in the litany I realized I hadn't thought of this or that in the preparation. And then we cry out to the Lord." "It's powerful because you are naming sin and at the same time asking forgiveness." For many the litany opens up other realizations, other acknowledgments of sin: "There are real sins of omission that you do without really knowing it until you're again jarred into the reality by the kinds of reflections in the litany — the naming of sin." And another added: "It was all so concrete. It's not just generic sin. It's mean-spiritedness, it's gossip, it's overindulgence and broken promises. And so much is true that the community's 'Lord have mercy' seems to build as we all say 'yes!' and ask for God's mercy."

Everything seemed to converge for people in the litany: kneeling, the growing volume of the plea for forgiveness, the specificity of the examination so "you couldn't wiggle out of it," the experience of being sinner and saved together: "The litany made me so conscious of the enormity of sin and also the all-encompassing love of God. I don't often reflect on all of those things, especially the sense of social sin, how we're all in that together, but then we're all forgiven together as well."

SILENCE
Then, as one woman remarked, "What's most important about the litany of sin is the profound silence at the end. There is time to reflect on one's own life and one's own sin. The quiet is hard to describe. Something is happening when you have hundreds of people, even the children who are normally quite noisy, become so incredibly still." Individuals spoke of a deep recollection, a contemplative attitude, an experience of being before God. "In that moment of silence, it's almost the silence of God, but it's so permeating that it in itself transforms."

INDIVIDUAL CONFESSION, ABSOLUTION AND LAYING ON OF HANDS
The two communal rites, to this point identical, now diverge. If rite two is being celebrated, individuals approach one of the priests for confession and absolution. In rite three, some general acknowledgment of sin — in the celebration described here, coming forward for the laying on of hands in silence — is followed by general absolution. In both communal rites there are procession, touch, care, a one-at-a-time deliberateness, the community itself in all its diversity moving as one. The relationship of this procession to that other weekly procession for the bread of life was also the subject of attentive reflection during and after the prayer: "It always reminds me of the story of Jesus and how much time he took with the individual. The man that was let down through the ceiling and Jesus took the time with the man right there in the middle of his proclaiming the word. He always took time with each individual. I think the amount of time we spend on each person is very important. It is so seldom that we do this in the Catholic church and there are so few times that we go forward and do something other than receive eucharist. Eucharist and the kissing of

the cross and the ashes and blessing . . . it's a very unique time in our liturgical year to have hands laid on."

Many report being drawn to the ritual action, riveted by the meaning of the rite, the story lived by each person, the solidarity of one with another, the promises which this silent procession was speaking: "Watching the procession really touched my heart. There were elderly, there were young people. There were government officials and people from all walks of life. And we all walk up there together. Each one has a different story. We have a lady who wears a scarf because she lost her hair. And she takes her scarf off so that Father can lay hands on her. And I know that she is very self-conscious about her bald head, but that always touches my heart and I feel very close to her."

The laying on of hands was of particular significance for many: "I was thinking about all this wounded healer business, that even though I've sinned, I can still be touched. A person who is wounded or has a terrible scar on the body gets healed if the one who loves him or her is able to touch the scar. It's not enough just to say that God loves you and all that. The touch is what makes a difference." And the touch was perceived by many as the touch of the divine, either God or Christ: "There is a real experience of the presence of Christ, that somehow this is Christ. We always say that about priesthood, but really it comes together in that moment of the laying on of hands for me." "When I close my eyes and Father lays his hands on me, just for those few seconds, it's like God is all there is for me." Another insight stirred up by the laying on of hands was this: "I felt a wonderful connection with the sacrament of the sick, with people who experience the same gesture of laying on hands in both sacraments and it made me think 'this is God's tender touch.'"

Confession, too, stirred deep reflection: "To me that's like a burden lifted, your yoke is all gone — that's the feeling after that." "It's as if your whole body has just gone away and everything that's inside is just cleansed, and you're just completely taken by God." "When I got back and knelt down again I felt absolute forgiveness."

One person compared her previous experience of confession with the communal rite: "What happens when we are together is so much more of the embodiment of the incarnation. We need one another for the sacraments. I don't know how much people would articulate it, but there is a real understanding that humanity, and each of us, have a whole lot to do with what the sacrament is. There is no such thing as magic."

SATISFACTION

"As a sign of the conversion we celebrate, let us enter the sacred three days of the Triduum with a deep sense of the awesome mysteries into which we are invited. Let us keep these days as the holiest days of the year. In doing this may we be led to more authentic love and service of neighbor and then to discover again the precious gift of life which we have been given." Such was the satisfaction invited of one assembly, the keeping of the holy days of Lent as well as possible. Some commented on this: "To enter deeply into Holy Week and Triduum as far as possible — now, that is strong medicine. Our Fathers you can toss off, but you can't just toss off that kind of penance."

"Penance suggests that by doing this thing we enable forgiveness. But that's not true. Forgiveness is a gift. Really what we are being called to is a change of heart. And the grace that we receive at that point in time helps us to make a change. 'Penance' somehow got away from any of those more significant things. It gave the wrong impression."

"It was called a 'satisfaction' and it's more a challenge than a penance. There is a role model for us to follow, Jesus Christ, and the challenge is to follow him. And we do the best we can. And when we don't, we get together as a group and acknowledge that."

SIGN OF PEACE

Often the exchange of peace concludes a communal celebration. Those who have experienced it as part of the rite find it very helpful: "I think it is particularly important that there is a sign of peace. You're reconciling yourself to God, but you're recognizing that sin is through relationships you have with other people. And in sinning against other people, you're sinning against God. And when you reconcile yourself to God you have to reconcile yourself to your neighbor. You have to forgive and ask for forgiveness. You forgive those who have injured you and you ask their forgiveness. To me, that's what the sign of peace is in that kind of a relationship. It's not so much a greeting as it is a forgiveness."

LEAVE-TAKING

The experience of the celebration was named forgiveness, faith, fresh starts, journey, humility, change, community and healing. It was named by as many words as there were participants gathered to reaffirm and deepen friendship with God, the goal of the sacrament. "Am I changed for having been to reconciliation? I don't know. I do know I try harder. Some things that I do that I name as sins are things that will happen again no matter how hard I try. But every year I try a little bit harder." Every year, trying harder—that spoke to another of the relationship of the sacramental event to life: "It's a whole journey kind of thing. It's a ritualization of a whole experience that is more than just this moment or this hour."

Commitment to an ongoing process of conversion was in a number of hearts: "I had a sense of a fresh start, a sense of energy that I am loved and healed and forgiven, and let's get on with it!" "Getting on with it," for another, had to do with gospel living: "From the beginning, all the way through, I felt being emptied and at the same time being filled. I looked around and I saw people's faces and I thought: It's up to each individual person how we want to finish the gospel story."

Solidarity with others helped one participant to be as forgiving of herself as she realizes God is: "I was amazed at the number of people who came to reconciliation. What I realized tonight is that a lot of times I consider myself as the only person who has sinned. But what I felt tonight was that we have all sinned and that we are forgiven. I have to realize we are forgiven. I am the hardest person on me, not God. God forgives me." The community experience put another in touch with the transcendent: "What we celebrated and experienced was faith. There is a deep sense of faith, and a trust, and a recognition of the need to be forgiven and to express that need. There is a certain humility in that huge gathering of people; there's a sense of something beyond us. It was quite a profound experience for me."

Perhaps most simply, as one person said upon taking leave: "It seems to me that I learned more and I love more and I understand more where I am going and what is my life every day. I'll be back."

Amen

How did the participants name their commitment? How did they specify what Amen meant? Some could express it in just a few words: "a change of heart," "recommitted," " invited to change again," "peace that I haven't had for a while," "Jesus as redeemer." A woman who had been away from the church for a number of years declared: "I'm committed to following Christ and staying the course this time and not dropping out like I've done in the past." Another woman identified the action of the Spirit: "To me there is no better feeling than coming to church. I would imagine what it is to me is the Holy Spirit. We come to church and we are filled with the Holy Spirit when we leave the church."

A man linked his Amen with the gospel: "Amen . . . that's the Father's Amen first of all, the Father already half-way down the road greeting us." To which another man added: "The overwhelming feeling for me with the Amen is that I know where I belong . . . and to whom."

For many, the following comments faithfully name the experience and the commitment: "Amen to me was being reconciled with being more human and more aware of my shortcomings and praying and continuing in faith." "Sometimes I sit there at liturgy and hear what the questions are that are posed to catechumens and I think to myself if I were one of them, would I just be terrified? And it's no longer terrifying for me because I feel like I'm moving into it more deeply. It's more a piece of my life." "I guess for me Amen is another step in the whole thing. It's moving ahead. It's being able to let go of some things — maybe not everything but some things." "The Amen is a hopeful Amen. But it is still on the way because it is a journey that is still going on. . . . It's not being static and it's not being finished." "It's a sense that I can try again. I've identified some areas that I know are really sinful patterns in my life. I got a sense of such strength and support in the community experience. We're praying for each other. We support one another in our journey to God, in our putting on Christ. So it's like a new beginning for me."

"Yes, Lord. That's what the Amen means. To what? To my following and to his love and my love for him."

Reflecting on the Options

In conclusion, the reflections of participants about the different sacramental options in celebrating reconciliation are instructive. Regarding Rite I, for the Reconciliation of Individual Penitents, one woman mused about the value of the rite and her own reluctance: "Individual confession is available. We don't take advantage of it very often. I'm ashamed to say that the last time I went, I only went because I brought one of my sons who I thought needed it. And Father said, 'Did you want to go to confession, or are you making him go?' But on the way into the church the bargain was, 'Well, Mom, if I'm going, aren't you going?' I didn't really anticipate going, but it was wonderful. And I thought afterwards, I know this is available every Saturday, and it was a big part of my life when I was in grade school, so how come if it feels so good and it's available, why don't I take advantage of it?"

Another person commented about the opportunity for spiritual guidance in the individual rite: "For the individual, you don't just sit there and name all your sins. Father asks if there is something that is troubling you and you talk about that. I really felt good about it." And a third person noted: "I think there is a place for both individual and communal reconciliation. There are some people who need to go individually, who just need to talk and have their sins forgiven privately. Sometimes what they need is someone to help them unravel what is happening. You have to know what will help you be a better person."

The church now offers three distinct ways of celebrating reconciliation, depending on circumstances and need. Communal and individual reconciliation appear to be very different rituals and many may feel, because there is no "formula," that they are no longer at home in the individual, one-to-one encounter, whether it is in the dark confessional or in a face-to-face encounter in prayer. But, in fact, the pattern of all the rituals is the same: a word of greeting, prayer for God's mercy, reading from scripture, the acknowledgment of sin, the opportunity for counsel and spiritual conversation in the individual rite, the prayer of the penitent, the words of absolution, and in conclusion, praise for God's mercy. Whether alone or with others, we are drawn to the sacrament because of the mercy of God who first loved us, Christ who gave himself up for us, and the Spirit who has been poured out on us abundantly and who stirs us to love God completely and commit ourselves completely to God (#5).

What is new in our day is the opportunity for communal celebrations and the remarkable new insights that communal reconciliation stir up in us. In general, communal celebration is responsible for a new sense of church, of the power of ritual, of the responsibility of a sacramental way of life, and of the need to prepare so that the rites genuinely celebrate an experience of God's healing, forgiving presence. "Not only are we forgiven but we feel it with this kind of liturgy. It's one thing to hear it, but it's another to be so engrossed by it." Another agreed and added: "I get far more out of a community celebration and participation ever than going to a confessional-type situation. I get more out of sharing with a friend where we can mutually deal with each other and talk about things. Communal penance in terms of a sacramental experience within the church has always been far more fulfilling for me and there's always been a lot of deeper things happening because we're doing it as a group of people."

The power of the communal celebration is well summed up in this story: "I have three young children, three boys. My little son is coming up to his first communion. We went to the Advent communal penance and on the way home he said, 'All those people. Think of all those sins that were forgiven. We're going to go every single time.' He got it. And he's only eight years old. I think if you prepare, you really do get it."

If we prepare, if we live the experience before bringing it to celebration, if we pay attention to the movements of our heart and then the movements of the rite, we won't miss the meaning. We really will get it.

Chapter Eight
Pastoral Care of the Sick

Lord, the one whom you love is ill.
John 11:3

PRELUDE

Something puzzling happens these days when the church celebrates a communal anointing of the sick. Nearly *everyone* identifies themselves as needing the church's ministry to the sick — or so it seems. If the presider issues what even appears to be a general invitation, for example, "I now invite those of you who experience a need for Christ's healing to come forward for the anointing of the sick," the aisle fills up with people. The seriously ill and those who suffer the debilitation and diminishment of old age are joined by the apparently healthy, the latter in large numbers. This scene — and even this attitude — was inconceivable prior to Vatican II. A sacrament once reserved for those at the point of death has been so thoroughly revised that its regular celebration and frequent reception are no longer uncommon.

What's going on here? Who is the sacrament for? How did it move from the deathbed to the parish church? Why do so many people experience a need for this kind of sacramental ministry from the faith community? And how can such an expansive and welcoming attitude toward the Anointing of the Sick celebrated in common co-exist with the lingering hesitancy about its individual use as suggested by the following comment: "I've been anointed several times, even in this last year, not that I was absolutely in danger of death or anything like that, and I think it is just too bad so many people still believe that the point of death is when anointing should be administered. I feel bad when people don't go ahead and intercede for family or friends who might be helped by the sacrament. I've heard people say, 'Oh, I couldn't do that, she'd be scared to death.'"

"Scared to death!" Many of us can remember that feeling — or, if not fright, at least apprehension — surrounding the sacrament that we once called extreme unction. The very title *extreme unction* identified the focus of the sacrament as the church's dying members, those who were in *extremis*, or at the point of death. And because the mystery of death was so immediate, extreme unction bore all the weight of wonder, awe and fear that imminent encounter with God conjured up. Most Catholic homes were equipped with a "sick-call kit" — a linen cloth, a standing crucifix and two blessed candles. These were arranged on the bedside table next to the dying person in preparation for the pastor's arrival. When he entered the room he placed the holy oil and the blessed sacrament before the lighted candles, turning the bedside table into a quasi-altar.

Extreme unction included confession, anointing and viaticum. "You had to say the act of contrition," one woman recalled with some mystification. "Here you are dying, and you're supposed to be remembering the act of contrition. And then the priest would say 'I absolve you of all your sins.'" The anointing followed — the anointing of the eyes, ears, nose, mouth, hands and feet — together with prayer that any sins committed by those parts of the body would be forgiven. Lastly, holy communion was given. This communion we called *viaticum*, or "food for the way." Viaticum was the last food for the journey, the last meal before one's home-going. "Last rites" became the shorthand name for the sacrament of extreme unction.

Now a new name designates a different reality. *Pastoral Care of the Sick* (PCS) is the designation for the complex of rituals that have been amply expanded to incorporate care for the sick and the dying. A first section of the ritual book includes pastoral notes and prayers for visits to the sick, communion of the sick and the rite of anointing. The church's pastoral care of the dying is found in a second section of the book: prayer, viaticum and the commendation of the dying to the embrace of an all-merciful and compassionate God. The sick and the dying both are the subjects of the church's pastoral care, and the church's ministrations to the sick and dying are now the work of all of us. Family and friends, pastoral care workers, medical professionals and extraordinary ministers of communion join priests and deacons in enacting God's tender care for the suffering among us.

This public and ecclesial focus is very like the experience of the post-apostolic church. The early church's care for the sick included a variety of practices. Sometimes families presented oil for the bishop's blessing and then anointed the sick within their households; sometimes deacons and priests were involved in the care of the sick; sometimes the blessed oil was self-administered. It appears from early church writings that the blessed oil was applied externally and also taken internally, and that the rite took place in church or at home, depending on the condition of the sick who were the subjects of the church's ministry. The hoped-for effect of the sacrament was the healing of the whole person, body, mind and spirit, and restoration to full health and well-being.

Gradually, a shift of focus from the sick to the dying occurred, largely because of the growing practice of death-bed penance. Anointing became reserved for those who had been reconciled to the church through the sacrament of penance. Anointing, then, was part of the death-bed scenario and, associated as it now was with penance, a priest was the proper and sole minister. This empirical shift from the sick to the dying had theological ramifications. Since anointing was regularly followed by death, the theological focus shifted from physical health and well-being to spiritual salvation. Quite simply, the sacrament of extreme unction prepared its recipient for encounter with God. Such was the sacramental practice of the church redressed by the bishops at Vatican II:

> "Extreme unction" which may also and more properly be called "anointing of the sick," is not a sacrament for those only who are at the point of death. Hence, as soon as any one of the faithful begins to be in danger of death from sickness or old age, the fitting time for that person to receive the sacrament has certainly already arrived. (CSL, 73; emphasis added)

Some old habits and attitudes die slowly, however. One woman recently recalled an invitation to receive the anointing of the sick, to which she had reacted with surprise and some alarm: "Does this mean the end?" "Not at all," responded her pastor. "It will help you to be better."

"Help to be better" is the thrust of the anointing of the sick — understood in many different ways. The rite provides a way of naming the anxieties and fears associated with sickness even as the community prays for restoration to health, for trust in God, for strength against temptation, for the courage to bear suffering more patiently and for the faith and tranquillity to believe that the mystery of suffering — both Christ's and ours — is ultimately redemptive. The church's ritual makes another series of commitments to those who are dying. It embraces them with care, brings comfort and strength in their dying moments, helps them renew their baptismal faith and join themselves to Christ in communion as they anticipate their final passage from this life to life with God. Anointing and viaticum complete the process of conformity to the death and resurrection of Christ Jesus, just as baptism began it.

These are some of the themes of the church's ritual care for the sick and the dying, themes that gather up their diverse experiences of faith and doubt, fear and hope in the face of illness, and bring all these — when the time is ripe — to ritual expression.

When someone is first diagnosed with a terminal disease or has an accident that radically alters their state of health and well-being, there is a shock to be lived through. Perhaps in no other instance is the invitation to let go and to turn to God more apparent and at the same time more fearsome. There often follows a period of denial, anger, helplessness, utter vulnerability, loss of the sense of self and despondency.

It takes time to be ready to hear a word of life and hope, of faith and consolation, in the midst of the experience of grave illness. It takes time to be able, in some measure, to join oneself to the sufferings of Christ. Moreover, it often takes the ministry of others, of family and friends, health-care professionals and pastoral-care ministers, to bring the sick person to the point of readiness for the sacrament. This genuinely sacramental ministry of the whole community to its suffering members, an extension of the ministry of Christ to the sick, is described in the introduction to *Pastoral Care of the Sick*:

> The concern that Christ showed for the bodily and spiritual welfare of those who are ill is continued by the Church in its ministry to the sick. This ministry is the common responsibility of all Christians, who should visit the sick, remember them in prayer, and celebrate the sacraments with them. The family

and friends of the sick, doctors and others who care for them, and priests with pastoral responsibilities have a particular share in this ministry of comfort. Through words of encouragement and faith they can help the sick to unite themselves with the sufferings of Christ for the good of God's people. (#43)

The rites are celebrations with and for the sick; they are also celebrations of the whole church, making all of us aware, because of the presence of the sick and dying in our midst, of the fragility of the human condition, of the many modes of suffering, of the body as sacrament, of the gift that is life and health. The sick and those near death make manifest and tangible the suffering and uncertainty and experience of limits which each one of us, in our fast-paced life, may choose to ignore or to deny. Furthermore, according to the introduction to the rite, it is the role of the sick "to be a reminder to others of the essential or higher things. By their witness the sick show that our mortal life must be redeemed through the mystery of Christ's death and resurrection" (#3).

The sick and the dying are powerful icons; they have a ministry among us if we will attend carefully to their experience.

Experience: Being Joined to the Sufferings of Christ

What is the experience of the sick and the dying? How is it possible to generalize about unique human lives, each belonging to a network of relationships, each with a different history and spiritual geography, each with particular gifts and graces? In the following pages the sick will speak for themselves, as will families and friends who cherish and care for them and a health-care worker who provides a striking testimony of the sacramental witness of the sick. In each case, as the sick and their loved ones name their experience, they offer a glimpse of the conversion journey that sickness may prompt, the conversion invitation to redefine suffering, to join one's suffering to that of Christ, to make up in one's body for what is wanting in the suffering of Christ, and to be willing, in some measure, to say Amen to that vocation for however long its duration. These experiences, some raw and some refined, are all brought to the sacramental celebration.

The Experience of the Sick and Dying

Through sickness a person is put in crisis. Suddenly, relationships — to others, to self and even to the earth — are ambiguous. Relationship with God becomes equally tenuous for many. As one man recalled, "I wanted to cry out like Christ on the cross, 'Why have you abandoned me.'" Even for those who have prayed regularly, the relationship with God undergoes profound transformation. "I didn't have a pious thought," one priest acknowledged of the hours following a life-threatening accident. And a woman spoke of three months of pain-filled recuperation when she could not experience the presence of God nor, "for the first time in my life," could she find the words for prayer.

Serious sickness, a disruption of the status quo, is an experience of being betwixt and between. It places the one who is stricken at a threshold whose meaning has yet to unfold. Some have known only robust health all their lives, with colds and flu and the occasional headache their only experience of illness, their only brush with medication and bed rest. Most newly diagnosed patients do not understand technical medical terminology. Many feel alienation from their body and experience the examinations and tests as somehow happening to someone else; they become powerless spectators. "My body betrayed me," said one. Another noted how apathetic she felt about medical decisions being made for her because "I was too sick to participate in the discussion and decisions. If he wanted another test, 'that's fine, okay,' I'd say."

Many sick people speak about the helplessness involved in sickness, the sense of utter vulnerability. Often the sick experience themselves as objects to be taken care of and ministered to, but without their active participation. People speak about them to others in the third person, or by the name of their disease: "I was the mastectomy in 312," one woman reported, "and I wanted to scream that I was more than my diseased breast. I was still a person!" Another described a visiting priest more intent on arranging the furniture than on making their exchange human and hope-filled.

Helplessness and vulnerability extend beyond the physical condition. People who pride themselves on being dependable and conscientious are no longer able to discharge their responsibilities to others. Busy, active people who identify themselves with their profession, their reputation or their success are distressed by enforced idleness and feel a resultant loss of self-worth. Many are troubled by possible loss of income while they are sick or the possibility of losing their jobs. They worry about the expense of treatment at the very time they are incapable of doing anything about it. They worry about the burden their sickness places on their families, physically and psychologically as well as financially.

For many, this is the first time in months or years that they have prolonged time with loved ones and friends. There are alienations large and small, old hurts, breaches of family bonds or friendship, words to be reeled back in or deeds to be forgiven that come to the forefront of consciousness. But how can people find the words to talk about what matters, how can they get below the surface of things and shift from talk of current events and the weather to matters of consequence when the family has no pattern, no permission to speak about all that now looms so large yet remains unspoken? There are words of gratitude and love, tender exchanges that come so easily for some but catch in others' throats, words of praise for deeds well done and testimonies to faithful presence that need to be invited and received. There are, above all, thoughts of God to be shared, questions and doubts to be probed, fears to be expressed and hopes to be claimed. Sometimes it is only ritual and prayer that can overcome this reticence and give a language to these experiences.

A different experience altogether is the experience of the person in old age who longs for God. As one woman said, "After ninety years of life, heaven is very desirable. I think about death with considerable joy." Another woman drew on her childhood memories of boarding school to find an analogy for the experience of her waning years and her desire for God: "I loved school, but when vacation came I went home with great enthusiasm. I think my parents would have been devastated if I didn't look forward to going home. I think that's true also of God."

For some, this imminent home-going offers a new opportunity for intimacy with God unknown or unrealizable earlier in life. A man described how a priest he knew and admired had confided in him shortly before he died about a lifelong inability to pray as he thought he ought: "His illness gave him a time when he could really learn how to connect with God. He was a priest and an extremely intelligent man, and he had always had difficulty. He told me he had difficulty with private prayer and that towards the end of his life, during his illness, he had made a breakthrough—he was going home to God. It was an incredible revelation to me that someone that I thought was so close to God already could admit first of all that there was this problem, and then get on with it."

Analogies, metaphors, images, dreams . . . what can we use but these to try to imagine eternal life? A childhood dream about death continued to sustain one elderly woman's faith: "I was being propelled through a dark tunnel, and all the time I was going through the tunnel, I saw a little glimmer of light. Just a little glimmer. And it got a little broader. I think of the sacrament as a preparation for the breakthrough. The sacrament is the thing that makes us realize that death, which is fearsome, is not just fearsome. I think it brings God into the picture so that the most important experience of our lives, which is our dying, is not so terrible, is not so awesome."

This reflection prompted another: "A lot of people describe death as a tunnel, but I really think that God is very close to us, and there's just a veil. God is there, and when death comes I think we may get a surprise as the veil is lifted and God is right there."

Many of the elderly attest that the longer they live, the easier it is to speak openly about death, both the mystery of it and the wisdom gleaned from others. One friend reported a conversation with a very holy old woman in her final days who, to the surprise of her companion, acknowledged, "I'm frightened." "What are you frightened of?" asked the friend, and the woman replied, "I think I'm frightened of the unknown." And then she added: "We can't escape it and we don't know how to resist it and we don't know how to give ourselves over to it." A man recalled a very frank discussion about death when the whole family was assembled at his father's bedside: "Father Jack said to Dad, 'Are you ready?' And Dad said, 'I guess so.' And then he said, 'Are you afraid?' And Dad said, 'Maybe a little.' And Father Jack said, 'Well, we don't know. It's okay to be a little uneasy.'"

The idea of letting go, of relinquishing control, of stepping into the unknown occupies the imagination of many older people as death draws near. A woman who had witnessed the deaths of both her parents said, "They wanted to face death squarely and to embrace it gracefully. It takes a lot of faith to make that offering," she concluded, "and I know they drew strength from us and the whole community of faith."

The community's ministry to the seriously sick, to the chronically ill and to those whose death is imminent is strikingly analogous to our ministry to those preparing for initiation. Visits to the sick, prayer, reception of communion, conversations about the things of God—these are so many ways that family, friends and ministers of care help the sick and the dying to negotiate this new conversion journey, joining their sufferings to those of Christ for the life of the world, bringing them to the point of readiness for sacrament.

THE SACRAMENTAL MINISTRY OF FAMILY, FRIENDS AND COMMUNITY

There is a mutual ministry that takes place between the sick or the dying and those who accompany them. Sometimes it is carried out in presence and simple gestures, sometimes in conversation, often in prayer when traditional words and sacramental signs support and sustain us in ways beyond our own capacities to name.

The importance of touch has been noted earlier in these pages: the hand of the sponsor on the shoulder of the initiation candidate, the hand of the priest on the head of the penitent, the hands of parents and siblings signing the forehead of the infant, the hand of the minister extending bread and the cup to the neophyte—so many ways that the touch of another communicates the sustaining presence of a loving, forgiving, generous, tender and consoling God. The sick and the dying are particularly sensitive to touch. A man recalled his vigil at his mother's bedside thus: "One thing I was conscious of during the whole time was just holding my mother's hand, or putting my hand on her forehead. When I was a kid, one thing she used to do when I was sick that I found most comforting was that she would put her hand on my forehead. It was good medicine." Others describe long hours of silence where support and love were communicated mostly in holding hands, the occasional cool cloth on the forehead, a sign of the cross traced on head and hands, even the sprinkling of holy water—all of these tactile ways of presence, strength and support.

Even more importantly, touching the sick with gestures that speak of faith and affection reduces the sense of alienation, isolation and worthlessness. One man spoke of being at his father's bedside and being himself very consoled by blessing his father. He commented on how natural he found the experience: "Increasingly, people are aware of these gestures in other contexts in their experience of the church and the more we encourage people to use them in their regular life, the basic touchstones of all of our sacramental gestures, then I think they will be encouraged to do that at moments when they are the only ones there to do it for their loved one. We shouldn't discount the reality of touch." The bedside ministry of touch is mirrored in the church's laying on of hands and anointing with oil. The experience of the one reinforces and prolongs the experience of the other.

Remembering is another gift we give to the sick and dying and to one another as we accompany them. "I shall never forget my father's testimony when my mother was dying, remembering his first meetings with my mother when she was only thirteen years old and getting married about six and a half years later. They lived on the same street, so it was a sixty-five-year relationship. His words were a renewal. He knew she was dying, and this was a renewal of his life with her. I was struck by the ability of my father, who was a somewhat reticent man, quite unexpectedly to say the most astounding things and to take the most astounding moments to bring something to bear—which is really the power of ritual."

We probably cannot overestimate the importance of speaking from the heart about things that matter, memories shared, moments of loss, favorite stories, challenges overcome—all the joys and sorrows that make up a life and give it meaning, all the ways in which lives intertwine and thus live on in one another.

Speaking honestly about an imminent death may also be a great gift to the one who is near death. Inviting their participation in planning their own funeral is one way to broach the subject of death and to make it a reality for all involved. Planning the funeral together can be an occasion for story-telling—and for some, wonderful humor. "My mother was asked 'What would you like sung at your funeral?' And she said, 'What about that old song your father used to sing, "We're glad to see you go, you old rascal you"!' It was a few days before she died. Actually, I found it consoling to be doing the planning with her."

Sometimes when prayer seems difficult or impossible for the sick or the dying, family and friends help them find the words by praying with them and in their name. In these instances, the predictable, the traditional, the cherished patterns of prayer take their place alongside newer rituals. One elderly and infirm couple loved the Our Father and expected its recitation at key moments, such as before their reception of holy communion. Their son recalled one time when "I tried to give communion to them without saying the Our Father and they reacted strongly— what are you trying to do to us! It was a very comforting thing for both of them to have the ritual of it. I think having that structure is very important."

Often families and close friends gathered at the bedside include some who have drifted from the church. Then more traditional prayers become the way of including everyone. The Our Father, the Hail Mary and the rosary enable everyone's participation and even occasional leadership. "I found the rosary an extremely sustaining prayer, especially that part about 'Holy Mary, Mother of God, pray for us sinners, now and at the hour of our death.' Those words take on an immediacy and a meaning even after saying that prayer a million times. Here it is now, the hour of a death. We started the glorious mysteries, which were very appropriate. That's what we prayed at the last."

A nephew described the prayer at the bedside of his dying aunt. He had access to the ritual book *Pastoral Care of the Sick* and made ample use of its scripture passages, litanies and other prayers: "We went through those prayers over and over and it was a very uplifting experience, praying all through the day. Those prayers that are in the church's ritual were immensely consoling and immensely satisfying to us. We were a community gathered in faith."

Friends often find the church's ritual a powerful and binding experience. One woman described the anointing of a friend as a way that everyone present at her bedside could "circle the wagons and stand beside our friend, communicating love and strength and the power of communion to face this thing." A member of a community of women religious described the day a friend was facing major surgery and was anointed at eucharist: "It was such a wonderful experience of what it means to be part of a group that lives together and worships together at a very key moment in a person's life. We do not abandon one another in times of need. I was more deeply moved by that than I sometimes am at the services that we have for the whole community, I suppose because there was, for me, a tangible, immediate need in it." Another person had thought deeply about the role of the community in caring for its suffering members: "We're really all giving the sacrament as well as receiving it." Yet another recognized the role of family and friends in the care of loved ones and said: "It's not only the ordained ministers of the church who pray with the sick. Religious are taking more and more of these roles, sisters in the hospital, extraordinary ministers from the parish, both women and men. We're all learning how to be with the sick and the suffering and how to be the consoling presence of the community in these situations of need."

One man, talking with others who had all had the experience of accompanying a dying family member in the final hours of life, had this realization: "We ourselves were the ministers as baptized people. The discovery of that touched me deeply. Maybe people have always prayed around the dead, but I don't think that people fifty years ago in an Irish household would have had the sense that they could pick up the rite and use it. But we feel that we have a right to take these books and to read and to pray the Commendation of the Dying. Ministry has widened. Priestly ministry is part of this and necessary, but sometimes it's those who really love and know the person who are going to be the most effective pastoral ministers."

On the one hand, then, family and friends have a genuine sacramental ministry to their loved ones. They help those who may feel out of control, ambiguous, helpless, worthless and fearful to know the tender care of the church and the presence of a loving God. Through their ministry they both prepare for and prolong the experience of sacramental anointing and viaticum.

On the other hand, the sick and the dying can be a theophany of grace for those of us privileged to be near them and really willing and able to pay attention. A hospice care worker gave this testimony about the sick: "I think that taking care of bodies is the holiest thing I have ever done. It is prayer and it is eucharist in a real and most profound sense. There may be people who know all this already. But I did not know it because nobody ever told me. I learned it by caring for people's bodies and, most especially, by caring for dying people's bodies. I offer my skill when it is needed. Patients give the gift of trust — and countless other gifts besides. The result is eucharist — a sacrament of love and union. This experience of love and union is not highly emotional, nor is it emotionally satisfying as a rule. It is quite austere, and feels like a quiet inner nagging to get on with the job of reconciliation and of dying. which is not just for the dying but for all of us all the time."

The job of reconciliation and of dying is for all of us. Dying to sin, dying to selfishness, dying to our culture's denial of death in all its forms, dying to all that is not of God in our lives — these forms of death make up the life-long journey of the Christian. When we attend with love to the sick and to the dying they help us to remember this vocation.

Celebration: Rites of Anointing and Viaticum

OUTLINE OF RITE: ANOINTING	OUTLINE OF RITE: VIATICUM
Introductory Rite	Introductory Rite
Liturgy of the Word	Liturgy of the Word
Liturgy of Anointing	Liturgy of Viaticum
• *Litany*	• *Lord's Prayer*
• *Laying on of Hands*	• *Communion as Viaticum*
• *Prayer over the Oil*	• *Silent Prayer*
• *Anointing and Prayer*	• *Prayer after Communion*
• *The Lord's Prayer*	Concluding Rite
Concluding Rite	

It is impossible to generalize about the content of the rites of anointing and viaticum because these rites must always be adapted in length and in choice of specific options to the condition and the experience of the sick or dying person. Communal anointing, for example, is now a regular feature of parochial life. In many places it is celebrated within the eucharist on a monthly or quarterly basis. On the other hand, for someone who faces major surgery in the coming days, individual anointing may take place at a weekday eucharist or it may be quasi-private, in a hospital room. The sick person may be strong enough to participate in selecting from among the proposed scripture passages and prayers, or the anointing may have to be much abbreviated because of the circumstances of the patient or the dictates of an emergency situation.

In all cases, as the experience of this woman suggests, it is important to attend to the heart of it with reverence, no matter the circumstances: "We were standing, it was quiet, there was nobody else around. Father Chris sort of recollected himself before God and it was obvious and that made me do the same thing. It wasn't hurried. He looked at me in the middle of the prayer and again during the anointing and the prayer after. It wasn't formal, but you couldn't miss the fact that he knew that he was administering a sacrament by the grace of his ordination, and that it was a gift of God to me, and he was the intermediary. And I went out, certainly just as inspired, prepared for whatever was coming, as I could have gone out from any big ceremony. And I think that is important. And it's the same thing if I had been in bed. There is a certain reverence, solemnity, sacredness that I think should be nurtured. Just because the details of a deathbed are somewhat prosaic, you need to be pulled in, your body isn't the only thing. You've got a soul, and that's what's up now. That's what God is interested in."

No matter the context, the length of the rite or the degree of formality, three elements of anointing stand out in the experience of those who participate: the laying on of hands, the prayer over the oil and the anointing proper.

LAYING ON OF HANDS

When people reflect on the laying on of hands they often draw on their ritual memory of other times and places when hands were laid on them, and they remark that the accumulated meaning of the rite becomes part of the new experience. One woman commented, "The laying on of hands is very significant for me. Sometimes it happens because a person is sick, sometimes because they need strength, sometimes it is because the person is in deep distress, or at a moment of conversion, and it is to invoke the power of God." Another likened this laying on of hands to the gesture of calling down the Spirit during the eucharistic prayer: "I think the laying on of hands is the presence of the Spirit. You see it, for example, in the eucharistic prayer when we say 'bless these gifts and transform them, and transform us into the body of Christ.' So it is the sanctifying power of the Spirit which comes to change us in the laying on of hands." A woman religious joined to all of these meanings yet another: "The laying on of the hands has always impressed me very much. I feel that Our Lord is really there putting his hands on my head. It began when I was clothed in the habit and then the veil was placed on my head. That was such a powerful experience of the presence and touch of the Lord, and with the anointing, too, the Lord is always right there putting his hands on my head."

What does the touch communicate? "I believe God's power comes right through our hands and into anybody we touch. I have great devotion to that, to God using my hands. And I feel it is God's touch, too, and God's power coming through when hands are placed on my head." Another suggested: "It's a communication of the healing strength from the well person to the one who is asking for the healing, who might be ill. It's like we're sharing this element of good health and I'm giving it to you through this laying on of hands. Isn't that what happened when people touched Jesus and power went out from him?"

The power of the Spirit moving among the community and out across the world was the experience of one participant in a communal rite of anointing as she paid attention to the presider touching one person after another: "The gesture that stood out for me was when Father Anderson just touched, with a gentle touch. It felt like the movement of the Spirit over each person there and over the whole world. I looked up at that canopy over the altar, the baldachino, and there was an image of the Holy Spirit as a dove and that really spoke to me of the Spirit moving among us and throughout the world. I thought of people I love across the Atlantic and my family in Illinois and my cousin Charlie in Peru—I don't mean to give a geography lesson, but all these people came to me because of the breeze of the Spirit moving around the chapel and over the face of the earth."

PRAYER OVER THE OIL

Remarkably, although the words of prayers rarely come to mind when people reflect on different sacramental celebrations, the prayer over the oil received a good deal of comment. What follows here is the prayer of blessing over the oil and then a meditation on the text composed from the reflections of several people.

God of all consolation,
you chose and sent your Son to heal the world.
Graciously listen to our prayer of faith:
send the power of your Holy Spirit, the Consoler,
into this precious oil, this soothing ointment,
this rich gift, this fruit of the earth.
Bless this oil + and sanctify it for our use.
Make this oil a remedy for all who are anointed with it;
heal them in body, in soul, and in spirit,
and deliver them from every affliction.
We ask this through our Lord Jesus Christ, your Son,

who lives and reigns with you and the Holy Spirit,
one God, for ever and ever. Amen. (PCS, 123)

These are the words I heard. First of all, consolation, "God of all consolation." That went right to my heart.

"Listen to our prayer of faith." Faith. I remember the first time I realized that the sacraments are an encounter with Christ and that this comes through faith.

And the title of the Spirit, "the Consoler."

And I love the way we talk about the precious oil. As a person interested in ecology, I'm aware that this oil comes from fruit, peanuts, olive oil, whatever. It is soothing — consoling and soothing. When I don't feel well I like to be consoled and soothed with the fruit of the earth.

And "sanctify it for our use." Well, it's already holy because it belongs to God, but we ask a special blessing because it's for our use as a remedy "to heal body, soul and spirit." It helps me very much that my spirit that I bring with its burden will be cleansed and the burden removed.

"And deliver us from every affliction." I have arthritis and I have different kinds of afflictions, here and there and everywhere in my body. So the word affliction spoke to me.

And again, the Trinity at the end of it, always the love of the Trinity.

ANOINTING

Especially for those who are sick, touch is important physically, psychologically and spiritually: "There is a commercial, I think for some kind of baby lotion, and it says, 'This is meant for touching,' and you see the different mothers touching the babies, the hands and the little cheeks. It's perfectly beautiful. And when we are anointed I think of that, the beauty of the human person no matter what the physical condition — 'this is meant for touching.'" She concluded that the gesture had to be deliberate and loving for its power to be released.

Anointing was the source of a deep sense of well-being and peace for some, " . . . that great peace that comes to you, even more than the sacrament of penance." It gave energy to others. "Actually, you feel different because you're anointed. You're anointed and ready for a journey, strengthened for what you're going to do. It's like having a cup of coffee and then getting up again refreshed and going out!" For a good number, the experience of anointing is one of soul-deep healing: "What I know of ancient civilization is that oil was such a strength-giving thing and that it was comforting, soothing and healing for body and spirit. That's the way I would like to think of the sacrament."

And what of the experience of viaticum and the final journey? Perhaps the insight of one family member at a deathbed gives us some glimpse: "I started to think of the nine months in the womb and then there is a birthing into the world, and sometimes labor is easy and sometimes it is excruciating, sometimes it is short, sometimes prolonged, but there is new life and joy beyond words at the end of it. Then I thought we could see earthly life as a second womb and death is like labor, getting out of the womb and coming into life that is eternal. And there is suffering and sometimes groaning but all of it is prologue to the redemption of our bodies and to a life that knows no end with God. It's what we've been straining after all our life long."

In the midst of that final "labor" all those who surround the dying act as midwives, commending them to God when the moment of death seems near. In words of urgency, they invite the dying to let go and to surrender to the mystery: "Go forth, Christian soul, from this world . . . go forth, faithful Christian. May you see your Redeemer face to face, and enjoy the vision of God for ever." (PCS, 220)

Amen

"Saying that word Amen made me more serious about my commitment. In other words, I can't take it lightly, I can't trivialize what's going on. I can't allow myself, if I have any control over it, to be distracted. It says I really am present to this thing that is going on."

And when we are really present, paying attention, the celebration of anointing and all the attendant rites and prayers surrounding anointing and viaticum give rise to a whole range of commitments. There is, first of all, the realization of the care we assume for one another and for ourselves: "There are many modes of healing, and there is the anointing with blessed oil and the prayer of the whole community, but there are many other elements that lead up to and prolong the sacrament and that are genuinely part of the sacrament, like our own laying on of hands when we care for one another in the day to day." "The sacrament is really the way we touch one another and I think it makes us promise to care for each other." "The sacrament made me promise to lead a healthy life and to change spiritually as well. I really think we're committing ourselves to take care of our health. After all we're asking God to make us healthy, so how do we participate in that for as long as we have on earth." "I promised to really let Christ work in me and through me, to become a healing presence."

Anointing and viaticum also turn one Godward: "We're committing ourselves to think about heaven a little more. I really think we don't desire heaven enough, we don't think about it enough." "We're committed to mystery." "We're committed to trust, to a healing of our spirits, our souls, so that we are more and more ready to meet God face to face." "During the anointing ceremony I felt a great deal of the pain of loss, which seems part of old age, but this was countered by joy and being prepared by a ritual that is real and literally consists of touching a body in order to heal it, as well as the spirit, for the great moment of entering eternal life. That is what I experienced. That is my Amen."

One woman who had been a professed religious for nearly fifty years said, "I think we've often talked about marriage as a celebration of the bride and groom, who give each other the sacrament all the rest of their lives through their mutual love until they are parted by death. I'd like to add something because it surprised me so much. The sacrament of anointing deepened my religious vows to follow Jesus Christ, as I said, 'until death.'"

POSTLUDE

The opening image of this chapter was of a communal celebration of the anointing of the sick with large numbers of people presenting themselves as candidates for this sacrament. We posed two questions, which remain to be answered as best we can: Who is the sacrament for? and Why do so many people experience a need for this kind of sacramental ministry from the faith community?

The answer to the first is easier than the second. According to *Pastoral Care of the Sick*, candidates for anointing include "those of the faithful whose health is seriously impaired by sickness or old age. . . . A prudent or reasonably sure judgment, without scruple, is sufficient for deciding on the seriousness of an illness; if necessary a doctor may be consulted" (#8). A footnote to this text indicates that the word *seriously* was chosen rather than *gravely, dangerously* or *perilously* so that it would include anyone whose health is seriously impaired. In other words, the sacrament is not to be restricted, as in the recent past, to those who are at the point of death. On the other hand, the footnote also states that the sacrament is not to be given indiscriminately or to any person whose health is not seriously impaired.

The candidate for anointing is someone who is seriously sick or someone facing major surgery or someone whose health is generally fragile, as would be true of people in old age. The category under consideration is the *physical state* of the body. Yet body and spirit are so intertwined that neat distinctions easily break down.

Medical science is recognizing the interdependence of *psyche* and *soma*, of mind and body, and recognizing, too, that numerous patterns of behavior once thought of as character weakness—for example, alcoholism, excessive gambling, drug dependency and other addictions—now appear to have some biological basis.

The rite too recognizes that when a person is physically ill he or she is usually also in spiritual crisis, hence the emphasis on bringing consolation and peace to the whole person. Surely the opposite is also true, namely, that profound spiritual crisis produces physical symptoms.

Who of us is able to judge in these instances whether anointing of the sick is appropriate and opportune except the individual?

That being said, it may also be true that there is a direct correlation between the decline in individual reconciliation and the increase in numbers needing the church's healing ministry. The two speakers who comment next may actually be candidates for the sacrament of reconciliation rather than the sacrament of anointing: "It occurred to me that sometimes I like to ask to be healed of wounds that I don't even know I have, or that I haven't acknowledged because somehow or other they haven't been brought to the forefront of my consciousness. So very often that is what I pray for." "I'm becoming more and more prayerfully aware that I need healing, physically, emotionally, spiritually and intellectually, healing at every level. Shall we say I'm very much aware of that."

Only the individual is able to judge whether he or she is seriously ill. At the same time what is needed today is a broader catechesis of the healing aspects of each of the sacraments, especially the eucharist. The eucharist has been called the primary sacrament of reconciliation. Perhaps it might also be recognized as the primary sacrament of healing—soul healing. We actually make that claim every time we celebrate the eucharist. Before we approach the table, we say: "Lord, I am not worthy to receive you, but only say the word and my soul shall be healed."

Chapter Nine

Funerals

Precious in the sight of the Lord is the death of his faithful ones.
Psalm 116:15

PRELUDE

With the death of a Christian, the sacramental life comes full circle. Having been baptized into the life, death and resurrection of Christ, the faithful Christian has made the lifelong journey of growing in conformity to Jesus Christ. In these pages we have called this journey a process of conversion and transformation, of "putting on Christ." For most Christians, the journey has its ups and downs and probably a number of detours over the years. It has taken many different forms and been celebrated in many different ways: the baptized Christian has been sealed in the Spirit, nurtured at the table, healed of the wounds of sin and division, supported by the sacramental graces of vocation, and most immediately, prepared to be gathered into the embrace of God by anointing and viaticum. When a Christian dies in Christ, the journey is over. The transformation begun at baptism is complete. The veil is lifted. The mystery of God is fully revealed. There is no more need of sacrament.

The Christian funeral liturgy is not a sacrament in the strict sense. Nevertheless, it is included in these reflections because it is one of the most beautiful of all the revised rites and because it occupies a central place in the liturgical life of the church. There is no more eloquent symbolic statement about the meaning that Christians attach to life and to death, no more profound enactment of the communion of the church unbroken even by death, no more consoling portrayal of the love that connects us and the mysteries that bind us to one another in faith than there is when Christians gather both in anguish and in hope to give their sister or brother into the arms of God.

Pastoral Care of the Sick (PCS) and the *Order of Christian Funerals* (OCF) together constitute the community's sweeping pastoral care of its sick, dying and deceased members and those who love them. *Pastoral Care of the Sick* concludes with the commendation of the dying and prayer after death; the *Order of Christian Funerals* pick ups seamlessly with additional prayers at the deathbed, prayers for the first gathering of loved ones in the presence of the body, vigil prayers for the deceased, prayers for the transfer of the body to the church, the funeral liturgy and the rites of committal at the final resting place. Every stage of this transition has been anticipated; the crossing of each new threshold is eased by the church's ministry of care, both for the dying and for those who journey with them in their final illness. That comprehensive care was experienced by one man: "I think in both my parents' cases I was able to see how closely the church cared for them during the different points of their months of illness. It just had so much of a sense of a transition. It was a gentle transition between their life on earth and the afterlife. The prayers, the rituals, the sense of community are all just a marvelous part of our faith."

Not only does the church surround its suffering and grieving members with words of hope and gestures of consolation, but it entrusts this ministry to each one of us who claims membership in the body of Christ.

"If one member suffers in the body of Christ which is the Church, all the members suffer with that member" (1 Corinthians 12:26). For this reason, those who are baptized into Christ and nourished at the same table of the Lord are responsible for one another. When Christians are sick, their brothers and sisters share a ministry of mutual charity and "do all that they can to help the sick return to health, by showing love for the sick and by celebrating the sacraments with them" (see *Pastoral Care of the Sick: Rites of Anointing and Viaticum*, General Introduction, 33). So too when a member of Christ's Body dies, the faithful are called to a ministry of consolation to those who have suffered the loss of one whom they love. Christian consolation is rooted in that hope that comes from faith in the saving death and resurrection of the Lord Jesus Christ.

Christian hope faces the reality of death and the anguish of grief but trusts
confidently that the power of sin and death has been vanquished by the risen
Lord. The Church calls each member of Christ's Body — priest, deacon,
layperson — to participate in the ministry of consolation: to care for the dying,
to pray for the dead, to comfort those who mourn. (OCF, 8)

Familiarity with the rites of the church and greater access to these rituals among lay
Catholics will make this ministry possible. Paying attention to the experience of
those who are bereaved will ensure that our ministry is believable and trustworthy.

But beyond the ministry of consolation there is a deeper invitation here. Paying
attention — really attending — to the movements of our own hearts as we grieve the
death of another will teach us much about God and faith and about the many ways
we are being called, even now, to die for the sake of our own journey into God. The
author Muriel Spark once stated that life without an ever-present sense of death is
insipid, "a little like living on the whites of eggs." Paying attention as we stand before
the mystery of death may be one of the clearest invitations we ever receive to live a
converted life.

Experience: Returning One Whom We Love to God's Tender Care

Two different kinds of experience are mirrored when we gather for the funeral rites.
There is, most immediately, the experience of the mourners, of family and friends, of
colleagues and co-workers, and, in the case of an infant or small child, even the
uncomprehending grief of playmates. There are people gathered who barely know
the deceased, but are there because of a connection, perhaps business or social, to
one of the bereaved. There are people of all faith traditions and those without faith.
There are people of diverse ages with their particular attitudes to death, and people
of different cultures with their different patterns of grieving and letting go. We shall
call all these people the mourners and attempt to offer some generalizations about
their experience.

There is also the experience of the church as a community of faith, an experience and a set of beliefs on which to lean in days of sorrow. The experience of the
church is reflected in the rites it offers.

EXPERIENCE OF THE MOURNERS

For those immediately affected by a death there is, first of all, shock. It does not matter if the person who has died is elderly and in frail health. It does not matter if the person is ravaged by disease and already beyond the doctor's prognosis of survival. Death is always shocking. But sudden death, death without warning, without the sedative of anticipation, throws family and friends into convulsions of unanticipated grief. Such is the experience following a fatal accident or a death that results from violence. And always, the death of an infant or a child shocks us by its subversion of nature's patterns. "Was it sudden?" seems a meaningless question in the face of the always unpredictable. The shock of death is always present; it is only a question of degree. Even the way we die cannot be predetermined: "Everybody dies in a different way, and the idealization we have that they're all going to be saying the name of Jesus with their last breath like all those stories we used to read — that just doesn't happen."

The type of death endured and the closeness of our relationship to the one who has died are only part of the story of the upheaval that death brings in its wake. The death of one close to us can be like the shifting of tectonic plates. Our small world changes radically. The death of the second parent, for example, means a renegotiation of relationships and of leadership among brothers and sisters. It means there is no more "home" to return to, no more "switchboard central" to rely on for family news. There is the need for "orphaned" siblings — an apt title no matter the age — to establish new bonds and work out a different set of connections with one another. Similarly, the death of a spouse or a child or a best friend leaves a massive hole in one's home and in one's heart, a hole never to be filled — not in the same way. In *Encounters with Silence* Karl Rahner said it well: "As death has trodden roughly through our lives, every one of the departed has taken a piece of our heart . . . and often enough the whole heart."

That hole in the heart lingers long, and with it a sense of profound loss: "I was sixteen years old when I went to my first real funeral," said one man. "My grandfather died, and I could feel myself being pulled away. I knew there was this separation. I could no longer talk to this person, relate to him. And that was a very hard thing." Mourners go through a variety of experiences. There is deep grief for many, a sense of loss, sometimes an incomprehension of the reality and the finality of this death. At the same time, there is, in the face of such separation and dislocation, a need to stay connected to one another and to the one who has died through the long hours following death — especially by touch and by physical proximity. "A number of my brothers and sisters went up and touched my mother's hand and then we remained quiet for a little while. Just standing near the coffin was important." Assistance in preparing the body for burial is an important and grounding experience for some; being able to pray in the presence of the body, especially at wrenching moments such as the closing of the coffin is another antidote to this sense of separation. Proximity to the bereaved is an equally important ministry for the rest of the community — not leaving the mourners in ritual isolation in the church or at the funeral home.

Sometimes in the way we relate to the body of the deceased we give each other glimpses of the communion that transcends loss and separation. One man had such an experience as he watched the mother of a friend after the death of her husband: "Something that really struck me when we walked into the funeral home on the first day of the vigil was how comfortable she was with his death. She walked right up to him as if she was just walking up to him at the kitchen table, and put her hands on him. It was just like they were together. It was beautiful to watch that. It changed everything I had thought about that separation thing. It doesn't always have to be that way." No, it does not, not in a church that believes in the communion of saints, although that felt sense of communion is a matter of time and is a gift.

There are always conflicting emotions that batter the bereaved: anger when death is by suicide, relief when long suffering has ended, devastation at the seeming meaninglessness of it all. Gratitude for the gift of this life and a sense of tragic waste that it ended when it did can co-exist. Unfinished business nearly always preoccupies some of the mourners who have gathered; some feel guilt because of a ruptured relationship. Regret because I did not do more or say more or cherish our times together can cause great agitation at one moment; alternatively, memories and storytelling can restore a sense of peace.

The raw emotions that afflict the bereaved are further complicated by the awkwardness of families gathered in grief who have not been close or who have been estranged from one another by hurts half-forgotten. Other families, while close to one another, are at various stages of relationship to the church — with different degrees of participation and different levels of ease with the church's ritual patterns and expectations. Said one respondent: "Active participation in the church and its liturgy varies in my family from non-existent to irregular to very regular. And there are people, too, from different generations who have different, even conflicting, ritual needs and expectations."

Perhaps the overarching experience in the face of death is the desire that this person be remembered for who she was and what she did, that her death and new life be celebrated in a way that is fitting and appropriate. As one woman remarked: "There is no such thing as generic death. There is no Joe or Jane Christian for whom we can roll out the 'same old same old' for a funeral. There is only *this* child, *this* son, *this* mother, *this* spouse who happens to be cherished by somebody." Remembering plays itself out in a variety of ways in the days after death, ritual remembrance foremost among them. Remembering, the anamnesis of the church, takes on a whole new meaning in the various moments of the funeral liturgy. As Christians we gather to make memorial of Christ, dead and risen; during the funeral we keep the memory, too, of the one who died in Christ.

Our faithful remembering is a continuation of the life and ministry of Christ in our midst. We are the presence of Christ for one another, a reality expressed beautifully in the pastoral notes of the funeral rite:

> The participation of the community in the funeral rites is a sign of the compassionate presence of Christ, who embraced little children, wept at the death of a friend, and endured the pain and separation of death in order to render it powerless over those he loves. Christ still sorrows with those who sorrow and longs with them for the fulfillment of the Father's plan in a new creation where tears and death will have no place. (#239)

Precious in the sight of the Lord is the death of his faithful ones. Christ comes and lingers long. Throughout the unfolding of the funeral rites, Christ, whom we know as high priest and leader of prayer, is also the preeminent mourner among us.

EXPERIENCE OF THE CHURCH

There is a beautiful symmetry in the patterns of prayer we use to welcome Christians and to return them to God, the author of life and the hope of the just. Baptisms and funerals, well celebrated, illuminate each other. One man reflected on his experience of funerals and baptisms intertwined: "We had a couple of baptisms in the larger family soon after a funeral, and we used many of the same readings. It was just astounding to me how the baptism works through all of this stuff so that the next generation — those of us who have been at the funerals — during the readings could recall the generation we have just sent forth."

Let us look more closely at this symmetry between baptisms and funerals. Recall that the rite of infant baptism begins at the door of the church with a word of welcome and a prayer, a ritual signing of the cross and the crossing of the threshold of the church both literally and metaphorically. Accompanied by loved ones, the infant is brought into the church in procession, the beginning of his or her pilgrimage in faith. Tender care marks the baptism of a child — touching, holding, bathing, anointing and clothing with the white baptismal garment.

As the child is "clothed in Christ" the whole community is reminded of the significance of this garment: "See in this white garment the outward sign of your Christian dignity. With your family and friends to help you by word and example, bring that dignity unstained into the everlasting life of heaven" (RBC, 99).

Then as the candle is given, the celebrant proclaims: "Parents and godparents, this light is entrusted to you to be kept burning brightly. This child of yours has been enlightened by Christ. She is to walk always as a child of the light. May she keep the flame of faith alive in her heart. When the Lord comes, may she go out to meet him with all the saints in the heavenly kingdom" (#100).

At the conclusion of the baptism, the community brings the infant to the altar, marking our hope that the initiation will come to completion when the child is welcomed to the banquet of Christ's sacrifice (#103).

At the funeral liturgy we do very much the same for the one we love. We gather at the door of the church, crossing the threshold in procession together, marking the end of the journey of the one we give back to God. Signs of tender care for the body abound. Holy water is sprinkled on the coffin as an explicit reminder of baptism and the words have a new depth, finality and hope: "In the waters of baptism [Susan] died with Christ and rose with him to new life. May she now share with him eternal glory" (OCF, 185).

Then the pall, a large white cloth signifying the baptismal garment, the outward sign of Christian dignity, is placed on the casket by family and friends. The connection of the two was brought home to the one who offered this reflection: "I remember when my uncle, who was also my godfather, had died. I was asked to be a pallbearer then. The pallbearers were the ones who were invited to put the pall on. I remember at that moment thinking that he had given the white garment to me and now I was placing it on his body — it was really a poignant moment."

The procession continues, the way lighted for us by the paschal candle, the symbol of Christ in our midst and the symbol of the vocation of each one to walk as a child of light, with the flame of faith alive in Christ Jesus. The body is brought before the altar, the banquet table where faithful Christians are nourished throughout their lives. The table is also the altar of sacrifice where, week after week for their lifetime, Christians have offered themselves with Christ Jesus to the One he called Abba, begged for the transformation of the Spirit, and joined themselves to the death and rising of Jesus for the life of the world. Water, pall, paschal candle, procession — all of it a stunning reminder of one journey and many, all of it a faithful depiction of the promises of God. It is our most deeply held beliefs that we enact in the rites of the funeral liturgy, above all, that God who began the good work in us will bring it to completion.

The rites surrounding the death of a Christian form a single motion, a single ritual with many different movements, very much like a symphony. The individual ritual moments encompassed in the *Order of Christian Funerals* mirror the way we understand and celebrate the Easter Triduum, not as three separate and discrete events but as the passage from death to life of the Lord Jesus, the event we call the paschal mystery. It is a single event. But because we need to tell the story slowly, we do it over several days. The same thing happens in the death of a Christian. We are telling a single story of a Christian life and death and of God's action in this life. It is a story about one whom we love, whose life can only be told by degrees. These different ritual moments of remembering were felt by one mourner as "this little piece of structure that keeps the whole thing together and makes it go forward."

Planning

A final note before turning to the rites: The participation of the mourners in the planning of each of these rites — to the extent that they are able — is critical in assuring that this funeral will be a faithful reflection of a particular life well lived. One man who assisted in planning for the funeral of his mother said that "planning gave me an opportunity to think about her life and to choose things, or think of things that would apply to her life, or how she lived her life." Another recalled that the very working through the readings and the prayers "was a wonderful opportunity to grieve and to realize more deeply what was happening." A third person talked about selecting the readings, the prayers and the music, and about deciding which of the members of the family would fulfill various liturgical ministries. Throughout this process, he said, "the choices that we were making became our prayer."

The invitation to take key roles in the preparation of the rites, one person concluded, is an invitation essential to the mourners: "Their readiness and willingness to do it is up to them, but the invitation should be written into the laws of the church, that they should be invited." Families have fundamentally good instincts about how they need to ritualize death. One man recalled, with gratitude, how his mother's wishes were respected in this regard: "My mother, without any doubt and without any hint from me at all, was really clear she wanted the body lowered at the grave-side service, and that was a non-negotiable. But it was absolutely unheard of in the cemetery and to the funeral home and to most of the Atlanta archdiocese. And that parish went to bat for her and made sure it happened."

The experience of talking through the various moments of the funeral "cemented us and grounded us in reality." That is the overwhelmingly positive effect of family involvement in the preparations and planning. On the other hand—after having taken the time and care to plan for two evenings of vigil and the rite of transfer—the experience of being disenfranchised, first by the parish deacon, then by the Knights of Columbus and finally by the funeral director, still lingers in one family's memory. This is contrary to both the letter and the spirit of the *Order of Christian Funerals*, which presumes that it is the family who is most actively involved and whose wishes and needs must be respected.

As will become apparent, the insights about the rites to which we now turn are the reflections of people who took an active part in preparing and celebrating the home-going of one they loved.

Celebration: Order of Christian Funerals

OUTLINE OF THE RITE

> Gathering in the Presence of the Body
>
> Vigil for the Deceased
>
> Transfer of the Body to the Church or the Place of Committal
>
> Funeral Liturgy
>
> Rite of Committal

GATHERING IN THE PRESENCE OF THE BODY

The first gathering in the presence of the body and the final leave-taking often prove to be the most wrenching experiences for family and friends. As the *Order of Christian Funerals* has recognized, at this first gathering around the one who has died family members confront in a most immediate way the fact of their loss and the mystery of death. The rite provides the possibility of prayer and gesture — a simple pattern of scripture, sprinkling with holy water, a psalm, the Lord's Prayer, a concluding prayer and blessing with a gesture such as marking the body with the sign of the cross — to enable those present to "show reverence for the body of the deceased as a temple of the life-giving Spirit and ask, in that same Spirit, for the eternal life promised to the faith" (#110). The pattern is completely adaptable to the desires and needs of the mourners and the particular circumstances of the gathering.

One person recalled that the scripture verses were very short, for example, "Come to me, all you who labor and are heavy burdened," and that they were "so familiar and consoling — just right." After the scripture, the priest who knew the family well and was leading them in prayer made a judicious selection: "He added some prayers from the old ritual, for example, Saints of God, and he said some of the other traditional prayers and that added something important, because there were people there who were from that generation that would have heard that at a wake service. The combination of what the new rite offers and the living tradition was perfect."

In practice, this first gathering includes family from near and far, arriving a little before others, coming from different places — all of them taking time to touch and say goodbye to the body. Often, extended families are intergenerational and the youngest members are having their first experience of death. This gathering becomes particularly important for them. "My children hadn't seen their grandfather for months. For them to be invited to stand around the coffin, as you would in a family gathering around the body, was very important." And, as for the children for whom this was the first encounter with death, "they were watching me very closely to see what to do in this situation. This is a dead body, this was Grandpa. I think the ability to surround that prayer moment with simple touch and familial affection toward the body was as important as the prayer."

VIGIL FOR THE DECEASED

The vigil is the principal celebration of the community prior to the funeral liturgy. Depending on the times of celebration, the vigil often attracts more people than the funeral Mass. "The beauty of it," remarked a family member of the deceased, "is that, often more so than the Mass, the vigil draws a greater variety of people, and for them all to have a liturgy of the word with some care for song and preaching made it an event that gathered everyone in." It also prepares close family and friends for what is to follow. "Those of us that returned for the funeral Mass felt a little more ready to enter into it and a little more part of the community. The fact that it was word and not some other devotional exercise really worked — word and song."

The purpose of the vigil, according to the pastoral notes of the rite, is to meet the needs of the often bewildered, shocked and grieving mourners. "The ministry of the Church at this time is one of gently accompanying the mourners in their initial adjustment to the fact of death and to the sorrow this entails" (#52). Thus the focus of the vigil rites — which include an introductory rite, a liturgy of the word, intercessory prayer, and a concluding prayer and blessing — is to assist mourners to express their sorrow and to find strength and consolation through faith in Christ and his resurrection. What once we called the "wake" is now called a "vigil": The community keeps watch with the family in prayer, reading, song and story-telling. Attentive participants may find a resonance in this vigiling rite to that of Easter eve when, annually, the community turns to God's word "as the source of faith and hope, as light and life in the face of darkness and death" (#56).

A vigil well prepared and well celebrated is enormously sustaining for family and friends: "What really struck me was the participation level, the participation of people. That was very, very helpful. They purposely provided time during the vigil service for people to get up and remember. I think that the key is participation." By all reports, the opportunity to remember, to tell stories, to reminisce together about important events and defining moments in the life of the deceased is a very important element of the vigil. One family member spoke about the blending of prayer and reminiscing: "Without that dimension of remembering the prayers lose a whole lot. They don't become cemented in reality and grounded." Remembering takes a variety of forms: music, tapes, pictures, mementos and, most often, stories: "After the readings and song, some of my sisters wanted to say something about my mother, so right after the intercessions four of them got up and spoke. It made her so present. Concluding the evening that way was perfect."

TRANSFER OF THE BODY TO THE CHURCH OR THE PLACE OF COMMITTAL

The time of the transfer of the body is another occasion of great emotion for the mourners. Often it includes the closing of the coffin for the last time. Some brief form of prayer — possibly a scripture verse, a litany, the Lord's Prayer and a concluding prayer — eases this moment of grief. The use of holy water, blessing prayers, the familiar "Eternal rest" prayer: all of it is source of great consolation. Use of these options at the closing of the coffin would also fill the vacuum of ritual that one man found horribly jarring: "It was decided as they transferred the body that the casket should be closed. All these people were milling about the room and not realizing that this was happening. I had wanted to do the closing of the casket with prayer. It was wrenching. It was very wrenching to see that lid go down. It was not celebrated with any kind of a rite." In another situation the opposite was true, to the great consolation of the onlookers: "I placed my hand on my mother's forehead as I sang 'May the choirs of angels' and then as some of the people started to leave the room, I said, 'Do you want to stay for the closing of the coffin?' and most of the Catholics said 'Yes.' And I read the gospel about 'In my Father's house.' It was powerful. Again, the accompaniment of the words and ritual led you through it."

The transfer rite concludes with a beautiful invitation to begin the final journey. "The Lord guards our coming in and our going out. May God be with us today as we make this last journey with our sister." The importance of prepared and prayerful leadership at this moment makes what we say and what we ask believable. "Father Jack had internalized this whole rite. He held the book, but he didn't need it. The words were just coming out. And they weren't forced. You could tell he meant it. And when he got to that part it was very, very moving."

FUNERAL LITURGY

The funeral Mass is the central liturgical celebration of the Christian community for the deceased. This is the heart of it. This is where we make the most condensed statement of all that we believe about death and life. This is the time when we most clearly join our remembering of the deceased to the community's great memorial of Christ, dead and risen, and find new strength and hope in God's promises.

> At the funeral liturgy the community gathers with the family and friends of the deceased to give praise and thanks to God for Christ's victory over sin and death, to commend the deceased to God's tender mercy and compassion, and to seek strength in the proclamation of the paschal mystery. Through the Holy Spirit the community is joined together in faith as one Body in Christ to reaffirm in sign and symbol, word and gesture that each believer through baptism shares in Christ's death and resurrection and can look to the day when all the elect will be raised up and united in the kingdom of light and peace. (#129)

The funeral liturgy is able to bring to ritual expression all of the experiences previously described and, with the support of a believing community, mourners are able to enact in word, gesture and song that sure and certain hope claimed aloud by one mourner: "This life continues in a way that we can only glimpse at and hope for."

RECEPTION AND INTRODUCTORY RITE

Family and closest friends accompany the body across the threshold of the church for the last time. They carry the body of the one they love, clothe it with a baptismal garment and may place a sign of their loved one's faith on the top of the casket. One man recalls watching his mother's Bible placed on top of the pall: "I found the placing of the symbol to speak so loudly. She had read the Bible all her life, and there was that battered, thumbed, thoroughly used book on top of her coffin as a witness of her love of the word. It spoke volumes."

These gestures of carrying, clothing and presenting their loved one's body to the church for the last time are very human gestures, in addition to being gestures of faith. Beyond their theological significance, they are deeply meaningful from a human point of view. They make that moment in the funeral rite stand out as different from any ordinary celebration.

The procession is equally significant, especially when accompanied by song. One mourner explained that it is a thunderous sort of support and sustenance to hear many voices accompany you and your loved one up the aisle: "We chose 'Lord of all hopefulness' for the opening hymn—such a beautiful metaphor for the whole rite, especially the line 'be there at our homing.'"

It is important that the funeral rite be adapted to this person, this family and these very particular circumstances of death. After the fact, mourners are sometimes able to cite a line or two of the funeral texts that helped them name their loss and claim their faith. One man participated in the selection of texts and said: "Choosing the prayers with the presider was important—having prayers that were true. We used that prayer about 'the bond that had been forged in our lives and not destroyed' and the presider took that up in the homily, which was deeply consoling."

LITURGY OF THE WORD

For many families, selecting the readings is very important, both at the time of preparation and long after the funeral is over, when lines from the readings return to memory and imagination. "The souls of the just are in the hands of God" was a line that echoed again and again for one man. Another man was deeply consoled by the reading from Romans: "Are you unaware that we who were been baptized into Christ Jesus were baptized into his death," and, in fact, he had memorized the passage. Similarly, good service music done responsorially and well can support those who mourn in a magnificent way. A responsorial psalm, for example, allows time not just to sing, but to listen to the singing and then to sing again, creating a prayerful, meditative and grief-aware atmosphere that allows faith and grief together. Responsorial music has this power even more than hymns, according to musicians who have heard that experience often related by mourners.

One family member reflected on the importance, as well, of the homily: "It was my experience that the homilist, having some awareness of the deceased person, and ideally the family, too, is indispensable. If it's the liturgy of the word with the preaching centered on the readings and the prayers, and if there is attention to the real person who has died and to the family, then it works. In my dad's case, the man had great affection for my dad, so there was even another layer to it. If some real contact comes through, then it moves hearts." Another person commented on a homilist's effort at the vigil the night before to talk to every one of the children of the deceased. Then he used their reflections in the homily, an experience that meant the world to the family. Said one of them: "It takes time but it can really help people and draw people in if it's done, and it expresses in a way well beyond words that the church loves and cares for each one."

The intercessions, too, may be personalized for this person and this family: "During the intercessions we noted the people like my dad and other people in the family who had died and that's very important. A family can compose its own 'Litany of Saints,' and I think it is very powerful. I had a great sense of the communion of the whole church — living and dead."

LITURGY OF THE EUCHARIST

What amazes and deeply moves some mourners, especially those who regularly participate in the celebration of the eucharist, is the unmistakable sense of being held and carried by the very familiarity of the eucharistic rite. One person described it this way: "It's an indication, to me, of the importance of ritual. We know how it is going to unfold. It immerses you and holds you, because it's the familiar. It's what you know from Sunday to Sunday. And there it is again to sustain you and cradle you and lead you through with all of those expected words and parts of the eucharistic prayer leading up to the intercession for the dead. It brings you forth, it carries you in a very beautiful way. It's another example of how the church's ritual speaks to human experience."

KISS OF PEACE

The exchange of peace is another familiar ritual that takes on a different dimension in the context of a funeral. "We can be embraced, we can be kissed, we can be consoled by all these people that we love coming together and saying 'The peace of Christ.'" The kiss of peace works at a funeral in ways that we cannot predict, because family members come together in all their complexities and degrees of association with the church and some, in larger families, with no association whatsoever. Somehow the exchange of peace speaks at all those levels. It is an act of solidarity in this moment. In larger families sometimes a whole set of relationships is renegotiated at that point. One mourner recalled of the experience: "Somehow you can't always do it with words, but at that moment you can perhaps bring about the possibility of reconciliation with the past and the promise of being a better family in the future. It speaks in ways that words couldn't possibly." Especially in families of mixed belief and practice, the exchange of peace helps mitigate the division that is experienced at communion: "The peace began the healing process where there had been alienation in my own family among some siblings, and that has all been transformed since then. Certainly when people have to come together and at least acknowledge each other's presence, it probably is a moment in many families where that begins the healing process. In larger families, and in families in which religious practices are mixed, some will not go to communion perhaps, but you can see the unity of coming together as the Body of Christ when they share the peace of Christ, even though they will not join us at the table. So that helps, I think too, so that they won't feel completely left out at that particular moment just prior to communion."

FINAL COMMENDATION

How different the new prayers of commendation are from those of the past! In the old requiem Mass, things ended a bit too abruptly. We have discovered the importance of closure, a word and gesture of farewell, especially as many are not going to go to the committal. For many, it is the Song of Farewell that brings closure. "The setting we used was 'May the choirs of angels.' I had a sense of the community passing that person on to heaven. It was so palpable. The people apparently had sung it in the parish before, so they were already familiar with it and really sang it. It was very beautiful." Choice of music, familiar prayers and careful gestures of farewell combine in the final commendation to express the church's unwavering hope. These simple concluding rites also sustain the mourners as they take their loved one to the final resting place: "The priest took his time with the sprinkling of the coffin and the incensing of the coffin. It was done with reverence and dignity and that was another sign of the community's care for my mother. I found that extremely moving, the final commendation." Another found these closing ritual moments "the high point of the funeral liturgy. It was tremendously powerful and I was very grateful for that. The closing hymn, 'I know that my redeemer lives,' was so strong. As my brothers and I walked with my mother's body down the aisle, to hear all of those people singing — That was a tremendously uplifting, faith-filling, sustaining experience."

RITE OF COMMITTAL

We turn now to the conclusion of the funeral rites at the grave, tomb or crematorium. The rite of committal is the final ritual act of the community. We give back the one whom we love to God's tender care.

> In committing the body to its resting place, the community expresses the hope that, with all those who have gone before marked with the sign of faith, the deceased awaits the glory of the resurrection. The rite of committal is an expression of the communion that exists between the Church on earth and the Church in heaven: the deceased passes with the farewell prayers of the community of believers into the welcoming company of those who need faith no longer but see God face to face. (#206)

The issue of closure arises again. The rite of committal is a simple, some say too brief, ceremony that includes an invitation to prayer, a verse from scripture, a prayer over the place of committal, the prayer of committal, intercessions, the Lord's Prayer, concluding prayer and prayer over the people. If celebrated in this way, it may take only five or six minutes. Nearly everyone who was interviewed found the need to adapt this ritual to incorporate song and some ritual gesture that each one could perform — everyone sprinkling the coffin with holy water, for example, placing a flower on top of the coffin or marking the coffin with a sign of the cross — some last sign of love and farewell to augment the words of the prayer.

> One person reported, "It is really worth considering the importance of lowering the body, of being at the grave and not just leaving the body in the chapel, not just keeping this ritual distance that is set up away from the family, but coming right up and being able to touch the coffin." Another concurred, "It is unsettling just to walk away and leave the body."

Far more satisfying was the experience of the burial of a woman religious surrounded by her community and family: "They have the custom of singing the Salve Regina, and then people just stood, as often happens at funerals. They didn't want to leave. I think that our greatest weakness is our committal rite. It is bald, and unless you find some ways to make something more of that, it is really unsatisfying. In a lot of circumstances people don't want to leave. The six or seven minutes of committal isn't enough. I decided to say spontaneously that prayer, 'Protect us, Lord, as we stay awake, watch over us as we sleep . . .' and then 'May the Lord bless us, protect us from all evil . . .' and we sang one verse of 'May the choirs of angels.' The priest had left. It was just the sisters and my family. And an eighty-five-year-old sister standing to the side said, 'That put the icing on the cake!'"

A final comment about the committal rite really applies to all of our ritual behavior. Children are constantly being formed by what they observe from adults. The attitudes and patterns they see in us form them in habits of ritual behavior, and even more importantly, in the habits of the heart that our ritual behavior signifies. At funerals, children discover and are formed in what we believe about death: "The children are taking it all in right from the word go. They are really watching, trying to figure out how they feel about this. And all the way through they were watching their parents and the other adults to try and figure out how they are supposed to be there. They are being ritually formed even by watching the behavior adults take on. At the heart of it, from the Christian point of view of these rites, is our understanding of the body as a sacrament to that person. Everything we do gives our children cues. We say here, 'This is the burial of a Christian who was a temple of the Spirit.'"

Amen

> For the Son of God, Jesus Christ, was not "Yes and No"; but in him it is always "Yes." For in him every one of God's promises is a "Yes." For this reason it is through him that we say the "Amen," to the glory of God.
> (2 Corinthians 1:19–20)

When the Christian community gathers to return one we love to the embrace of God, we say Amen, first of all, in the name of the deceased, gathering up and handing over every Amen she uttered throughout her life. Our Amen joins the one we love to the perfect Amen who is Christ to the glory of God. That's what we long for. That's what we hope for. That's what we pray for.

Our prayer of Amen is, secondly, for and with the bereaved. Here is a remarkable account of an experience of the community's embrace through presence and prayer: "My experience was of community and assembly. I felt embraced by the community and its representatives. I immediately felt them drawing me in. I could lean back and let the community take care of me and my family. It was the community embrace at the beginning of the experience and then it was the assembly in action in all the ritual throughout. We're just hungry in those situations for the very words and the bread of life. It's like a very needy creature for whom anything addresses the thirst and hunger. To me the strongest ritual symbol was not any one of the physical things that we did towards that body, but it was all of that caught up in a community action. That is one of the beauties of these rites. They are about people doing it together and symbolizing their unity. That is the human experience of death. In the end that assembly speaks to me that we're not just saying goodbye, we're expressing faith for a future reunion."

Our prayer is, finally, for ourselves. Amen, we say, to shore up our own belief, to stand by one another in a time of profound sadness, loss and grief, to say by our words and gestures, our prayer and praise that we really believe the words of the preface: "Lord, for your faithful people life is changed, not ended. When the body of our earthly dwelling lies in death we gain an everlasting dwelling place in heaven." Amen.

Chapter Ten
Eucharist

... our desire to thank you is itself your gift.
Preface, Weekdays IV

PRELUDE

We come, finally, to the heart and center of our lives as Christians, to the sacrament that constitutes the community and has bound us together, one with another and with Christians of every age, of every place, race and tongue, of every way of life. We come to the sacrament that has been like a wave of grace rolling over the community again and again across the centuries of Christendom, hollowing out spaces for the divine in the midst of the everyday.

We come to the eucharist, a sacrament so familiar to us, an action we do so instinctively that it is in our blood and our bones — the movements and the gestures, the oft-repeated words and phrases, the sights and sounds and tastes and smells that frame this miracle of graced relationship. We come to listen and to love and, having loved, we come in order to be sent — to complete Christ's work on earth. We do it over and over. In a way, it is like the air we breathe — absolutely essential for life but often taken for granted. And yet, frequent and familiar as it is, it is also and always mysterious to us that God would choose such simple elements as story-telling and table-sharing to move among us and to touch and transform our hearts. Eucharist is familiar in its every contour; it is mystery at its core.

We have placed the eucharist last in these mystagogical reflections on the sacraments for several reasons. First of all, every sacrament is a celebration of one or another facet of the journey of conversion, and the eucharist keeps us going and provides us with necessary nourishment along the way. Second, every sacrament is a celebration of the paschal mystery — Jesus' life, death and rising — and the eucharist is its most condensed and perfect expression. Third, the eucharist is the sacrament that connects, recapitulates and intensifies the promises we have made in every other sacrament. And finally, eucharist so clearly illustrates the fundamental structure in every sacrament, the structure of word and response, of listening and loving, that it serves as a model and summary of the whole of the sacramental economy. Let us look at each of these realities in turn.

First, the relationship of eucharist to the ongoing journey of conversion.

Most of the sacraments come at crossroads moments of the human journey. They are the faith community's intervention and blessing at times of birth and coming of age, of vocation, of rupture and reconciliation, of sickness and debilitation and death. These are the critical passages of human life, each of them a new invitation to join ourselves to Christ, a new call to conversion as turning to God or moving more deeply into the life of God.

Eucharist is that repeatable sacrament which sustains us on this lifelong journey of conversion. Each time the community assembles for the celebration of the eucharist, it celebrates its own conversion journey as well, and it acknowledges the paradox of the Christian life: that we are saved yet sinners, liberated yet ever in need of deeper conversion. Each time we gather we rehearse the wonderful works of God and give praise and thanksgiving that we have been counted worthy to stand in God's presence and serve. At every celebration we acknowledge that God never ceases to call us to a new and more abundant life, that as sinners we are invited to trust in God's mercy, that the covenant of friendship with God is a bond that need never be broken, and that now, today — the always present *hodie* of the liturgy — is the day to listen for God's voice, to return and to be renewed in Christ. A time of grace and reconciliation is always at hand. With each celebration of the eucharistic liturgy we beg that the Spirit of God, the sanctifying Spirit, the Spirit of transformation, will change the elements of bread and wine and will change each one of us to be the very holiness of God. This slow, even imperceptible, transformation happens when we are faithful to the journey and it happens because we are surrounded by a believing community and the grace of God who always draws us to a new and more abundant life. It is, in the last analysis, the eucharist that shapes us and transforms us week after week as we rehearse Jesus' attitudes and values in the presence of the one he called Abba.

Second, every sacrament is a celebration of the paschal mystery; the eucharist is its most perfect expression. In post-conciliar theological reflection, the language of paschal mystery looms large. The life, death, rising and exaltation of Christ in glory is the cornerstone of contemporary sacramental theology. The *Constitution on the Sacred Liturgy* (CSL) points to the foundation of the church's sacramental patterns of prayer in the paschal mystery of Christ and in the church that continues his saving presence. The constitution states that Christ the Lord

> achieved his task of redeeming humanity and giving perfect glory to God, principally by the paschal mystery of his blessed passion, resurrection from the dead, and glorious ascension, whereby, "dying, he destroyed our death and, rising, he restored our life." For it was from the side of Christ as he slept the sleep of death upon the cross that there came forth the sublime sacrament of the whole Church. (#5)

Once born of Christ and empowered by the Spirit, the church completes Christ's saving work principally through word and sacrament. In the sacrament of baptism, each of us is plunged into the paschal mystery, dying with Christ for the sake of life. Every other sacrament, in turn, continues to join us to the redemptive activity of Christ's life, death and rising: conforming us to Christ in confirmation; teaching us his pattern of loving and dying in response to his divine vocation; joining us to his redemptive sufferings in anointing and viaticum; restoring us to his friendship and making us his ambassadors of forgiveness and new life in reconciliation. Every sacrament lives out that cycle of death and life which is the paschal mystery; every sacrament works the gradual transformation of the human person into the glory of God.

Third, the eucharist is the sacrament that connects, recapitulates and intensifies the promises we have made in every other sacramental moment. The eucharist is the culmination of Christian initiation. Bathed in the waters of regeneration and sealed with the Spirit, we are invited to the table, there to offer ourselves to God with Christ, to share in the eucharistic sacrifice and to rehearse the attitudes and values of God's reign until we gather in communion at the great end-time banquet. The eucharist is the primary sacrament of reconciliation, for in the celebration of the eucharist "the passion of Christ is made present; his body given for us and his blood shed for the forgiveness of sins are offered to God again by the Church for the salvation of the world. In the eucharist Christ is present and is offered as 'the sacrifice which has made our peace' with God and in order that 'we may be brought together in unity' by his Holy Spirit" (*Rite of Penance*, 2). Furthermore, eucharist is a sacrament of healing, a gift and grace we acknowledge before approaching the table: "Lord, I am not worthy to receive you, but only say the word and I shall be healed." And if marriage, and indeed every vocation, is a matter of loving and dying, it is the eucharist that allows that dynamic of our lives to be celebrated together with other Christians, themselves engaged in the same cyclic pattern—the dying and rising of those who love deeply and give themselves away for the sake of others.

Eucharist connects all of the sacraments and recapitulates them as it continually invites us to remain faithful to the promises elicited from us in every other Amen. The effect of our sacramental promises, we might say, is cumulative and we celebrate the eucharist as promise-makers—and as those who know they need the grace of God and the nourishment of holy food and drink to live a faithful life. The eucharist empowers our promise-keeping. That sense of the ebb and flow of the sacramental cycle and the interconnection of our promise-making and promise-keeping across the sacramental spectrum was captured in this man's experience week after week at the Sunday eucharist: "The sense of dying and rising affects me personally because of the death of an adult child and having that child buried from this church. When we entered that church and that baptismal water was sprinkled on her casket, it was a renewal and I then had that sense that from baptism to death, it was a connection, and death was just an intermission. The life goes on. And it was very powerful for weeks afterward, as I stood in the choir and looked out at our baptismal font, which is the focus of the main part of our community. I was just overcome with, again, that feeling that I didn't need to worry, that my daughter's death was only an intermission in her total life with God."

A total life with God. What a wonderful insight about the sacraments—so many ways to celebrate our total life with God: coming to faith, being newborn and beloved of God, gradually being conformed to Christ, the loving and dying of vocational choice and fidelity, reestablishing friendship with God after the rupture of sin, being joined to the sufferings of Christ, and, in the end, being returned by those who love us to God's tender care. All of these are elements of a total life with God, a life sustained and celebrated regularly at the table of God's word and the table of sacrifice and meal.

Finally, the eucharist has been left as the last of our sacramental reflections because it perfectly illustrates the fundamental structure of all sacraments: the structure of listening and loving. In each of our sacraments the community is first gathered to hear again the invitation of God and then, and only in the power of God's life-giving Spirit, are we able to respond in loving. The holy life is, after all, a matter of God's initiative. The Preface of Weekdays IV makes this point emphatically:

All powerful and ever-living God,

we do well always and everywhere to give you thanks.

You have no need of our praise,

yet our desire to thank you is itself your gift.

Our prayer of thanksgiving adds nothing to your greatness,

but makes us grow in your grace,

through Jesus Christ our Lord.

This preface underscores the mystery of our life with God—all is gift, all is God's utter gratuity. We do well to give God praise and thanks, but even our desire to do so is because God has planted that desire in our hearts and continually nurtures us in divine life. Our liturgy, our prayer and praise, is deep within us; it is drawn out of us because of God's initiative, God's summons, God's desire to be in communion with us, God's longing to draw us into deeper union. It is for us to respond to the initiative of God. Eucharist and every other sacrament play out this cyclic pattern: first God's initiative, then human response; first our listening and then our loving. These are the two basic movements every time we gather for the liturgy. They are in clear relief as the fundamental structure of eucharist.

Experience: All Is Gift

What do we celebrate when we gather for eucharist? How can we name the personal experience we bring to public expression?

One way that eucharist differs from other sacraments is that with the other sacraments it is possible to be fairly precise about the journey of the candidate and his or her particular experience of conversion. In every other sacrament we can look for signs of readiness for celebration, signs that an individual has come to some new threshold in their life with God and has negotiated that threshold in faith and love. The concept of readiness for sacrament is predicated on that kind of precision. We can say, for example, that coming to faith will take some recognizable shapes and will have some common features: A person will have come to know Christ in a personal way, will be ready to join a community and participate in its liturgical prayer and will understand that faith issues forth in mission in the church and in the world. When candidates give evidence of this way of life we discern that they are ready for initiation. Similarly, when a couple present themselves for the sacrament of marriage, their love for each other must give some evidence of mature freedom, a capacity to remain faithful until death and an openness to expand their world beyond themselves. That is the point of the questions about freedom, fidelity and acceptance of children asked of them at the beginning of the marriage ceremony.

With the eucharist there is no such precision possible or even necessary. The eucharist does not mark a particular and momentous threshold; it is not reserved for a once-in-a-lifetime celebration. The eucharist celebrates all of our experiences, small and great alike. The eucharist is an opportunity to join ourselves anew to Jesus' death for the life of the world and to know in our own daily dyings a faint replica of his death. As one respondent expressed this reality, "If I'm having something happening in my life that is really taking all the faith I have to deal with, always something will happen in the liturgy that brings it home to me and makes it real for my life. And if your liturgy doesn't do that, then you might as well not bother because the liturgy is about life and death."

Eucharist, then, has a way of gathering up and bringing to expression our life and death issues. But it also is the celebration of the ordinary. The eucharist is an opportunity to bring to liturgical expression all the personal, internal experience that is ours — experience of new life and growth and celebration, joys large and small, times we know love and friendship, gifts given and received, hopes realized, faith deepened. The eucharist marks the dailyness of our lives, the routine, the small triumphs and tiny fidelities, the little disappointments, the disturbing words, the broken dreams, the deepest longings.

Catholics of a certain age grew up reciting the morning offering, handing over all the "prayers, works, joys and sufferings of this day." It was a shorthand for all our experience, all the people we carried in our hearts, all the actions of our day, all our work for the reign of God — mostly just trying to live a faithful and discerning life in the humdrum of the day-to-day. The morning offering was a prayer that consecrated our day and transformed it by joining it to the perfect offering of Christ. Everything about our experience was able to be caught up in this one great act of self-donation. It is the same totality of experience that we bring with us when we come to the eucharist. It is the material of our offering when we join ourselves to the gifts of bread and wine. We have no other.

Readiness for eucharist, then, has to do with paying attention. In chapter two we spoke about becoming attentive in a cyclic process of awareness, reflection, reception and transformation, and we applied these stages of attentiveness to our own experience and to the unfolding of the liturgical event. Eucharist is uniquely able to mirror our experience back to us even as it transforms that experience, but it does so to the extent that we learn to pay attention to the interior movements of our lives and to the unfolding of the eucharistic celebration. The more deeply we become aware, reflective and receptive to these inner and outer worlds, the more possibility that transformation happens.

Celebration: Eucharist

The Second Vatican Council's recovery of word and eucharist as the principal parts of the celebration has important consequences. Prior to the Council we spoke about the offertory, consecration and communion as the three principal parts of the Mass. The liturgy of the word was also part of the celebration, but a bit like an appendage. We didn't call it a principal part nor did we think it was absolutely essential to the integrity of the whole. In the days when the obligation to attend Mass carried the threat of mortal sin should we miss it without serious cause, we could skip the whole entrance rite and liturgy of the word without incurring grave sin. Now, the council reforms include the recovery of the ancient pattern of word and table, a two-part structure achieved by the end of the first century when Christians definitively joined the word service of the synagogue to their celebration of prayer and the breaking of the bread. Our post-conciliar reform was recovery, then, of this simpler and earlier pattern, and recovery in general of the power of the word of God to draw forth human response.

In this last chapter we shall highlight the twofold dimension of the eucharist, word and table, listening and loving, by actually exploring the parts of the celebration under the headings of the many actions that make up our listening and our loving. In focusing on the actions of the eucharist we take our cue from a wonderful insight contained in the United States bishops' document on *Environment and Art in Catholic Worship*:

> The most powerful experience of the sacred is found in the celebration and the persons celebrating, that is, it is found in the action of the assembly: the living words, the living gestures, the living sacrifice, the living meal. This was at the heart of the earliest liturgies. Evidence of this is found in their architectural floor plans which were designed as general gathering spaces, spaces which allowed the whole assembly to be part of the action. (#29)

Actions then, are what we shall highlight, actions that blend together to constitute our active participation.

Listening

Assembling, Processing, Singing, Signing, Greeting, Acknowledging, Praising, Praying, Hearing, Interceding, Giving

ACTS OF LISTENING

Assembling. • The first act of listening is simply coming together and discovering God already active in the assembly of believers before a word is spoken. "The building is not the church; the people are the church," said a young woman, "and when you get there and the place is full of people, it's a beautiful place—we are like stained-glass windows!" God speaks a powerful word if we attend to who it is that comes together, people of every age, race, gender, ability, educational background—the oddest assortment of people, the loveliest collection of stained-glass windows—drawn together by a little miracle of God's grace.

Listening begins by looking on the faces of the others and by paying attention to what is happening in our own and in one another's lives and in this parish, city, country, world. There are natural disasters and job lay-offs, ethnic divisions, fighting and racial tensions across the globe. We all carry all of this with us as members of the global community. But there is more. We can read the traces of God on the faces of those we know well: the joys and sufferings of every day. Some have entrusted more to us: concern about their children, about drugs, sex and violence; the biopsy being done on a spouse; the heartache of aging parents; the anxieties about finances; the joy of their daughter's early acceptance into college; the fear of losing a job; the marital difficulties; the baby on the way.

"I try to get there on time because this is what I've figured out: The priest isn't the center of attention, the altar is not the center of attention, but we as a body, a family, are the center of the action with Christ among us and within us. We're the ones who are there to do all the celebrating together, not individually."

Assembling is like a miracle, the gathering of this motley crew, coming together because it is God who draws us, "black and white, young and old, well-to-do and not so well-to-do, every social spectrum . . . there's a real attempt to include everyone." God is already speaking to our hearts if we would listen, speaking through the daily ups and downs, joys and struggles of other faith-filled Christians. If we listen we will hear a word: compassion, delight, perseverance, faithfulness, struggle, loneliness, kindness, heroism, suffering, peace. Listening to God present and active in ourselves and others can be a cause of invitation to a new and deeper response.

Why attend to the presence of others? A good question, especially for those raised on the theology that tried to leave ordinary life concerns at the door and enter into silent communion with eyes closed in prayer before Mass. Yet God finds us and saves us in a common life; God reveals Godself through those at our right and our left; God will speak and act through this assembly of believers. Our first act of listening then is simply coming together and becoming attentive to the revelation of God in the presence and action of one another.

Processing. • The action of processing signals the beginning of the celebration. The point of the procession of ministers is not just to move them into position, like staging a play before the curtain is raised. Processing is not simply functional. It provides an image for us of our own journey, in this case condensed to a dance down the aisle. Those in the procession, the presider and assistant ministers, identify with the assembly as they move among us. They are, in a way, being deputed for ministry from the assembly, for the assembly, even as they signal to us that all life is journey into God.

The cross is at the head of the procession and serves as a primary symbol, linking this liturgy with every other. That insight came from a man who had witnessed years of cross processions: "That cross for me is so significant because we use that same cross for weddings, funerals, every Mass. And we venerate the cross on Good Friday. We put it in a place of honor. There's no place to sit in that building where it can't be seen, where you won't have to reverence it, at least by eye."

Candles, too, form part of the procession and find a resonance in the deep ritual memory of some participants — of baptismal candles and wedding candles and Easter Vigil candles and the one great paschal candle: "The community will bring the candles forward and put them on the pillars in the sanctuary. And it's wonderful, because if we are Christ's hands and body and eyes and feet on this earth, then we are also Christ's light."

Singing. • Most often, music and song accompany the procession, the fusion of voices into one voice; the fusion of hearts and lives into one body giving God glory; the search for words adequate to name the feast or season and to set the tone. "Sometimes the words and music just flow over me," stated a woman, "and then I join this choir of angels. I didn't used to sing, didn't like it, couldn't do it very well — but that's not the point, is it? The point is praise." This once-reluctant singer has discovered that music is integral to liturgy, that it assists us in expressing our faith, adds joy to the celebration, imparts a sense of unity and sets the tone for the particular feast or season. It helps us be whole persons at worship. Joining heart and voice, Augustine taught, is praying twice.

Signing. • Now a series of other words and actions follows, demanding every skill of listening that we can muster. We begin the celebration by tracing a cross on our bodies, marking ourselves with the sign of our salvation. In so doing we claim once again our belief in the triune God and we promise that all that we do will be done "In the name of the Father and of the Son and of the Holy Spirit." Above all we act in the name of the Son and under his leadership, Jesus our high priest and leader of prayer who stands before the throne of grace, interceding on our behalf. With the mark of Christ's cross, that sign of utter vulnerability traced on our bodies, we acknowledge that all ministry is that of Christ as we participate in his one great sacrifice.

Greeting. • The miracle of this motley assembly is recognized. "The grace and peace of our Lord Jesus Christ, and the love of God, and the fellowship of the Holy Spirit be with you." Grace and peace are gift to us no matter what we come from; the love of God is offered, no matter the distance we experience; the Spirit's communion is ours, bound together by a love so strong and consuming that the outstretched arms of the presider are like a great embrace gathering us into one mystical body.

Acknowledging. • We come to the celebration as loved sinners, and we go no further without naming our need for God's healing. First we are invited into silence. How much our world needs stillness. So do we, as we learn again to pay attention to the movements around us and within us. We cherish this time for God to reach to our inmost self. We are invited to pause, to pray, to call to mind our sin and to let the healing power of God prepare us for eucharist. "I need this time," stated a young mother, a child fidgeting in her arms. "It puts me in right relationship. I try to remember why I am here and what I am doing." Whether it is a sprinkling rite to recall the purifying waters of baptism, or a group confession of sin, or a litany in praise of God for having rescued us from this body of sin and death, or the simple, even stark, "Lord have mercy" — whatever the form, we ask God to take us and shape us and make us ready to enter into this action of thanksgiving.

Praising. • Praising follows, at least most of the year, and it sums up for some why we come: "Some of my friends go to church to be wooed by the minister and to be entertained. I say, that ain't why you should go — to see the show. They don't realize that they are a part of the show! I really think that we go to church to praise the Lord with our fellow worshipers." We go to sing our praise. We sing the Gloria, the song of the angels, a hymn of praise once sung at morning prayer and only on Christmas at the eucharist. But now it is sung regularly on Sundays to praise God for this day and all that will fill it, to praise God for every good gift, above all God's perfect gift to humankind, the Lord Jesus Christ. We praise God for creating us and sustaining us, and rescuing us and allowing us to see this day and this hour, for God alone is the Holy One.

"We praise and then we fall silent," as one person described this progression. "The most powerful part of the prayer is 'let us pray' and 'Amen.' And when it follows the Gloria, there is this sequence: Gloria, Amen, Let us pray, silence . . . and it is a powerful moment."

Praying. • These introductory actions draw to a close with prayer. First we are invited again into silence and prayer, followed by an ample pause, a "time to connect," according to a young man, "a time to become inwardly engaged in the prayer of the church once we are in touch with our own prayer. It is a significant moment."

The opening prayer speaks the truth about our stance before God. We are essentially a needy people, and so, week after week, our first formal prayer is a petition. We name God under one of a variety of metaphors, all of them inadequate to capture the God of mystery, each of them hinting at the divine. We say more. We remind and thank God for past goodness to us and, on the strength of that and in confident hope, we ask yet again for God's gifts. And we make this and every prayer to God through Christ in the power of God's abundant and life-giving Spirit. It is such a short conclusion to prayer, but it expresses in a condensed way the essence of Christian prayer in Jesus' name. "I think the words are almost secondary. Each one of these prayers is like a doxology and each brings closure to some part of the rite."

Hearing. • Processing, singing, signing, greeting, acknowledging, praising and praying—all of it is an opportunity to begin listening to God moving within us and among us. Next we sit for the hearing of the word of God, a formal mode of listening to God as proclaimed from the pages of our sacred book. We turn to the Old Testament and the Psalms, the letters of the early church and the gospels, all of it the inspired word of God, all of it revealed, all of it revealing of human history and human life and the human heart. And even in the midst of our listening we need to respond with psalms and alleluias for the word in our minds and on our lips and in our hearts.

Word and homily fuse together into a word of consolation and a word of challenge, a word that reaches us, identifies us, touches our lives and consoles us for its very familiarity—but the word of God never leaves us where it finds us. It dares us to move beyond where we are. It provides a different vision, the longing of many: "You don't have to say it long—but it has to be engaging and there has to be challenge. That's my bottom line. I want to hear a challenge in a homily that forces me to look beyond or move beyond or think beyond or not be stagnant."

The homily, a word derived from the Greek word that means "familiar conversation" or "heart speaking to heart," is an integral part of the celebration, focused on this word just read and the lives of this people gathered here, weaving back and forth between one pole and the other, providing the nourishment so necessary for living a redeemed life. "The point of the homily, I think, is to draw you into the reading and then get out of the way." And to this insight, another was joined: "I'd say the readings and the homily draw you to action. The majority of the people are involved in some aspect of the community, social ministry or the different liturgical ministries. So a person who would rather just sit back and not be active probably would not be comfortable here. It's very demanding." Still another reflected on the delayed action of some readings and preaching: "Sometimes a day or two later the reading may hit me. Sometimes I don't hear the word or the homily. I might even be resistant to opening up to the word, and then, days later, something was triggered in my mind. It can leave a lasting effect."

Interceding. • We are a priestly people. It is our baptismal inheritance. The word stretches our hearts, our concerns, our cares. Our listening now makes us reach out to all God's people. We listen to the cry of the needy, to the plight of our world, to the anguish of sickness and death in this local community. "It's important to me that we bring the poor people and people in prisons and all of suffering humanity into our worship — it has made my Catholicism much more alive." Moreover, here we are most like Jesus, the high priest of our prayer. We stand with him before the throne of grace, interceding for all of humankind. Intercession is found in ancient synagogue patterns of prayer. It was borrowed by Christians and inserted into our celebration from the beginning. For us it is part of what it means to be Christian and to act, with Christ, for the life of the world.

Giving. • Giving is intimately linked with interceding. We bring the poor and the suffering and the needy of every kind before God. Then we do our part, giving of our substance, collecting together the offerings of this people for the sake of the church and the world, entrusting money to our leaders to care for the needy. And it has ever been thus. The earliest description of the eucharist, dating from the middle of the second century, mentions the collection — for orphans and widows, and those who are in want on account of sickness or any other cause, and those who are in bonds, and the strangers who are sojourners among us, and for all who are in need. The giving of gifts is simply another way of listening to God in those who are marginalized, those not present in this assembly save in our larger hearts. In the liturgy of the word we listen and then, emboldened, we make our needs known and back up our petitions with concrete manifestations of our loving concern.

These are the many ways of listening throughout the gathering and celebration of God's word. Now, a question: What prevents our hearing? Why is it possible not even to know what was read or what word was preached a few minutes after the celebration? How can we become more attentive to God's word stirring in our hearts and in the lives of those around us? How can we hear the invitation of God to a new and more abundant life whose passage is through death? How can we help one another to pay attention during these many actions, to become more and more aware and reflective and receptive so that the transformation God longs to work in us can have its sway? Is the word we act out believable and trustworthy? Do we expect to hear it in such diverse people and places? Do we provide enough silence to hear the still small voice? Can we learn, as communities, to calm and quiet our souls like children in their mothers' arms? Would it be good to prepare the readings ahead? Pray them at home? What choked the seed on the ground in Jesus' parable — and where do we find these in our listening: stones? weeds? no moisture? no roots? That parable of the sower and the seed is a story of the heart in real time.

Loving
Preparing, Remembering, Begging, Storytelling, Offering, Petitioning, Praising, Praying, Exchanging Peace, Dining, Leave-taking

ACTS OF LOVING RESPONSE

Listening is important because it leads to loving. Recall the twofold action of the sacramental economy: God's initiative joined to human response. It is the action of every sacrament. It is God's word that draws forth our repentance and desire to reactivate or deepen our friendship with God; it is God's word spoken in the scriptures and in those who surround us and minister to our fears and our pain that helps us become ready to join our suffering with that of Christ; it is God's word spoken by one we love or by a community of seekers that draws forth from us that self-dona-tion which is our acceptance of vocation and mission. It is because of the word of God which is the gift of God that we are able to respond, to join ourselves to Jesus dead and risen, to reciprocate in love, to receive and to return love.

Listening leads to loving. And we act out our loving as we turn to the table of the eucharist. Think of the actions that we perform, each one a different way of lov-ing: preparing, remembering, begging, storytelling, offering, petitioning, praising, embracing, dining and leave-taking—to love and serve the Lord.

Preparing. • We do not rush into our eucharistic action. First there is the rite of preparation—of the table and the gifts, and of ourselves, too, gifts all. Love is deliberate; it plans, it prepares, it takes its time until all is ready. To this point the table has been bare, uncluttered and unnoticed. The focus has been on the ambo for the proclamation of the word. Now everything that is needed is brought to the table; everything is set with care. The rite of preparation is a way of shifting our psycho-logical focus from ambo to altar. Indeed, it helps us shift our spiritual focus from lis-tening to loving. Our gifts are brought forward: another procession, but this time members of the assembly come forward with simple things, bread, wine, plate, cup, flagon—ordinary gifts, created gifts, transformed by the labor of human hands—creator and creatures in partnership. And there is prayer: "I love the way the priest prays over the food and the money collection. We bless these food offerings and the people for whom this money is given. May they know the love of God through us and we through them."

The preparation rite includes the readying of ourselves, of course, the prepa-ration of time and focus as we place ourselves with the gifts, make ourselves avail-able for the same action of God that will make the bread and wine into the body and blood. We prepare to be transformed. This preparation, a modest moment of the rite, is nonetheless very important, for through it we become ready, open, available for the transforming action of God.

Everything is ready. Next we turn to the eucharistic prayer, the heart of our celebration, the great prayer of praise and thanksgiving spoken in our name. In the course of the prayer we unite ourselves with Christ; we remember the great things God has done in Christ and in us; we offer the sacrifice and join ourselves to the one and only perfect sacrifice.

The eucharistic prayer is a long prayer. "Sometimes we move in and out, we hear a word, **a** phrase, we are present to parts of it, sometimes to the whole. But that's okay," said a man. His wife continued, "Your body can do the action and that leaves your mind then to free itself spiritually — to think or to pray or to enter into it more fully." Another woman described her strategy for entering into the prayer: "It's a struggle to be a participative listener . . . to really listen to what those words mean and to pray the prayer with the presider. Some time ago I realized I would pay better attention if I said the words. I know every eucharistic prayer by heart now, and I say them in my heart and sometimes even whisper them. My husband told me I was a closet concelebrant." So are we all as we join ourselves to the many actions of the eucharistic prayer, the many ways we express our love.

The dialogue of our love begins:

The Lord be with you.

And also with you.

Lift up your hearts.

We lift them up to the Lord.

Let us give thanks to the Lord, our God.

It is right to give God thanks and praise.

It is right, indeed. And it is right, first of all, to remember.

Remembering. • How could we begin except by joyous memory of all the ways that God has been active in our lives and in our world. In the preface of the eucharistic prayer we praise and thank God for the whole work of creation and redemption and then we mention some quite specific gift of God that corresponds to the season or feast. Now are the mighty acts of God spelled out. And having done so we cry out "Holy," and holy, too, we long to be.

Begging. • Here is our psychology at work. How like children is our strategy. We say to God: You did this and this and this and this for us. Now be faithful and generous again. Send your Spirit, the Spirit who sanctifies, the Spirit who transforms. Let your Spirit move over these gifts of bread and wine, and let your Spirit move among us as we pray. Let your Spirit act with power to change these gifts and to change us that we, too, become truly the body and blood of Christ for the life of the world.

Storytelling. • Every time we gather for eucharist we remember and we tell it again, the story about the night before he died when he took bread and cup and told us to keep his memory. We recount the words and the actions of Christ as if we had been there, "a little like the way we feel compelled to talk about what happened in the last hours of life of someone we loved deeply." What a wonderful insight, and how true. We want the details: Who was present? What did she say? What did he do? What was going on in those last hours that remains our legacy? How like us when it is someone we treasure. How important then, again and again, for us to repeat the story of Christ.

So we remember it was the night before he died and we rehearse the words and actions. We tell it simply. We keep the memory of Jesus' life and his passion, death and resurrection. We recall his ascension into heavenly glory, his exaltation at God's side. And we do all of it in fulfillment of Jesus' invitation: "Do this in memory of me." Was ever another command so obeyed?

Offering. • Storytelling and remembering make us bold. Now we stand in God's presence, counted worthy to serve. Now we stand in union with the Risen One and offer the one and only sacrifice. Now the whole church of which we are a small microcosm offers the living sacrifice, the spotless victim, to the one he called Abba, in the power of the Spirit. And as we offer this sacrifice, we offer ourselves, through Christ, our mediator before the throne of grace. We surrender ourselves to that same action of the Spirit. We beg for ever more complete union with God and with one another, so that God may be all in all.

Petitioning. • Again, we are bold. How can God resist us, joined as we are with God's beloved child? We pray for the church that we be holy, for all ministers of the gospel that we be faithful, for all faithful people living and dead. "We pray in ever-widening concentric circles," one person recognized of these petitions. We stand in communion with all the saints, joining our prayer to that of Mary and the saints in glory, that all the world will share in the salvation and redemption of Christ purchased by his body and blood.

Praising. • What is there left to say? Only that everything we do is through and with and in Christ for the glory of God. It is enough. And finally, having spent ourselves in responding to God with love, we give our assent to the whole and we make our promises again by saying Amen. So important was community participation in the great eucharistic action in the early church that Justin Martyr makes it the focus of his commentary. At the end of the presider's praise and thanksgiving, he tells us, ". . . we all say, 'Amen.'" Justin tells us precious little else. What the presider said is all very sketchy. But this word Amen Justin cannot pass over — the community's pledge to live what we have just proclaimed in word and ritual action.

It is worth pausing sometimes at the end of the eucharistic prayer and that which we have called "the Great Amen" to ponder what it is that we have promised. "There's something going on here that's a mystery," said one parishioner. "I feel it when the bread and wine are lifted up at the end and there is so much focused energy." And another tried to spell it out: "We call it the eucharistic prayer and I think it is the heart of the celebration and it has the summation of all the feelings and thoughts that we should be having at the time. We got rid of the bells because the whole of the prayer is important, not just when the priest raises the host and the cup. It's the central prayer and the priest is praying it for us and with us, and by our singing the responses we enter into it more deeply. One day I realized it was being said over bread and cup and us. I have never felt the same." The same insight was expressed in other words: "I always had this idea that the priest is up there and he says the Mass and there's this incredible thing that happens: The bread and wine become body and blood. And then all of a sudden one day I realized it's us, too, it's all of us doing this incredible thing and becoming this incredible thing."

Praying. • Now, what is there left to do? Only this. To say the words that Jesus left us, to embrace one another in an exchange of his peace among ourselves and then to turn to the table for the nourishment to continue this listening and loving when we leave. We will go in peace, but never the same — whether we know it or not, believe it or not, feel it or not, we are never quite the same. Prayer is not for the sake of God, said Thomas Aquinas, but for the sake of the community, to bring us to reverence, to form habits of the heart in us, to move us just a little bit further into our life with God.

Exchanging Peace. • "Look not on our sins but on the faith of your church and grant us peace and unity." We draw on the strength of one another, on one another's faith and hope, on one another's presence and participation, on one another's faithfulness. And somehow we know that the peace we exchange is not our own fragile peace but the peace of Christ which the world cannot give, but which nevertheless we know we have been given in trust and for one another. "People are very particular about their space," one man said. "So for someone to let you come into their personal space and hug them and say, 'The peace of God be with you,' that says to me we can break down all kinds of boundaries with the love of Christ." Another linked this action with what follows: "There's a great deal of joy that Jesus is there and we're going to partake of him with the entire community. There is joy as we give one another peace and I feel the joy and also a responsibility — of living up to that, living up to being Christ in the world. My actions make a difference and my thoughts and words make a difference. Then I say: 'Lord, I am not worthy, but you can change me,' and I know I will have the grace and stamina to make that difference."

Dining. • A shared meal is what is left. The sharing of food reminds us of the sharing of life that is ours. Our dining begins with a simple rite of preparation — the breaking of the bread: "I watch the bread be broken in pieces to share with the people. And yet in some mysterious way it is not something divided but it is bringing us together. Its strength is still there. It's like you have three children. You divide your love but it's not really divided."

Jesus' ministry of table fellowship was a scandal throughout his life. He sat down at table with the most disreputable types, outcasts and sinner and marginalized folks of every imaginable kind. Here at our Sunday table we can be most like Jesus, saying "everyone is welcome to this table, no exceptions." Said one participant: "I'm struck by the uniqueness of each one going up to receive the body of Christ. We're all unique, with different gifts and different problems, and yet we're all one people and I'm struck by that especially when I'm giving out communion and see the different shapes and sizes of the hands and the eyes."

The table is the place of universal reconciliation and the place where the unworthy are healed; it is the place of deepest conformity to Jesus as we are transformed from the inside out; it is the place where the sacrifice is consumed — an image of the loving and dying that is our life choice. The table is the place where we are fed in order that we will have the courage and the strength to live out a lifetime of Amens.

Leave-taking. • One last moment of loving is that of leave-taking well choreographed. We are poised to return to ordinary time. Reflecting on her experience, one woman summarized her many actions: "I feel I have completely worshiped God in every way I would want to — in song, in prayer, in the word, at the table, every kind of song, you know, from laments to psalms to anthems, all of it." All of it, body, mind and spirit engaged in our action of thanksgiving, our listening and loving and serving.

But the Mass never ends, or so I was told by the group of teens who were confirmed. You must live it. And that sentiment was also expressed by an elderly woman: "Liturgy isn't just what happens on Sunday. It's a whole lot more than that. The liturgy creates something, but the way people relate during the week seals it. It's a good expression of what the Vatican Council said in terms of liturgy being the source and summit. Everything flows from it." Life and liturgy become one. Perhaps that's the deepest meaning of the injunction to make of our lives a living worship.

Amen

The whole of the eucharist is like a dress rehearsal. We have done it countless times. We will do it again and again until we get in right — and that will be at the great end-time banquet. But short of that heavenly banquet our rehearsal can be decidedly ragged: "It is my experience and my sense that people are moving on a similar journey to my own and we try to celebrate those journeys. It doesn't always happen, and it doesn't always relate to how well the different pieces of the liturgy worked together. There's always that mystery of grace that cuts both ways. Sometimes you have all the pieces and it just didn't happen and it may have been just a bad day for everybody. Or it was a clumsy procession and the microphone was off and someone had to plug it in, and there was a baby crying all during the homily and I felt totally out of sorts by the eucharistic prayer and then God broke in and the Spirit moved among us. Grace is unpredictable and uncontrollable."

It is, all of it, a mystery of God's grace, unpredictable and uncontrollable. And each of us says Amen to life and to liturgy in our own way and in hundreds of different ways. The sacraments help us to say it and keep us faithful to the One to whom it is uttered.

All the assembly said, "Amen,"

and praised the Lord.

And the people did

as they had promised.

Nehemiah 5:13b

Further Reading

Chapter One: Mystagogy as Method

Gerard F. Baumbach, *Experiencing Mystagogy: The Sacred Pause of Easter*. New York/Mahwah, New Jersey: Paulist Press, 1996.

Anne Field, *From Darkness to Light*. Ann Arbor, Michigan: Servant Books, 1978.

David Regan, *Experience the Mystery: Pastoral Possibilities for Christian Mystagogy*. Collegeville: The Liturgical Press, 1994.

Edward Yarnold, *The Awe-Inspiring Rites of Initiation*. Collegeville: The Liturgical Press, 1971/1994.

Chapter Two: Paying Attention

Eleanor Bernstein, ed., *Words, Gestures, Objects*. Notre Dame, Indiana: Notre Dame Center for Pastoral Liturgy, 1995.

Leonardo Boff, *Sacraments of Life: Life of the Sacraments*. Washington: The Pastoral Press, 1975/1987.

Balthasar Fisher, *Signs, Words and Gestures: Short Homilies on the Liturgy*. New York: Pueblo Publishing Company, 1979/1981.

Romano Guardini, *Sacred Signs*. St. Louis: Pio Decimo Press, 1956.

Gabe Huck, ed., *A Liturgy Sourcebook*. Chicago: Liturgy Training Publications, 1994.

Frank Kacmarcik and Paul Philibert, *Seeing and Believing: Images of Christian Faith*. Collegeville: The Liturgical Press, 1995.

JJacques and Raissa Maritain, *Contemplation and Liturgy*. New York: P. J. Kenedy & Sons, 1960.

Gertrud Mueller Nelson, *To Dance with God: Family Ritual and Community*. New York: Paulist Press, 1986.

Padraic O'Hare, *The Way of Faithfulness: Contemplation and Formation in the Church*. Valley Forge, Pennsylvania: Trinity Press International, 1993.

David Philippart, *Saving Signs, Wondrous Words*. Chicago: Liturgy Training Publications, 1996.

Gail Ramshaw-Schmidt, *Letters for God's Name*. Minneapolis: Seabury Press, 1984.

Chapter Three: Christian Initiation of Adults

The Rite of Christian Initiation of Adults.

J. Robert Baker, et al., eds., *A Baptism Sourcebook*. Chicago: Liturgy Training Publications, 1993.

Mary Pierre Ellebracht, *The Easter Passage*. Minneapolis: Winston Press, 1983.

Maxwell E. Johnson, *Living Water, Sealing Spirit: Readings on Christian Initiation*. Collegeville: Liturgical Press, 1995.

Thomas Morris, *The RCIA: Transforming the Church*. New York: Paulist Press, 1989.

Ronald A. Oakham, et al., *One at the Table: The Reception of Baptized Christians*. Chicago: Liturgy Training Publications, 1995.

Gail Ramshaw, *Words around the Font*. Chicago: Liturgy Training Publications, 1994.

Mark Searle, "The Journey of Conversion," *Worship* 54 (1980): 35–55.

Victoria M. Tufano, ed., *Celebrating the Rites of Adult Initiation: Pastoral Reflections*. Chicago: Liturgy Training Publications, 1992.

Video: *Easter Vigil.* Chicago: Liturgy Training Publications, 2000.

Video: *This Is the Night.* Chicago: Liturgy Training Publications, 1992.

Chapter Four: Infant Baptism

The Rite of Baptism for Children.

Paul F. X. Covino, "The Postconciliar Infant Baptism Debate in the American Catholic Church," in Maxwell E. Johnson, *Living Water, Sealing Spirit: Readings on Christian Initiation.* Collegeville: Liturgical Press, 1995, 327–49.

Timothy Fitzgerald, *Infant Baptism: A Parish Celebration.* Chicago: Liturgy Training Publications, 1994.

Mark Searle, "Infant Baptism Reconsidered," in Maxwell E. Johnson, ed., *Living Water, Sealing Spirit: Readings on Christian Initiation.* Collegeville: Liturgical Press, 1995.

Victoria M. Tufano, ed., *Catechesis and Mystagogy: Infant Baptism.* Chicago: Liturgy Training Publications, 1996.

Video: *New Life: A Parish Celebrates Infant Baptism.* Chicago: Liturgy Training Publications/ Allen, Texas: Tabor Publishing, 1995.

Chapter Five: Confirmation

The Rite of Confirmation.

Gerard Austin, *Anointing with the Spirit: The Rite of Confirmation.* New York: Pueblo Publishing Company, 1985.

Timothy Fitzgerald, *Confirmation: A Parish Celebration.* Revised edition. Chicago: Liturgy Training Publications, 1999.

Paul Turner, *Confirmation: The Baby in Solomon's Court.* New York: Paulist Press, 1993.

James Wilde, ed., *When Shall We Confirm?* Chicago: Liturgy Training Publications, 1989.

James Wilde, ed., *Confirmed as Children, Affirmed as Teens.* Chicago: Liturgy Training Publications, 1990.

Chapter Six: Marriage

The Rite of Marriage.

J. Robert Baker, et al., eds., *A Marriage Sourcebook.* Chicago: Liturgy Training Publications, 1994.

Paul Covino, *Celebrating Marriage, Preparing the Wedding Liturgy: A Workbook for the Engaged Couple.* Portland: Pastoral Press, 1994.

Austin Fleming, *Parish Weddings.* Chicago: Liturgy Training Publications, 1987.

Michael G. Lawler, *Secular Marriage, Christian Sacrament.* Mystic, Connecticut: Twenty-Third Publications, 1985.

Michael G. Lawler, *Marriage and Sacrament: A Theology of Christian Marriage.* Collegeville: The Liturgical Press, 1993.

Video: *Our Catholic Wedding.* Chicago: Liturgy Training Publications, 2001.

Chapter Seven: Reconciliation

The Rite of Penance.

Kathleen Hughes and Joseph Favazza, eds., *A Reconciliation Sourcebook.* Chicago: Liturgy Training Publications, 1997.

Robert J. Kennedy, ed., *Reconciliation: The Continuing Agenda.* Collegeville: The Liturgical Press, 1987.

Robert J. Kennedy, ed., *Reconciling Embrace: Foundations for the Future of Sacramental Reconciliation*. Chicago: Liturgy Training Publications, 1998.

Chapter Eight: Anointing

Pastoral Care of the Sick: Rites of Anointing and Viaticum.

Genevieve Glen, et al., *Handbook for Ministers of Care*. Revised edition. Chicago: Liturgy Training Publications, 1997.

Charles W. Gusmer, *And You Visited Me: Sacramental Ministry to the Sick and the Dying*. New York: Pueblo Publishing Company, 1984.

Chapter Nine: Funerals

The Order of Christian Funerals.

William Cieslak, *Console One Another: Commentary on The Order of Christian Funerals*. Washington: The Pastoral Press, 1990.

Richard Rutherford, *The Death of a Christian: The Rite of Funerals*. New York: Pueblo Publishing Company, 1980.

Virginia Sloyan, ed., *A Sourcebook about Christian Death*. Chicago: Liturgy Training Publications, 1990.

Margaret Smith, *Facing Death Together: Parish Funerals*. Chicago: Liturgy Training Publications, 2000.

Chapter Ten: Eucharist

The Sacramentary.

The Lectionary.

Edward Foley, *From Age to Age: How Christians Have Celebrated the Eucharist.* Chicago: Liturgy Training Publications, 1991.

Gail Ramshaw, *Words around the Table.* Chicago: Liturgy Training Publications, 1991.

R. Kevin Seasoltz, ed., *Living Bread, Saving Cup: Readings on the Eucharist.* Collegeville: The Liturgical Press, 1982.

The Sunday Mass Video Series. Chicago: Liturgy Training Publications, 1995.
    The Roman Catholic Mass Today: Introduction and Overview
    We Shall Go Up with Joy: The Entrance Rite
    The Word of the Lord: The Liturgy of the Word
    Lift Up Your Hearts: The Eucharistic Prayer
    Say Amen! to What You Are: The Communion Rite

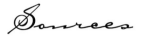

Sources